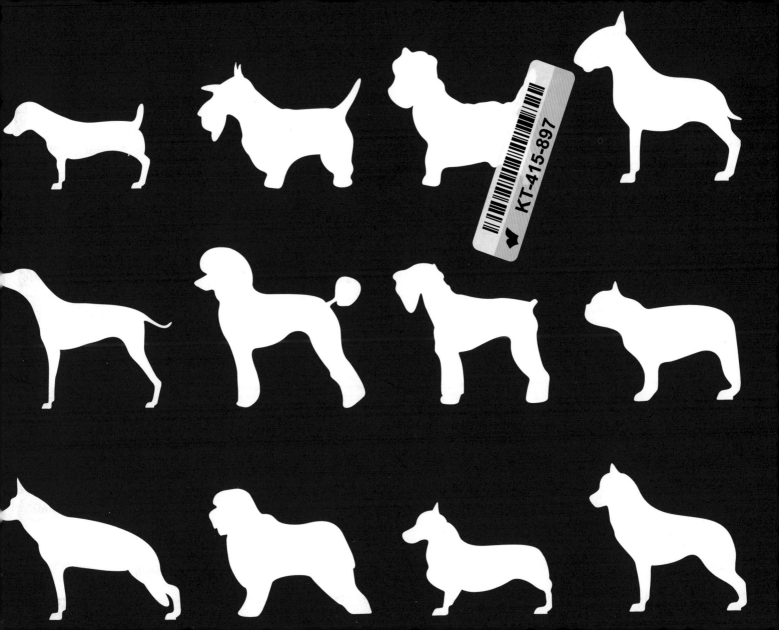

KT-415-897

Best in Show

knit your own dog

First published in the United Kingdom
in 2010 by
Collins & Brown
10 Southcombe Street
London W14 0RA

An imprint of Anova Books Company Ltd

Photography by Holly Jolliffe

ISBN 978-1-84340-573-3

A CIP catalogue for this book is available
from the British Library.

10 9 8 7 6 5

Reproduction by Rival Colour Ltd, UK
Printed and bound by
G. Canale&C.S.p.A, Italy

This book can be ordered direct from the
publisher at www.anovabooks.com

For Lily and Nell

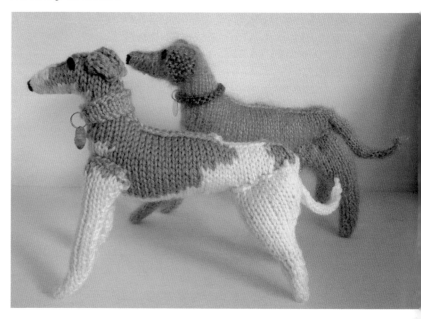

Best in Show

knit your own dog

Sally Muir & Joanna Osborne

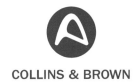

COLLINS & BROWN

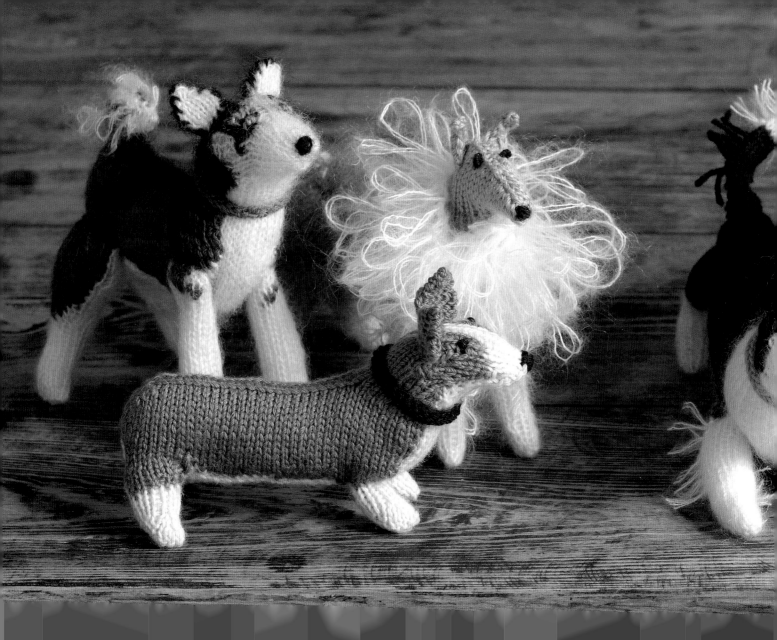

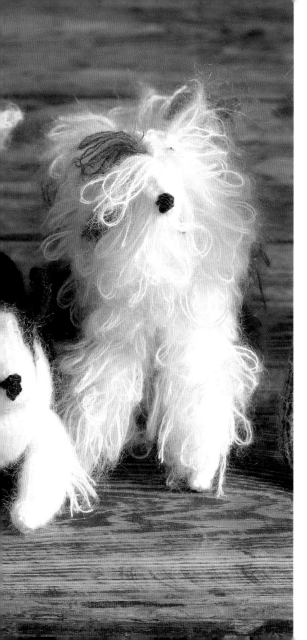

Contents

Introduction

We have both had dogs all our lives – between us we have owned eight Poodles, two Afghan Hounds, two mongrels, two Lurchers, one Dalmatian, one Whippet, one Spaniel and one Greyhound. We have also designed and made knitted things for almost as long, so it seemed like a good idea to combine the two and design knitted dogs.

The dogs aren't intended as toys, we have tried to make them as realistic as possible by including details specific to each breed. Once you have learned the basics of knitting you can make pretty much anything, so why not knit your own dog? You don't need to be an expert knitter, with just knit, purl and loopy stitches you can make all twenty-five dogs in this book. They are also fairly quick to knit, you don't need to be an expert and we have made them a manageable size so that they can be knitted in a few evenings.

The knitted dog is, of course, the ideal easy-care companion; it lives forever, there is no feeding, no barking, no moulting, no vets' bills – the perfect pet. With the help of our book you can now knit your precious pet, replace your long-lost friend, reproduce your favourite breed, or knit the dog your child has always desperately wanted.

We would also like you to feel that you can play around with the patterns. For instance, if you'd like a Golden Labrador or a black Pug you can change the yarn colour; if your dog is fatter than ours, add more stuffing. As you well know, each dog has its own personality and that can be influenced by where you place the ears, nose and eyes.

You could also mix and match, knit your own mongrel made from a random selection of pedigree dog parts. Take the legs and tail of the Poodle and put them on the Labrador and at a fraction of the price you have knitted your own Labradoodle.

Stitch your bitch.

Joanna and Sally

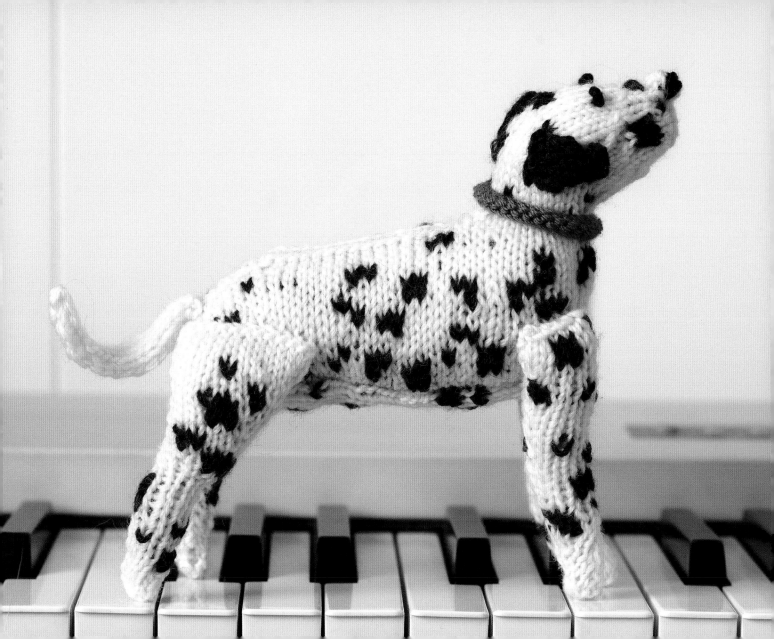

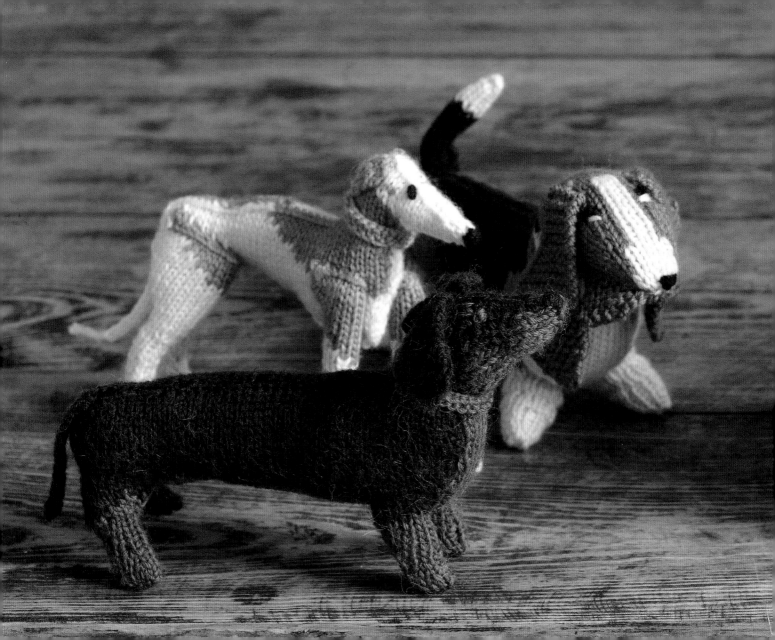

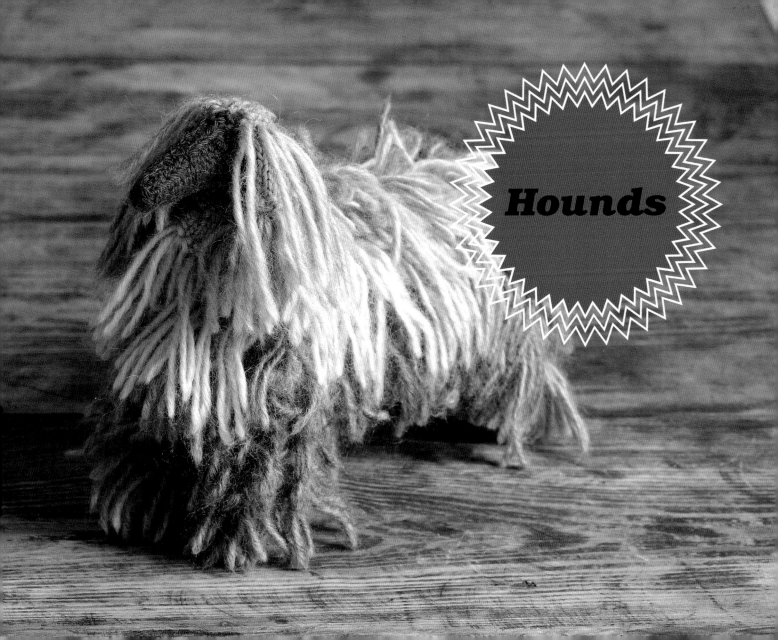

Hounds

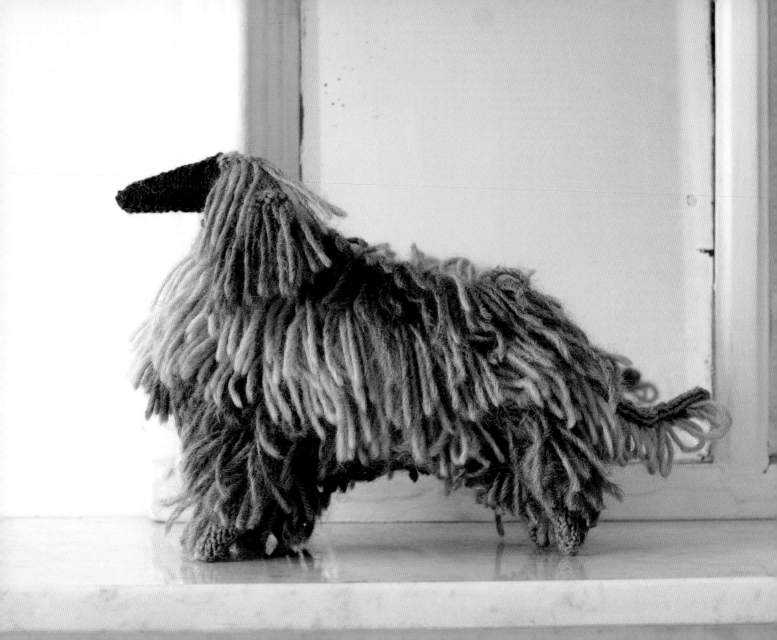

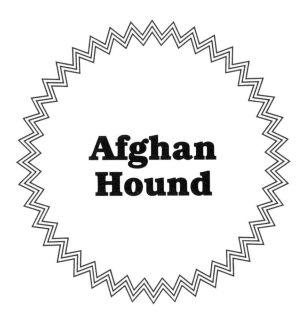

Afghan Hound

Hugely popular in the 1970s and now rarely seen,
the ridiculously beautiful and ornamental looking
Afghan Hound is a large game hunting dog and one
of the oldest of the sighthounds; they were reputed
to have had a berth on Noah's Ark. Afghans can
gallop at up to 40 miles (64km) an hour and can
leap 7 feet (over 2 metres) into the air from a
standing position. One of the earliest Afghan
Hound breeders was Zeppo Marx and an Afghan
was the hero of the *What-a-Mess* series of
children's books by Frank Muir.

Afghan Hound

A festival of loopy stitch, the coat is knitted in variegated-colour yarn to give a variety of tones.

Measurements
Length: 20cm (8in)
Height to top of head: 17cm (6¾in)

Materials
- Pair of 2¾mm (US 2) knitting needles
- Pair of 2¾mm (US 2) double-pointed knitting needles
- 20g (¾oz) of Rowan Pure Wool 4ply in Toffee 453 (tf)
- 30g (1⅛oz) of Rowan Tapestry in Country 170 (co)
- 5g (⅛oz) of Rowan Cashsoft 4ply in Bark 432 (ba)
- Small amount of Rowan Pure Wool 4ply in Framboise 456 (fr) for collar
- Tiny amount of Rowan Pure Wool 4ply in Black 404 for nose and eyes
- Pipecleaners for legs

Abbreviations
See page 172.
* before st indicates loopy sts, worked in k on p row with co and tf (see page 173).

Front and Back Leg
(make 4 the same)
With 2¾mm (US 2) knitting needles and tf, cast on 8 sts.
Beg with a k row, work 2 rows st st.
Row 3: Inc, k1, k2tog, k2tog, k1, inc. *(8 sts)*

Row 4: Purl.
Row 5: Inc, k6, inc. *(10 sts)*
Row 6: Purl.
Row 7: Inc, k8, inc. *(12 sts)*
Row 8: Purl.
Row 9: Knit.
Row 10: Purl.
Row 11: Inc, k10, inc. *(14 sts)*
Row 12: Purl.
Row 13: Inc, k12, inc. *(16 sts)*
Row 14: Purl.
Row 15: Knit.
Row 16: Join in co, p2, *k12, p2.
With tf, work 7 rows st st.
(Work st st rows in tf only and loopy st rows in co and tf).
Row 24: With co and tf, p2, *k12, p2.
With tf, work 7 rows st st.
Row 32: With co and tf, p2, *k12, p2.
Row 33: With tf, knit.
Cast (bind) off.

Coat
The loopy stitch technique makes evenly sized loops easy to produce. But don't worry if your loops are not all exactly the same size, any small differences don't matter.

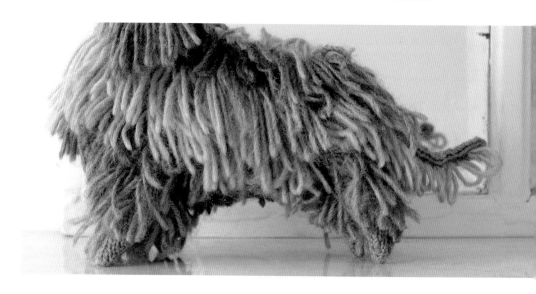

Tail

The Afghan's tail is worked as an i-cord on double-pointed needles. The loops are knitted in as the cord is worked and are deliberately made different sizes by winding the yarn around two or three fingers.

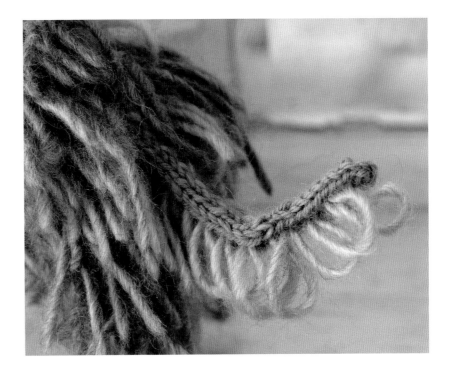

Right Side of Body and Head

With 2¾mm (US 2) knitting needles and tf, cast on 18 sts.
Beg with a k row, work 2 rows st st.
Row 3: Inc, k17, cast on 4 sts. *(23 sts)*
Row 4: Purl.
Row 5: Inc, k22, cast on 4 sts. *(28 sts)*
Row 6: Join in co, *k loopy st to end.
Row 7: With tf, inc, k27, cast on 4 sts. *(33 sts)*
Row 8: Purl. *(33 sts)*
Row 9: Inc, k32, cast on 6 sts. *(40 sts)*
Row 10: Purl.
Row 11: Inc, k39. *(41 sts)*
Row 12: With co and tf, *k loopy st to end.

Row 13: With tf, inc, k40. *(42 sts)*
Row 14: Purl.
Row 15: Inc, k41. *(43 sts)*
Row 16: P2tog, p40, inc. *(43 sts)*
Row 17: K41, k2tog. *(42 sts)*
Row 18: With co and tf, *k loopy st to end.
Row 19: With tf, k40, k2tog. *(41 sts)*
Row 20: P2tog, p38, inc. *(41 sts)*
Row 21: Knit.
Row 22: With tf, cast (bind) off 12 sts, with co and tf, *k29 icos. *(29 sts)*
Row 23: With tf, k2tog, k27. *(28 sts)*
Row 24: With tf, cast (bind) off 8 sts, with co and tf, *k18 icos, p2tog. *(19 sts)*

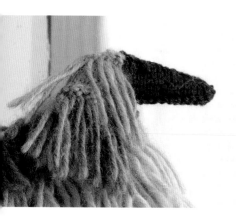

Head

The slim, elegant head is knitted in one piece with the body.

Row 25: With tf, k2tog, k15, k2tog. *(17 sts)*
Row 26: With tf, cast (bind) off 8 sts, with co and tf, *k7, p2tog. *(8 sts)*
With tf, work 3 rows st st.
Row 30: Join in ba, p8, cast on 13 sts. *(21 sts)*
Cont in ba.
Row 31: K21.
Work 2 rows st st.
Row 34: P2tog, p19. *(20 sts)*
Row 35: Cast (bind) off 6 sts, k to end.
(14 sts)
Row 36: P12, p2tog. *(13 sts)*
Row 37: Cast (bind) off 4 sts, k7 icos, k2tog.
(8 sts)
Cast (bind) off.

Left Side of Body and Head

With 2¾mm (US 2) knitting needles and tf, cast on 18 sts.
Row 1: Knit.
Row 2: Inc, p17, cast on 4 sts. *(23 sts)*
Row 3: Knit.
Row 4: Inc, p22, cast on 4 sts. *(28 sts)*
Row 5: Knit.
Row 6: Join in co, inc, *k27, cast on 4 sts.
(33 sts)
Row 7: With tf, knit.
Row 8: Inc, p32, cast on 6 sts. *(40 sts)*
Row 9: Knit.
Row 10: Inc, p39. *(41 sts)*
Row 11: Knit
Row 12: With co and tf, inc, *k40. *(42 sts)*
Row 13: With tf, knit.
Row 14: Inc, p41. *(43 sts)*
Row 15: K2tog, k40, inc. *(43 sts)*
Row 16: P41, p2tog. *(42 sts)*
Row 17: Knit.
Row 18: With co and tf, *k40, P2tog. *(41 sts)*
Row 19: With tf, k2tog, k38, inc. *(41 sts)*
Row 20: Purl.
Row 21: Knit.
Row 22: With co, p29, cast (bind) off *12 sts in loopy st.
Row 23: With tf, k2tog, k27. *(28 sts)*

Row 24: With tf, p20, with co and tf, cast (bind) off *9 sts in loopy st. *(19 sts)*
Row 25: With tf, k2tog, k15, k2tog. *(17 sts)*
Row 26: With tf, p8, with co and tf, cast (bind) off *9 sts in loopy st.
With tf, work 2 rows st st.
Row 29: Join in ba, k8, cast on 13 sts. *(21 sts)*
Cont in ba.
Row 30: P21.
Work 2 rows st st.
Row 33: K2tog, k to end. *(20 sts)*
Row 34: Cast (bind) off 6 sts, p to end. *(14 sts)*
Row 35: K12, k2tog. *(13 sts)*
Row 36: Cast (bind) off 4 sts, p7 icos, p2tog.
(8 sts)
Cast (bind) off.

Tail

With 2¾mm (US 2) double-pointed knitting needles and tf, cast on 2 sts.
Work in i-cord as folls:
Knit 2 rows.
Row 3: Inc into both sts. *(4 sts)*
Row 4: Knit
Row 5: Inc, k2, inc. *(6 sts)*
Row 6: Knit.
Row 7: Inc, k4, inc. *(8 sts)*
Row 8: Knit.
Knit 2 rows.
Row 11: K3, join in co and make *2-finger loopy st on 4th st only, k4 in tf.
Row 12: Knit in tf.
Rep last 2 rows 11 times more, working 2-finger loopy st on first 5 rows and 3-finger loopy st on next 6 rows.
Knit 2 rows in tf.
Cast (bind) off.

Ear

(make 2 the same)
With 2¾mm (US 2) knitting needles and tf, cast on 12 sts.
Row 1: Knit
Row 2: Join in co, *3-finger loopy st to end.

Row 3: With tf, knit.
Row 4: Purl.
Row 5: K2tog, k8, k2tog. *(10 sts)*
Row 6: Purl
Row 7: K2tog, k6, k2tog. *(8 sts)*
Row 8: Purl.
Row 9: K2tog, k4, k2tog. *(6 sts)*
Row 10: With co and tf, *3-finger loopy st to end.
Row 11: With tf, knit.
Cast (bind) off.

Collar

With 2¾mm (US 2) knitting needles and fr, cast on 26 sts.
Knit one row.
Cast (bind) off.

To Make Up

Sew in ends, leaving ends from cast on and cast (bound) off rows for sewing up. Using whip stitch, sew up legs starting at paw. Pipecleaners are useful for rigidity, as over-stuffing the loopy stitch legs makes them holey. Using whip stitch, sew along top of leg, leaving an end to sew leg to body. Using whip stitch, sew down back and tummy and across head and nose, using tf for body and ba for head and nose. Leave a 2.5cm (1in) gap in tummy for stuffing. Stuff then sew up gap.
Using whip stitch, sew on front legs straight with seams at back; back legs are at a slight angle with seams at back.
Sew tail to base of back with longest loops closest to body. Thread yarn from cast on end through tail to body and pull up slightly to make tail curve.
Sew ears to top of head as shown in photograph. Cut loops of loopy st on ears. Using black yarn, embroider the nose using satin stitch and make two French knots for eyes.
Put collar around neck and join ends.

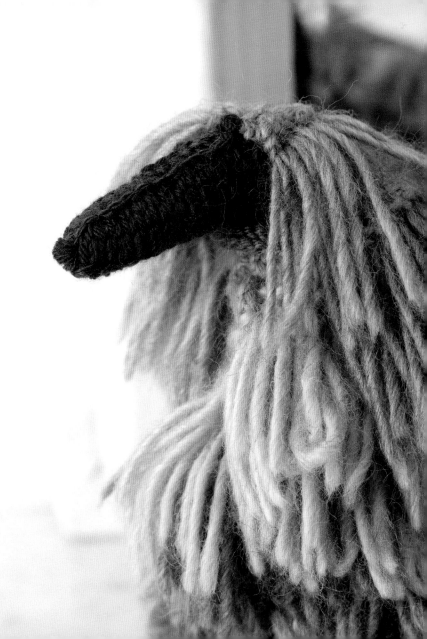

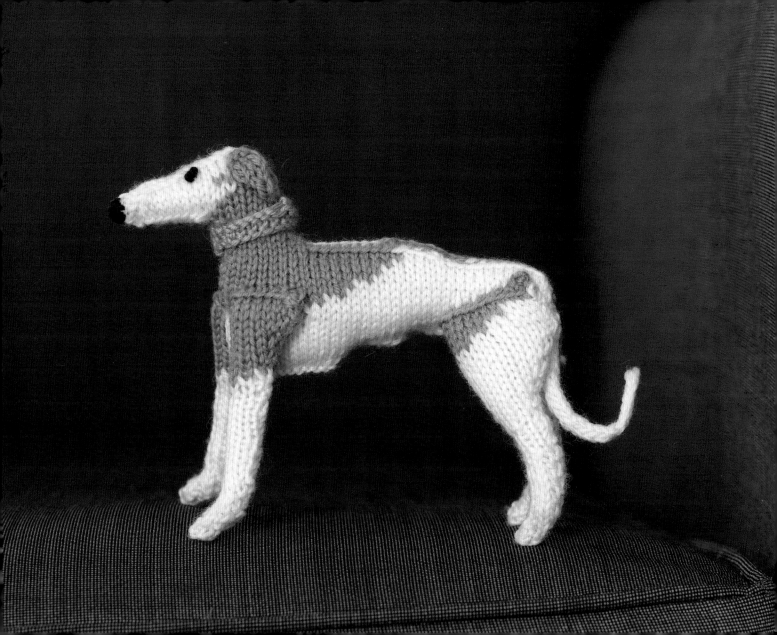

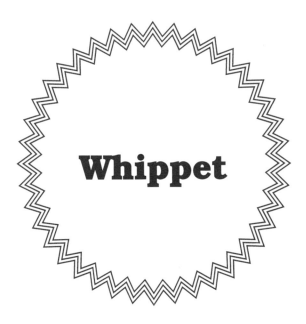

Whippet

The Whippet, known as 'the poor man's racehorse', is the perfect dog: friendly, gentle, loving and lazy. They like short bursts of exercise followed by a lot of lounging, stay close to their owners and will sleep in bed with them if at all possible; my Whippet also sings. Due to their elegant lines, Whippets feature in many paintings by artists from Pompeo Batoni to Lucien Freud. Well-known Whippets include Misse and Turlu who belonged to Louis XV, and my dog, Lily.

Whippet

To enhance the Whippet's fragility do not over-stuff any part, and do use pipecleaners in the legs.

Measurements
Length excluding tail: 15cm (6in)
Height to top of head: 12cm (4¾in)

Materials
- Pair of 2¾mm (US 2) knitting needles
- Pair of 2¾mm (US 2) double-pointed knitting needles
- 25g (1oz) of Rowan Pure Wool 4ply in Snow 412 (sn)
- 10g (¼oz) of Rowan Pure Wool 4ply in Shale 402 (sh)
- Small amount of Rowan Pure Wool 4ply in Eau de Nil 450 (en) for collar
- Tiny amount of Rowan Pure Wool 4ply in Black 404 for nose and eyes
- Pipecleaners for legs

Abbreviations
See page 172.

Back Leg
(make 2 the same)
With 2¾mm (US 2) knitting needles and sn, cast on 6 sts.
Beg with a k row, work 2 rows st st.
Row 3: Inc, k1, k2tog, k1, inc. *(7 sts)*
Row 4: Purl.
Row 5: Inc, k5, inc. *(9 sts)*
Row 6: Purl.
Row 7: Inc, k1, k2tog, k1, k2tog, k1, inc. *(9 sts)*

Row 8: Purl.
Rep last 2 rows twice more.
Work 2 rows st st.
Row 15: K2tog, k1, inc, k1, inc, k1, k2tog. *(9 sts)*
Row 16: Purl.
Row 17: Inc, k3, inc, k3, inc. *(12 sts)*
Row 18: Purl.
Row 19: Inc, k4, inc into next 2 sts, k4, inc. *(16 sts)*
Row 20: Purl.
Row 21: Inc, k14, inc. *(18 sts)*
Row 22: Purl.
Row 23: Knit.
Row 24: P6sn, join in sh, p12sh.
Row 25: Incsh, k10sh, k6sn, incsn. *(20 sts)*
Row 26: P10sn, p10sh.
Row 27: Incsh, k7sh, k11sn, incsn. *(22 sts)*
Row 28: P15sn, p7sh.
Row 29: K5sh, k17sn.
Row 30: P22sn.
Cast (bind) off in sn.

Front Leg
(make 2 the same)
With 2¾mm (US 2) knitting needles and sn, cast on 6 sts.
Beg with a k row, work 2 rows st st.
Row 3: Inc, k2tog twice, inc. *(6 sts)*
Row 4: Inc, p4, inc. *(8 sts)*
Row 5: Inc, k2tog, k2, k2tog, inc. *(8 sts)*
Row 6: Purl.
Row 7: Inc, k2tog, k2, k2tog, inc. *(8 sts)*
Row 8: Purl.
Row 9: Inc, k2, k2tog, k2, inc. *(9 sts)*
Row 10: Purl.
Work 10 rows st st.
Row 21: K4sn, join in sh, k5sh.
Row 22: P6sh, p3sn.
Row 23: K2sn, k7sh.
Cont in sh.
Row 24: Purl.
Row 25: Inc, k7, inc. *(11 sts)*
Work 3 rows st st.

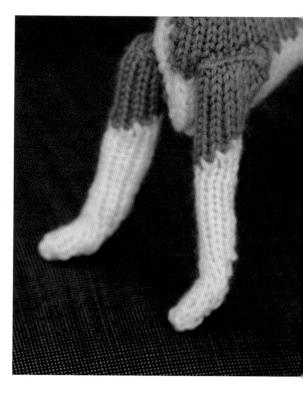

Legs
Make sure your leg seams are super-neat and firm; you don't want your Whippet to have lumpy legs.

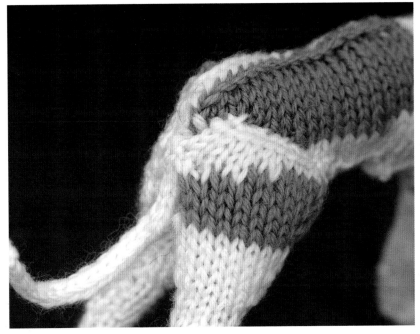

Body

Use the intarsia technique and a separate ball of each colour yarn, twisting the colours firmly over one another at the joins to prevent holes (see page 172).

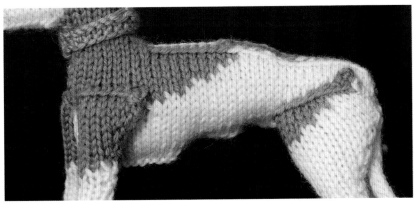

Row 29: Inc, k9, inc. *(13 sts)*
Row 30: Purl.
Row 31: Inc, k11, inc. *(15 sts)*
Cast (bind) off.

Right Side of Body and Head

With 2¾mm (US 2) knitting needles and sn, cast on 11 sts.
Beg with a k row, work 2 rows st st.
Row 3: Inc, k10, cast on 6 sts. *(18 sts)*
Row 4: Purl.
Row 5: K18, cast on 6 sts. *(24 sts)*
Row 6: Purl.
Row 7: K24, cast on 6 sts. *(30 sts)*
Row 8: Purl.

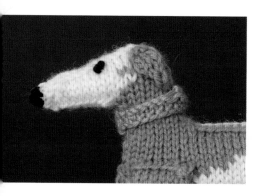

Head

The set of the ears is an essential part of a Whippet's character, so pin them in position first and only sew when you are sure they look right.

Row 9: K20sn, join in sh, k10sh, cast on 4 sts sh. *(34 sts)*
Row 10: P17sh, p17sn.
Row 11: Incsn, k16sn, k17sh. *(35 sts)*
Row 12: P19sh, p16sn.
Row 13: K16sn, k19sh.
Row 14: P2togsh, p16sh, p17sn. *(34 sts)*
Row 15: K17sn, k15sh, k2togsh. *(33 sts)*
Row 16: Cast (bind) off 10 sts sh, p6sh icos, p17sn. *(23 sts)*
Row 17: K18sn, k3sh, k2togsh. *(22 sts)*
Row 18: Cast (bind) off 12 sts sh, p4sh icos, p6sn. *(10 sts)*
Row 19: K6sn, k2sh, k2togsh. *(9 sts)*
Row 20: P2togsh, p2sh, p5sn. *(8 sts)*
Row 21: K4sn, k4sh.
Row 22: P4sh, p4sn.
Row 23: K2sn, k6sh.
Row 24: P8sh, cast on 10 sts sn. *(18 sts)*
Row 25: K11sn, k7sh.
Row 26: P2togsh, p5sh, p9sn, p2togsn. *(16 sts)*
Row 27: K2togsn, k8sn, k6sh. *(15 sts)*
Row 28: P2togsh, p4sh, p7sn, p2togsn. *(13 sts)*
Row 29: Cast (bind) off 4 sts sn icos, k4sn, k5sh. *(9 sts)*
Row 30: P7sn, p2togsn. *(8 sts)*
Row 31: Cast (bind) off 3 sts sn, k3sn icos, k2togsn. *(4 sts)*
Cast (bind) off in sn.

Left Side of Body and Head

With 2¾mm (US 2) knitting needles and sn, cast on 11 sts.
Row 1: Knit.
Row 2: Inc, p10, cast on 6 sts. *(18 sts)*
Row 3: Knit.
Row 4: P18, cast on 6 sts. *(24 sts)*
Row 5: Knit.
Row 6: P24, cast on 6 sts. *(30 sts)*
Row 7: Knit.
Row 8: P30, cast on 4 sts. *(34 sts)*
Row 9: K26sn, k8sh.

Row 10: Inc, p9sh, p24sn. *(35 sts)*
Row 11: K23sn, k12sh.
Row 12: P13sh, p22sn.
Row 13: K2togsh, k17sn, k16sh. *(34 sts)*
Row 14: P16sh, p16sn, p2togsn. *(33 sts)*
Row 15: Cast (bind) off 10 sts sn, k6sn icos, k17sh. *(23 sts)*
Row 16: P18sh, p3sn, p-2togsn. *(22 sts)*
Row 17: Cast (bind) off 12 sts sn, k4sh icos, k6sn. *(10 sts)*
Row 18: P8sh, p2togsh. *(9 sts)*
Row 19: K2togsh, k7sh. *(8 sts)*
Work 3 rows st st in sh.
Row 23: K8sh, cast on 10 sts sn. *(18 sts)*
Row 24: P11sn, p7sh.
Row 25: K2togsh, k4sh, k10sn, k2togsn. *(16 sts)*
Row 26: P2togsn, p10sn, p4sh. *(15 sts)*
Row 27: K2togsh, k4sh, k7sn, k2togsn. *(13 sts)*
Row 28: Cast (bind) off 4 sts sn, p6sn icos, p3sh. *(9 sts)*
Row 29: K2sh, k5sn, k2togsn. *(8 sts)*
Row 30: Cast (bind) off 3 sts sn, p3sn icos, p2togsn. *(4 sts)*
Cast (bind) off in sn.

Tail

With 2¾mm (US 2) double-pointed knitting needles and sn, cast on 4 sts.
Work in i-cord as folls:
Knit 10 rows.
Next row: K2tog, k2. *(3 sts)*
Knit 8 rows.
Next row: K2tog, k1. *(2 sts)*
Knit 4 rows.
Next row: K2tog and fasten off.

Ear
(make 2 the same)
With 2¾mm (US 2) knitting needles and sh,
cast on 4 sts.
Beg with a k row, work 2 rows st st.
Row 3: K2tog twice.
Row 4: Purl.
Row 5: K2tog and fasten off.

Collar
With 2¾mm (US 2) knitting needles and en,
cast on 20 sts.
Row 1: Knit.
Row 2: Cast (bind) off 5 sts, k to end. *(15 sts)*
Row 3: Knit.
Cast (bind) off.

To Make Up
Sew in ends, leaving ends from cast on
and cast (bound) off rows for sewing up.
Using mattress or whip stitch, sew up legs
starting at paw. Pipecleaners are useful for
rigidity as the legs are fairly thin. Using
whip stitch, sew along top of leg, leaving an
end to sew leg to body.
Using mattress or whip stitch, sew up all
around body, leaving a 2.5cm (1in) gap in
tummy for stuffing. Turn right side out, stuff
then sew up gap with mattress stitch.
Using whip stitch, sew legs to body as
shown in photograph, with back legs at
an angle and seams facing backwards.
Sew tail to base of back.
Sew ears to head as shown in photograph.
Using black yarn, embroider the nose
using satin stitch and make two French
knots for eyes.
Put collar around neck and sew ends
together at the front.

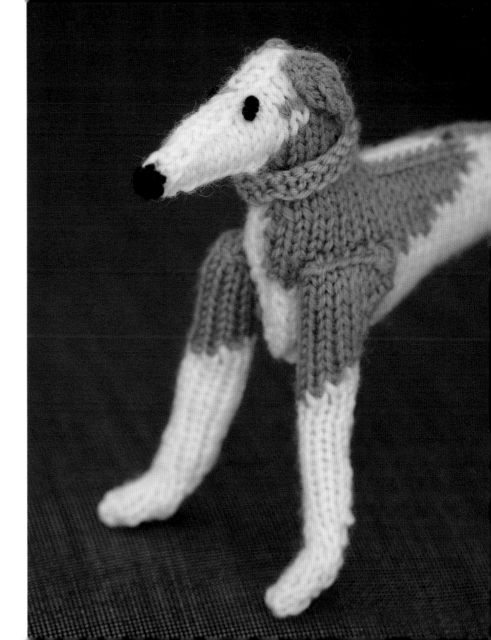

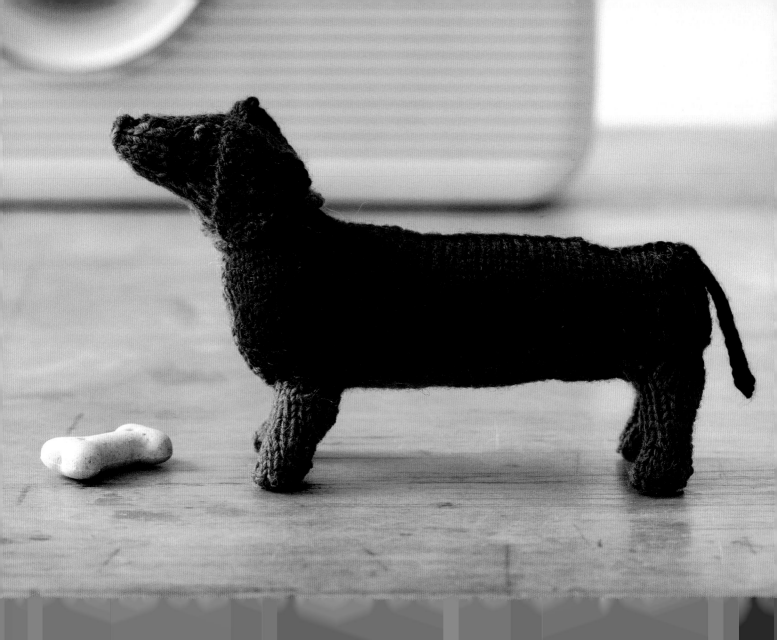

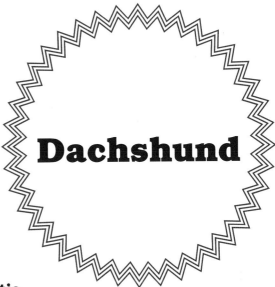

Dachshund

Instantly recognizable due to its idiosyncratic design, the Dachshund has extremely short legs and an elongated body and so has trouble getting up stairs, which can be a plus. They originated in Germany where the word *dachshund* means 'badger dog'. They have silky ears, enchanting faces, are lively, courageous and wonderfully portable, but they can be stubborn and vocal. Dachshunds are a popular choice with artists: Pablo Picasso, Andy Warhol and David Hockney have all owned Dachshunds, variously called Lump, Archie, Amos, Stanley and Boodgie.

Dachshund

Simple and rewarding to knit, with a very small amount of intarsia.

Measurements

Length: 19cm (7½in)
Height to top of head: 11cm (4½in)

Materials

- Pair of 2¾mm (US 2) knitting needles
- 4 spare 2¾mm (US 2) knitting needles or small stitch holders or safety pins
- 5g (⅛oz) of Rowan Pure Wool 4ply in Hessian 416 (he)
- 15g (½oz) of Rowan Pure Wool 4ply in Black 404 (bl)
- Small amount of Rowan Pure Wool 4ply in Framboise 456 (fr) for collar

Abbreviations

See page 172.

Right Back Leg

With he, cast on 11 sts.
Beg with a k row, work 2 rows st st.
Row 3: K3, k2tog, k1, k2tog, k3. *(9 sts)*
Row 4: Purl.
Row 5: K2, k2tog, k1, k2tog, k2. *(7 sts)*
Row 6: Purl.**
Row 7: Knit.
Row 8: Purl.
Row 9: Inc, k5, inc. *(9 sts)*
Row 10: Purl.
Row 11: Inc, k2, inc, k1, inc, k2, inc. *(13 sts).***
Row 12: Join in bl, p3bl, p10he.

Row 13: K5he, inche, k1he, inche, k5bl. *(15 sts)*
Row 14: P6bl, incbl, p1he, inche, p6he. *(17 sts)*
Row 15: K7he, inche, k1bl, incbl, k7bl. *(19 sts)*
Row 16: P10bl, p9he.
Row 17: Cast (bind) off 9 sts he, k to end in bl (hold 10 sts on spare needle for Right Side of Body).

Left Back Leg

Work as for Right Back Leg to ***.
Row 12: P10he, join in bl, p3bl.
Row 13: K5bl, inche, k1he, inche, k5he. *(15 sts)*
Row 14: P6he, inche, p1he, incbl, p6bl. *(17 sts)*
Row 15: K7bl, incbl, k1bl, inche, k7he. *(19 sts)*
Row 16: P9he, p10bl.
Row 17: K10bl, cast (bind) off 9 sts he (hold 10 sts on spare needle for Left Side of Body).

Right Front Leg

Work as for Right Back Leg to **.
Row 7: Inc, k5, inc. *(9 sts)*
Row 8: Purl.
Row 9: Inc, k7, inc. *(11 sts)*
Row 10: Purl.*
Row 11: Inche, k8he, join in bl, k1bl, incbl. *(13 sts)*
Row 12: P5bl, p8he.
Row 13: Cast (bind) off 6 sts he, k to end in bl (hold 7 sts on spare needle for Right Side of Body).

Left Front Leg

Work as for Right Front Leg to *.
Row 11: Join in bl, incbl, k1bl, k8he, inche. *(13 sts)*
Row 12: P8he, p5bl.
Row 13: K7bl, cast (bind) off 6 sts he (hold 7 sts on spare needle for Left Side of Body).

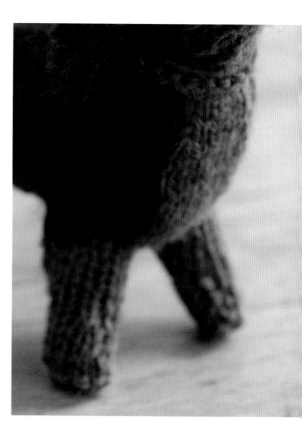

Legs

When sewing up match the curve of the tummy with the leg shaping, sewing up one side then the other.

Right Side of Body

Row 1: With bl, cast on 2 sts, with RS facing k7 from spare needle of Right Front Leg, cast on 7 sts. *(16 sts)*

Row 2: Purl.

Row 3: Inc, k15, cast on 6 sts. *(23 sts)*

Row 4: Purl.

Row 5: Inc, k22, cast on 6 sts. *(30 sts)*

Row 6: Purl.

Row 7: K30, cast on 2 sts, with RS facing k10 from spare needle of Right Back Leg, cast on 2 sts. *(44 sts)*

Work 3 rows st st.

Row 11: Inc, k43. *(45 sts)*

Row 12: Purl.

Row 13: K42, k2tog, k1. *(44 sts)*

Row 14: Purl

Row 15: K41, k2tog, k1. *(43 sts)*

Row 16: P1, p2tog, p40. *(42 sts)*

Row 17: K39, k2tog, k1. *(41 sts)*

Row 18: Cast (bind) off 8 sts, p to end. *(33 sts)*

Row 19: K11 (hold 11 sts on spare needle for neck and head), cast (bind) off rem 22 sts.

Left Side of Body

Row 1: With bl, cast on 2 sts, with WS facing p7 from spare needle of Left Front Leg, cast on 7 sts. *(16 sts)*

Row 2: Knit.

Row 3: Inc, p15, cast on 6 sts. *(23 sts)*

Row 4: Knit.

Row 5: Inc, p22, cast on 6 sts. *(30 sts)*

Row 6: Knit.

Row 7: P30, cast on 2 sts, with WS facing p10 from spare needle of Left Back Leg, cast on 2 sts. *(44 sts)*

Work 3 rows st st.

Row 11: Inc, p43. *(45 sts)*

Body

Stuff the body quite lightly so you don't detract from its length.

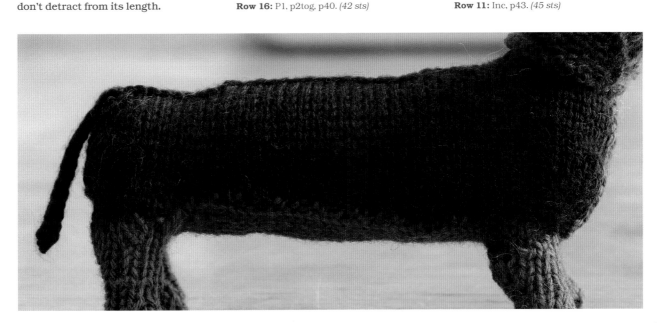

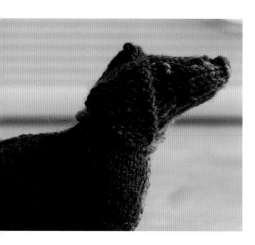

Head

Do make sure the stuffing is pushed into the tip of the nose.

Row 12: Knit.
Row 13: P42, p2tog, p1. *(44 sts)*
Row 14: Knit.
Row 15: P41, p2tog, p1. *(43 sts)*
Row 16: K1, k2tog, k40. *(42 sts)*
Row 17: P39, p2tog, p1. *(41 sts)*
Row 18: Cast (bind) off 8 sts, k to end. *(33 sts)*
Row 19: P11 (hold 11 sts on spare needle for neck and head), cast (bind) off rem 22 sts.

Neck and Head

Row 1: With bl, and with RS facing k2, k2tog, k5, k2tog from spare needle of Right Side of Body then k2tog, k5, k2tog, k2 from spare needle of Left Side of Body. *(18 sts)*
Row 2: Purl.
Row 3: K13, pult (pick up loop below next st on left needle by inserting tip of right needle from back through loop – this stops a hole forming when turning work – then turn, leaving rem 5 sts on left needle unworked).
Row 4: Working top of head on centre 8 sts only, p2tog (first st of p2tog is loop picked up at end of last row), p7, pult.
Row 5: K2tog, k7, pult.
Row 6: P2tog, p7, pult.
Row 7: K2tog, k7, pult.
Row 8: P2tog, p7, pult.
Row 9: K2tog, k12.
Row 10: Join in he, p2he, p14bl, p2he.
Row 11: K3he, k12bl, k3he.
Row 12: P3he, p12bl, p3he.
Row 13: K4he, k9bl, pult (leave 5 sts unworked on left needle).
Row 14: P2tog, p7bl, pult.
Row 15: K2tog, k7bl, pult.
Row 16: P2tog, p7bl, pult.
Row 17: K2togbl, k2he, k2bl, k2he, k2bl, k4he.
Row 18: P3he, p2togbl, p8bl, p2togbl, p3he. *(16 sts)*
Row 19: K3he, k2togbl, k6bl, k2togbl, k3he. *(14 sts)*

Row 20: P2he, p10bl, p2he.
Row 21: K2he, k10bl, k2he.
Row 22: P3he, p8bl, p3he.
Row 23: K4he, k2togbl, k2bl, k2togbl, k4he. *(12 sts)*
Row 24: P5he, p2bl, p5he.
Row 25: K5he, k2bl, k5he.
Row 26: P2toghe, p3he, p2bl, p3he, p2toghe. *(10 sts)*
Row 27: K4he, k2bl, k4he.
Row 28: P2toghe, p2he, p2bl, p2he, p2toghe. *(8 sts)*
Cast (bind) off 3 sts he, 2 sts bl, 3 sts he.

Tummy

With he, cast on 8 sts.
Beg with a k row, work 2 rows st st.
Next row: K2tog, k4, k2tog. *(6 sts)*
Next row: P2tog, p2, p2tog. *(4 sts)*
Work 6 rows st st.
Next row: Inc, k2, inc. *(6 sts)*
Next row: Inc, p4, inc. *(8 sts)*
Work 32 rows st st.
Next row: K2tog, k4, k2tog. *(6 sts)*
Next row: P2tog, p2, p2tog. *(4 sts)*
Work 4 rows st st.
Next row: Inc, k2, inc. *(6 sts)*
Next row: Inc, p4, inc. *(8 sts)*
Work 10 rows st st.
Next row: K2tog, k4, k2tog. *(6 sts)*
Work 7 rows st st.
Next row: K2tog, k2, k2tog. *(4 sts)*
Work 3 rows st st.
Next row: K2tog twice.
Work 2 rows st st.
Next row: P2tog and fasten off.

Tail

With bl, cast on 18 sts.
Cast (bind) off.

Ear

(make 2 the same)
With bl, cast on 3 sts.
Row 1: K3.
Row 2: Inc, k1, inc. *(5 sts)*
Row 3: Knit.
Row 4: Inc, k4. *(6 sts)*
Knit 3 rows.
Row 8: Inc, k5. *(7 sts)*
Knit 3 rows.
Row 12: Inc, k6. *(8 sts)*
Knit 5 rows.
Row 18: Cast (bind) off 3 sts, k to end. *(5 sts)*
Row 19: Knit.
Cast (bind) off.

Collar

With fr, cast on 26 sts.
Knit one row.
Cast (bind) off.

To Make Up

Sew in ends, leaving ends from cast on
and cast (bound) off rows for sewing up.
Using mattress or whip stitch, sew up legs
starting at paw. Stuff all four legs.
Using mattress or whip stitch, sew along
back and around bottom. At head, fold in
half and sew cast (bound) off edges of nose
together. Sew cast on row of tummy to
bottom end of dog and sew cast (bound)
off row to nose. Ease and sew tummy to
fit body, matching curves to legs, leaving
a 2.5cm (1in) gap in one side for stuffing.
Turn right side out, stuff and sew up gap
with mattress stitch. Ease body into shape.
Sew on tail just where dog's bottom begins
to curve.
With the cast (bound) off row, sew ears to
head as shown in photograph. Using black
yarn, embroider nose using satin stitch and
in hessian make two French knots for eyes.
Sew ends of collar together and slide over
head onto neck.

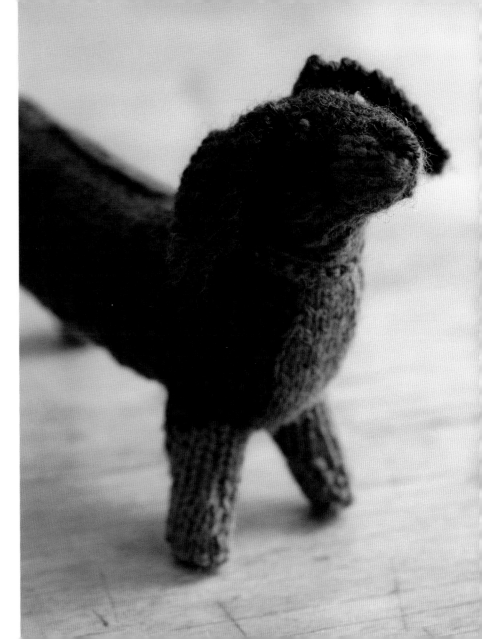

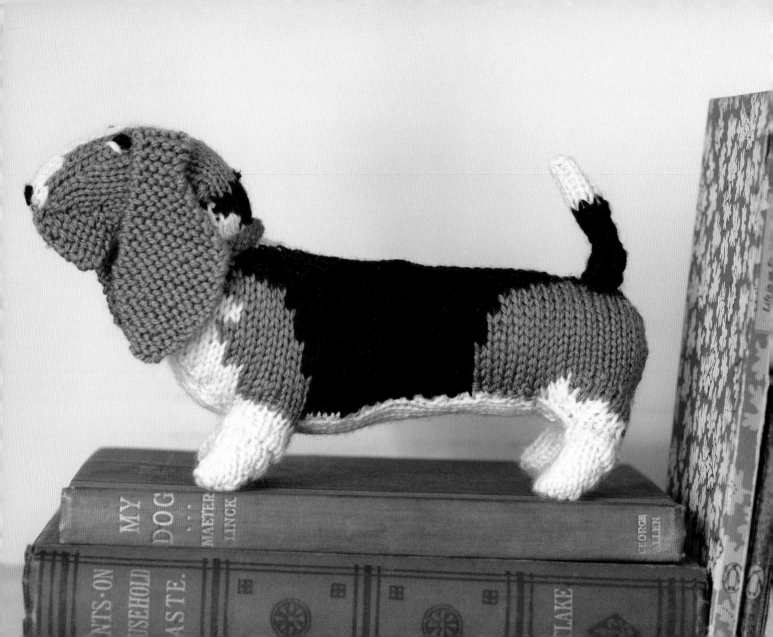

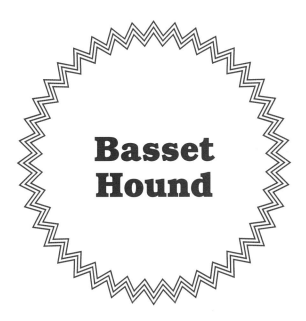

Basset Hound

The Basset is a very low-slung dog – in fact the name derives from *bas* meaning 'low' in French. They have extremely long ears and droopy eyes, which make them prone to numerous ailments. Although bred to hunt, they are friendly and child loving. They live for food and are champion beggars and stealers. Well-known Bassets include the stars of the Hush Puppie shoe advertisements and Fred Basset from the cartoon strip.

Basset Hound

The jowls and wrinkly legs give the Basset its classic hangdog look.

Measurements

Length: 21cm (8¼in)
Height to top of head: 12cm (4¾in)

Materials

- Pair of 2¾mm (US 2) knitting needles
- 4 spare 2¾mm (US 2) knitting needles or small stitch holders or safety pins
- 10g (¼oz) of Rowan Cashsoft 4ply in Cream 433 (cr)
- 10g (¼oz) of Rowan Cashsoft 4ply in Walnut 441 (wa)
- 10g (¼oz) of Rowan Cashsoft 4ply in Black 422 (bl)
- Small amount of Rowan Cashsoft 4ply in Bluebottle 449 (bu) for collar

Abbreviations

See page 172.

Right Back Leg

With cr, cast on 11 sts.
Beg with a k row, work 2 rows st st.
Row 3: Inc, k2, k2tog, k1, k2tog, k2, inc. *(11 sts)*
Row 4: Purl.
Rep last 2 rows once more.
Work 5 rows st st.
Row 12: Purl and pick up every 2nd st on 3rd row below (to make a ridge) as folls: [p1, p2tog (2nd st is the loop from 3 rows below)], rep to last st, p1.

Row 13: K2tog, k2, inc, k1, inc, k2, k2tog. *(11 sts)*
Row 14: P4, inc, p1, inc, p4.* *(13 sts)*
Row 15: K5cr, inccr, k1cr, inccr, k2cr, join in wa, k3wa. *(15 sts)*
Row 16: P6wa, inccr, p1cr, inccr, p6cr. *(17 sts)*
Row 17: K7cr, inccr, k1cr, inccr, k7wa. *(19 sts)*
Row 18: P7wa, p12cr.
Row 19: Cast (bind) off 9 st cr, k3cr icos, k7wa (hold 10 sts on spare needle for Right Side of Body).

Left Back Leg

Work as for Right Back Leg to *.
Row 15: Join in wa, k3wa, k2cr, inccr, k1cr, inccr, k5cr. *(15 sts)*
Row 16: P6cr, inccr, p1cr, inccr, p6wa. *(17 sts)*
Row 17: K7wa, inccr, k1cr, inccr, k7cr. *(19 sts)*
Row 18: P12cr, p7wa.
Row 19: K7wa, k3cr, cast (bind) off 9 sts cr (hold 10 sts on spare needle for Left Side of Body).

Right Front Leg

With cr, cast on 11 sts.
Beg with a k row, work 2 rows st st.
Row 3: Inc, k2, k2tog, k1, k2tog, k2, inc. *(11 sts)*
Row 4: Purl.
Rep last 2 rows once more.
Work 3 rows st st.
Row 10: Purl and pick up every 2nd st on 3rd row below (to make a ridge) as folls: [p1, p2tog (2nd st is the loop from 3 rows below)], rep to last st, p1.
Row 11: Inc, k9, inc. *(13 sts)*
Work 4 rows st st.
Row 16: Purl and pick up every 2nd st on 5th row below (to make a ridge) as folls: [p1, p2tog (2nd st is the loop from 5 rows below)], rep to last st, p1.**
Row 17: Cast (bind) off 6 sts, k to end (hold 7 sts on spare needle for Right Side of Body).

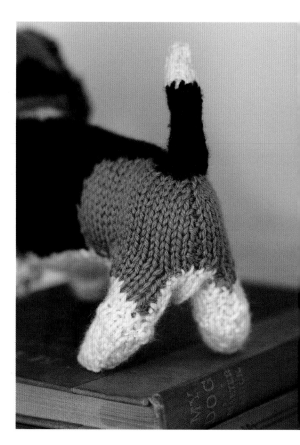

Legs

When sewing up the legs make sure you secure the ridge that emphasizes the folds of skin.

Left Front Leg

Work as for Right Front Leg to **.
Row 17: K7, cast (bind) off 6 sts (hold 7 sts on spare needle for Left Side of Body).

Right Side of Body

Row 1: With cr, cast on 2 sts, with RS facing k2cr from spare needle of Right Front Leg, join in wa, k5wa from spare needle of Right Front Leg, join in bl, cast on 7 sts bl. *(16 sts)*
Row 2: P7bl, p6wa, p2cr, inccr. *(17 sts)*
Row 3: Inccr, k2cr, k6wa, k8bl, cast on 6 sts bl. *(24 sts)*
Row 4: P14bl, p6wa, p3cr, inccr. *(25 sts)*
Row 5: Inccr, k4cr, k6wa, k14bl, cast on 6 sts wa. *(32 sts)*
Row 6: P6wa, p14bl, p6wa, p6cr.
Row 7: Inccr, k3cr, k7wa, k15bl, k6wa, with RS facing k10wa from spare needle of Right Back Leg, cast on 2 sts wa. *(45 sts)*
Row 8: P18wa, p15bl, p7wa, p5cr.
Row 9: Inccr, k4cr, k7wa, k15bl, k18wa. *(46 sts)*
Row 10: P18wa, p16bl, p7wa, p5cr.

Body

Use the intarsia technique and a separate ball of each colour yarn, twisting the colours firmly over one another at the joins to prevent holes (see page 172).

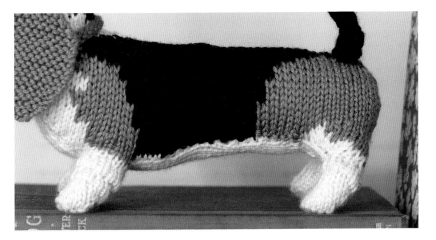

Row 11: Inccr, k4cr, k7wa, k17bl, k17wa. *(47 sts)*
Row 12: P17wa, p17bl, p5wa, p8cr.
Row 13: K8cr, k4wa, k18bl, k17wa.
Row 14: P16wa, p19bl, p5wa, p7cr.
Row 15: K2togcr, k3cr, k5wa, k21bl, k16wa. *(46 sts)*
Row 16: P15wa, p23bl, p3wa, p2bl, p3cr.
Row 17: K2togcr, k2cr, k2bl, k1wa, k26bl, k11wa, k2togwa. *(44 sts)*
Row 18: P2togwa, p8wa, p30bl, p4cr. *(43 sts)*
Row 19: K6cr, k35bl, k2togbl. *(42 sts)*
Row 20: P2togbl, p4bl (hold 5 sts on spare needle for tail) cast (bind) off 14 sts bl, p15bl icos, p7cr. *(22 sts)*
Row 21: K11cr, cast (bind) off 11 sts bl (hold 11 sts on spare needle for neck).

Left Side of Body

Row 1: With cr, cast on 2 sts, with WS facing p2cr from spare needle of Left Front Leg, join in wa, p5wa from spare needle of Left Front Leg, join in bl, cast on 7 sts bl. *(16 sts)*
Row 2: K7bl, k6wa, k2cr, inccr. *(17 sts)*
Row 3: Inccr, p2cr, p6wa, p8bl, cast on 6 sts bl. *(24 sts)*
Row 4: K14bl, k6wa, k3cr, inccr. *(25 sts)*
Row 5: Inccr, p4cr, p6wa, p14bl, cast on 6 sts wa. *(32 sts)*
Row 6: K6wa, k14bl, k6wa, k6cr.
Row 7: Inccr, p3cr, p7wa, p15bl, p6wa, with WS facing p10wa from spare needle of Left Back Leg, cast on 2 sts wa. *(45 sts)*
Row 8: K18wa, k15bl, k7wa, k5cr.
Row 9: Inccr, p4cr, p7wa, p15bl, p18wa. *(46 sts)*
Row 10: K18wa, k16bl, k7wa, k5cr.
Row 11: Inccr, p4cr, p7wa, p17bl, p17wa. *(47 sts)*
Row 12: K17wa, k17bl, k5wa, k8cr.
Row 13: P8cr, p4wa, p18bl, p17wa.
Row 14: K16wa, k19bl, k5wa, k7cr.
Row 15: P2togcr, p3cr, p5wa, p21bl, p16wa. *(46 sts)*

Row 16: K15wa, k23bl, k3wa, k2bl, k3cr.
Row 17: P2togcr, p2cr, p2bl, p1wa, p26bl, p11wa, p2togwa. *(44 sts)*
Row 18: K2togwa, k8wa, k30bl, k4cr. *(43 sts)*
Row 19: P6cr, p35bl, p2togbl. *(42 sts)*
Row 20: K2togbl, k4bl (hold sts open for tail), cast (bind) off 14 sts bl, k15bl icos, k7cr. *(22 sts)*
Row 21: P11cr, cast (bind) off 11 sts bl (hold 11 sts on spare needle for neck).

Neck and Head

Row 1: With cr, and with RS facing k11 from spare needle of Right Side of Body then k11 from spare needle of Left Side of Body. *(22 sts)*
Row 2: Purl.
Row 3: K2tog, k18, k2tog. *(20 sts)*
Row 4: P7cr, join in bl, p6bl, p7cr.
Row 5: K4cr, k2togbl, k8bl, k2togbl, k4cr. *(18 sts)*
Row 6: P2cr, p14bl, p2cr.
Row 7: Join in wa, k4wa, k10bl, k4wa.
Row 8: P6wa, p6bl, p6wa.
Row 9: K8wa, k2bl, k5wa, pult (pick up loop below next st on left needle by inserting tip of right needle from back through loop – this stops a hole forming when turning work – then turn, leaving rem 3 sts on left needle unworked).
Row10: Working top of head on centre 12 sts only, p2togwa (first st of p2tog is loop picked up at end of last row), p11wa, pult.
Row11: K2togwa, k11wa, pult.
Rep last 2 rows once more.
Row 14: P2togwa, p11wa, pult.
Row 15: K2togwa, k to end. *(18 sts in total)*
Work 3 rows st st in wa.
Row 19: K14wa, pult (4 sts wa on left needle).
Row 20: P2togwa, p9wa, pult.
Row 21: K2togwa, k3wa, k2cr, k4wa, pult.
Row 22: P2togwa, p3wa, p2cr, p4wa, pult.
Rep last 2 rows once more.
Row 25: K2togwa, k3wa, k2cr, k8wa. *(18 sts)*

Row 26: P8wa, p2cr, p8wa.
Row 27: Incwa, k7wa, k2cr, k7wa, incwa. *(20 sts)*
Row 28: Incwa, p8wa, p2cr, p8wa, incwa. *(22 sts)*
Row 29: Incwa, k9wa, k2cr, k9wa, incwa. *(24 sts)*
Start garter stitch jowls
Row 30: K5wa, p6wa, p2cr, p6wa, k5wa.
Row 31: Incwa, k6wa, k2togwa, k2wa, k2cr, k2wa, k2togwa, k6wa, incwa. *(24 sts)*
Row 32: K5wa, p6wa, p2cr, p6wa, k5wa.
Row 33: K7wa, k2togwa, k2wa, k2cr, k2wa, k2togwa, k7wa. *(22 sts)*
Row 34: K5wa, p4wa, p4cr, p4wa, k5wa.
Row 35: K2togwa, k7wa, k4cr, k7wa, k2togwa. *(20 sts)*
Row 36: K5wa, p3wa, p4cr, p3wa, k5wa.
Row 37: K2togwa, k3wa, k2togwa, k6cr, k2togwa, k3wa, k2togwa. *(16 sts)*
Row 38: K4wa, p1wa, p6cr, p1wa, k4wa.
Row 39: K2togwa, k3wa, k6cr, k3wa, k2togwa. *(14 sts)*
Cast (bind) off 4 sts wa, 6 sts cr, 4 sts wa.

Tail

Row 1: With bl, and with RS facing k5 from spare needle of Left Side of Body then k5 from spare needle of Right Side of Body. *(10 sts)*
Row 2: Inc, p2, p2tog twice, p2, inc. *(10 sts)*
Row 3: Knit.
Rep last 2 rows once more.
Row 6: P2tog, p6, p2tog. *(8 sts)*
Row 7: Knit.
Row 8: P2tog, p1, inc into next 2 sts, p1, p2tog. *(8 sts)*
Work 4 rows st st.
Join in cr.
Work 3 rows st st.
Row 16: P2tog, p4, p2tog. *(6 sts)*
Work 2 rows st st.
Row 19: K2tog 3 times. *(3 sts)*
Row 20: P3tog and fasten off.

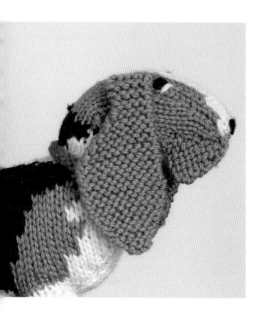

Head

The white stitch under the eyes enhances the droopy look.

Tummy

With cr, cast on 6 sts.
Beg with a k row, work 2 rows st st.
Row 3: K2tog, k2, k2tog. *(4 sts)*
Work 11 rows st st.
Row 15: Inc, k2, inc. *(6 sts)*
Row 16: Inc, p4, inc. *(8 sts)*
Work 30 rows st st.
Row 47: K2tog, k4, k2tog. *(6 sts)*
Row 48: P2tog, p2, p2tog. *(4 sts)*
Work 4 rows st st.
Row 53: Inc, k2, inc. *(6 sts)*
Row 54: Inc, p4, inc. *(8 sts)*
Work 2 rows st st.
Row 57: Inc, k6, inc. *(10 sts)*
Work 19 rows st st.
Row 77: K2tog, k6, k2tog. *(8 sts)*
Work 3 rows st st.
Row 81: Join in wa, k2wa, k4cr, k2wa.
Row 82: P3wa, p2cr, p3wa.
Cont in wa.
Row 83: K2tog, k4, k2tog. *(6 sts)*
Work 3 rows st st.
Row 87: K2tog, k2, k2tog. *(4 sts)*
Work 3 rows st st.
Row 91: K2tog twice. *(2 sts)*
Work 2 rows st st.
Row 94: P2tog and fasten off.

Ear

(make 2 the same)
With wa, cast on 4 sts.
Knit 2 rows.
Next row: Inc, k2, inc. *(6 sts)*
Knit 2 rows.
Next row: Inc, k4, inc. *(8 sts)*
Knit 2 rows.
Next row: Inc, k6, inc. *(10 sts)*
Knit 14 rows.
Next row: K2tog, k8. *(9 sts)*
Knit 1 row.
Next row: K2tog, k7. *(8 sts)*
Knit 1 row.
Next row: K2tog, k6. *(7 sts)*

Knit 1 row.
Next row: K2tog, k5. *(6 sts)*
Knit 1 row.
Next row: K2tog, k4. *(5 sts)*
Knit 6 rows.
Cast (bind) off.

Collar

With bu, cast on 30 sts.
Knit one row.
Cast (bind) off.

To Make Up

Sew in ends, leaving ends from cast on
and cast (bound) off rows for sewing up.
Using mattress or whip stitch, sew up
legs starting at paw. Stuff all four legs.
Using mattress or whip stitch, sew along
back, around tail and down bottom. At head,
fold in half and sew cast (bound) off edges of
nose together. Sew cast on row of tummy to
bottom end of dog and sew cast (bound) off
row to nose.
Using whip stitch, sew underside of
head to topside where st st changes to
garter st to make jowls (these hang down
below the seam).
Using mattress or whip stitch, ease and sew
tummy to fit body, matching curves to legs,
leaving a 2.5cm (1in) gap in one side for
stuffing. Turn right side out. Stuff and
sew up gap with mattress stitch. Mould body
into shape.
Sew on ears as in photograph, curved edge
facing towards tail of dog.
Using black yarn, embroider the nose using
satin stitch and make two French knots for
eyes. Using cream yarn, make a small
straight stitch under each eye, slightly
to the right/left of centre.
Sew ends of collar together and slide over
head onto neck.

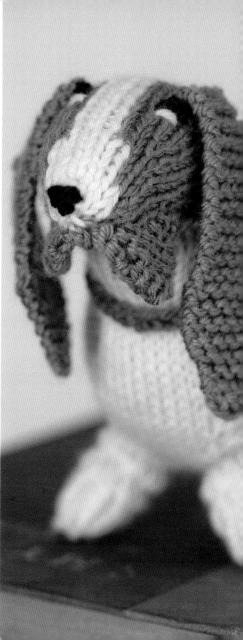

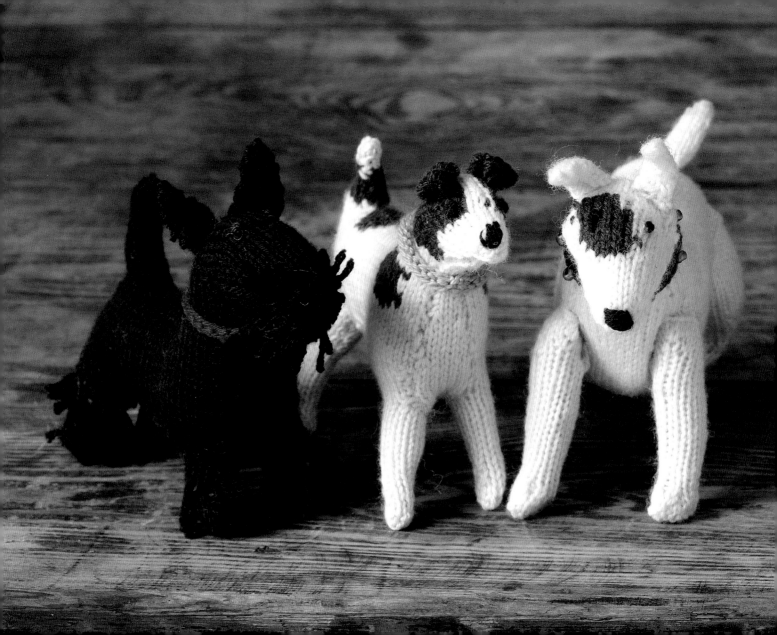

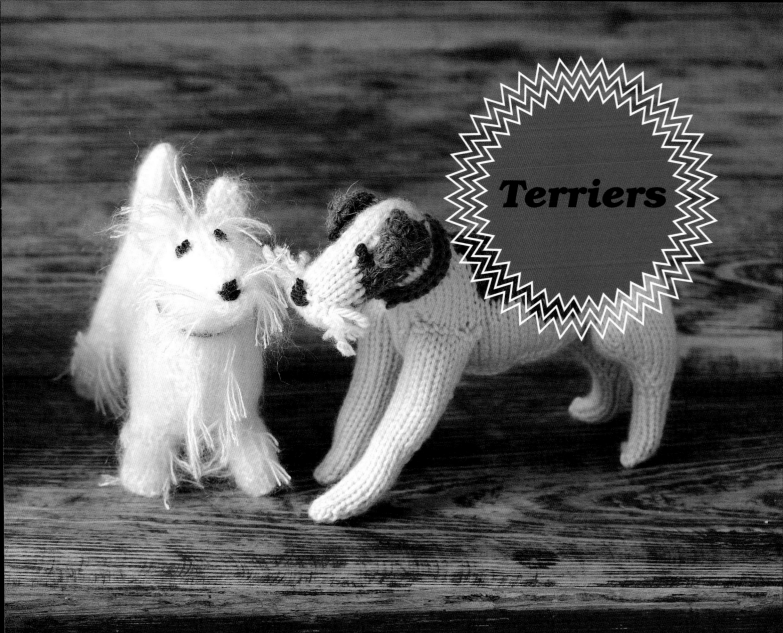

Terriers

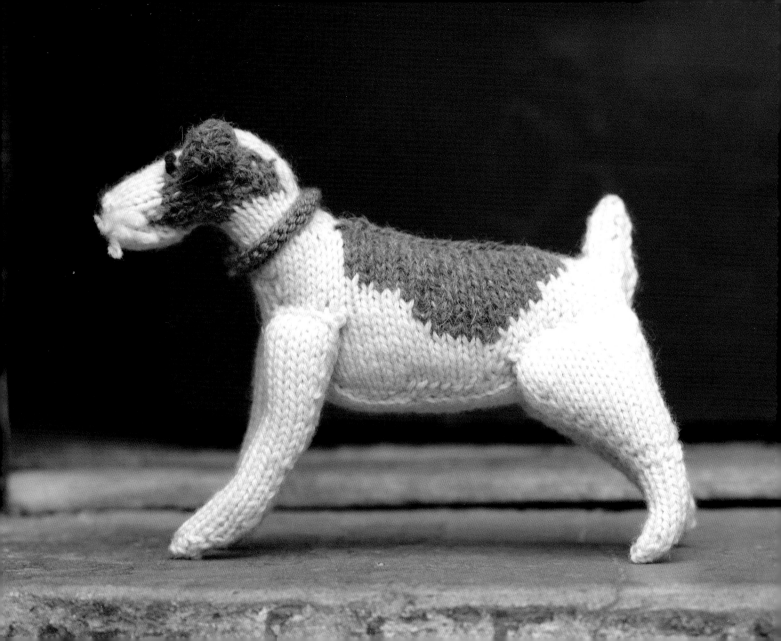

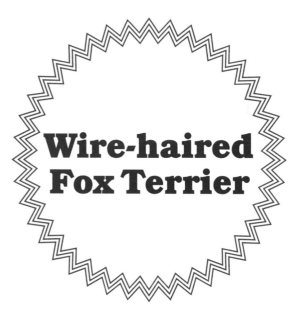

Wire-haired Fox Terrier

Clever and lively, Fox Terriers are bred to chase foxes into their burrows; the dogs' short tails are allegedly for pulling them out again. They will not tolerate nonsense from life forms whom they consider below themselves in importance, so be careful with children. Fox Terriers are also great escapers and need a lot of stimulation or will tend to naughtiness if bored. Famous Fox Terriers include Asta from *The Thin Man* films, the child's pull-along version on wheels and, of course, Tin Tin's chum, Snowy.

Wire-haired Fox Terrier

The characterful stance positively exudes energy and action.

Measurements

Length: 17cm (6¾in)
Height to top of head: 12cm (4¾in)

Materials

- Pair of 2¾mm (US 2) knitting needles
- 2 spare 2¾mm (US 2) knitting needles
- 25g (1oz) of Rowan Cashsoft 4ply in Cream 433 (cr)
- 5g (⅛oz) of Rowan Felted Tweed in Cinnamon 175 (cn)
- Small amount of Rowan Pure Wool 4ply in Glade 421 (gl) for collar
- Tiny amount of Rowan Pure Wool 4ply in Black 404 for nose and eyes
- Pipecleaners for legs

Abbreviations

See page 172.

Back Leg

(make 2 the same)
With cr, cast on 7 sts.
Beg with a k row, work 2 rows st st.
Row 3: Inc, k2tog, k1, k2tog, inc. *(7 sts)*
Row 4: Purl.
Row 5: Inc, k5, inc. *(9 sts)*
Row 6: Purl.
Work 6 rows st st.
Row 13: K2tog, inc into next 2 sts, k1, inc into next 2 sts, k2tog. *(11 sts)*

Row 14 and every alt row: Purl.
Row 15: K2tog, inc, k1, inc, k1, inc, k1, inc, k2tog. *(13 sts)*
Row 17: K5, inc, k1, inc, k5. *(15 sts)*
Row 19: K6, inc, k1, inc, k6. *(17 sts)*
Row 21: K7, inc, k1, inc, k7. *(19 sts)*
Row 23: K8, inc, k1, inc, k8. *(21 sts)*
Row 25: K9, inc, k1, inc, k9. *(23 sts)*
Row 27: K10, inc, k1, inc, k10. *(25 sts)*
Row 29: Knit.
Row 31: Knit.
Cast (bind) off.

Front Leg

(make 2 the same)
With cr, cast on 7 sts.
Beg with a k row, work 2 rows st st.
Row 3: Inc, k2tog, k1, k2tog, inc. *(7 sts)*
Row 4: Purl.
Row 5: Inc, k5, inc. *(9 sts)*
Row 6: Purl.
Row 7: Inc, k7, inc. *(11 sts)*
Work 7 rows st st.
Row 15: Inc, k9, inc. *(13 sts)*
Work 7 rows st st.
Row 23: Inc, k11, inc. *(15 sts)*
Work 7 rows st st.
Cast (bind) off.

Right Side and Tail

With cr, cast on 8 sts.
Row 1: K8, cast on 6 sts. *(14 sts)*
Row 2: P13, inc. *(15 sts)*
Row 3: K15, cast on 3 sts. *(18 sts)*
Row 4 P17, inc. *(19 sts)*
Row 5: K19, cast on 3 sts. *(22 sts)*
Row 6: P21, inc. *(23 sts)*
Row 7: K23, cast on 3 sts. *(26 sts)*
Row 8: Purl.
Row 9: K26, cast on 4 sts. *(30 sts)*
Row 10: Purl.
Row 11: K7cr, join in cn, 5cn, 18cr.
Row 12: P17cr, 7cn, 6cr.
Row 13: K5cr, 10cn, 15cr.

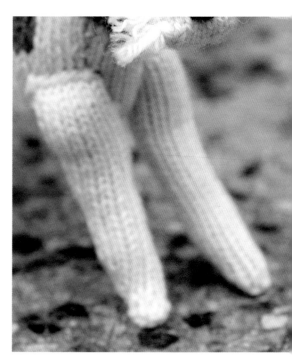

Legs

The Fox Terrier's front legs are sewn on at a slight forward slant and the back legs at a slight backward slant.

Body

Use the intarsia technique and a separate ball of each colour yarn, twisting the colours firmly over one another at the joins to prevent holes (see page 172).

Row 14: P14cr, 11cn, 5cr.
Row 15: K5cr, 13cn, 12cr.
Row 16: P12cr, 13cn, 5cr.
Row 17: Inccr, k4cr, 14cn, 11cr. *(31 sts)*
Row 18: P10cr, 15cn, 6cr.
Row 19: Inccr, 5cr, 15cn, 10cr. *(32 sts)*
Work in cr on first 5 sts only for tail.
Row 20: P5, turn.
Row 21: Knit.
Row 22: Purl.
Row 23: Inc, k2, k2tog. *(5 sts)*
Row 24: Purl.
Work 2 rows st st.

Row 27: K2tog, k3. *(4 sts)*
Row 28: Purl.
Row 29: K2tog twice. *(2 sts)*
Row 30: P2tog and fasten off.
Rejoin cr and cast (bind) off 6 sts cr and 12 sts cn (hold rem 9 sts on spare needle for head).

Left Side and Tail

With cr, cast on 8 sts.
Row 1: Knit.
Row 2: P8, cast on 6 sts. *(14 sts)*
Row 3: K13, inc. *(15 sts)*
Row 4: P15, cast on 3 sts. *(18 sts)*
Row 5: K17, inc. *(19 sts)*
Row 6: P19, cast on 3 sts. *(22 sts)*
Row 7: K 21, inc. *(23 sts)*
Row 8: P23, cast on 3 sts. *(26 sts)*
Row 9: K9cr, join in cn, 4cn, 13cr.
Row 10: P12cr, 6cn, 8cr, cast on 4 sts. *(30 sts)*
Row 11: K11cr, 7cn, 12cr.
Row 12: P11cr, 9cn, 10cr.
Row 13: K9cr, 12cn, 9cr.
Row 14: P8cr, 13cn, 9cr.
Row 15: K8cr, 15cn, 7cr.
Row 16: P7cr, 16cn, 7cr.
Row 17: K6cr, 17cn, 7cr.
Row 18: Inccr, p6cr, 17cn, 6cr. *(31 sts)*
Row 19: K6cr, 17cn, 8cr.
Row 20: Inccr, p7cr, 17cn, 6cr. *(32 sts)*
Work in cr on first 5 sts only for tail.
Row 21: K5, turn.
Row 22: Purl.
Row 23: Knit.
Row 24: Inc, p2, p2tog. *(5 sts)*
Row 25: Knit.
Work 2 rows st st.
Row 28: P2tog, p3. *(4 sts)*
Row 29: Knit.
Row 30: P2tog twice. *(2 sts)*
Row 31: K2tog and fasten off.
Rejoin cn, cast (bind) off 18 sts cn (hold rem 9 sts on spare needle for head).

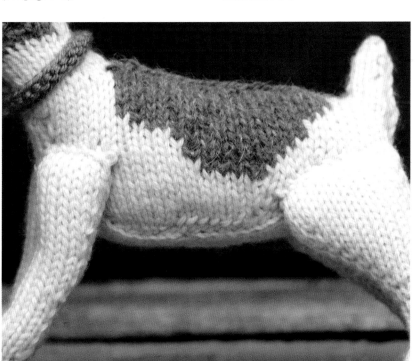

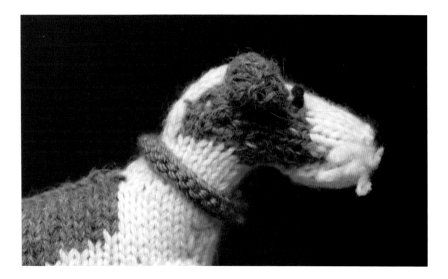

Head

Please note this terrier's idiosyncratic square muzzle.

Neck and Head

With cr, and with RS facing k9 from spare needle of Right Side of Body then k9 from spare needle of Left Side of Body. *(18 sts)*
Row 1: Purl.
Row 2: K6, k2tog, k2, k2tog, k6. *(16 sts)*
Row 3: Purl.
Row 4: K7, k2tog, k7. *(15 sts)*
Row 5: Purl.
Row 6: Join in cn, k6cn, 3cr, 6cn.
Row 7: P6cn, 3cr, 6cn.
Row 8: K6cn, 3cr, 3cn, pult (pick up loop below next st on left needle by inserting tip of right needle from back through loop – this stops a hole forming when turning work – then turn, leaving rem 3 sts on left needle unworked).
Row 9: Working top of head on centre 9 sts only, p2togcn (first st of p2tog is loop picked up at end of last row), p2cn, 3cr, 3cn, pult.
Row 10: K2togcn, 2cn, 3cr, 2cn, pult.

Row 11: P2togcn, 1cn, 3cr, 2cn pult.
Row 12: K2togcn, k1cn, 3cr, 1cn pult.
Row 13: P2togcn, p3cr, p1cn, pult.
Row 14: K2togcn, 3cr, 2cn, pult.
Row 15: P2togcn, 1cn, 3cr, 2cn, pult.
Row 16: K2togcn, 1cn, 3cr, 3cn, pult.
Row 17: P2togcn, 2cn, 3cr, 3cn, pult.
Row 18: K2togcn, 2cn, 3cr, 6cn.
Row 19: P6cn, 3cr, 6cn.
Row 20: K6cn, 3cr, 6cn.
Row 21: P2togcn, p4cn, 3cr, 4cn, p2togcn. *(13 sts)*
Row 22: K2togcn, k2cn, 5cr, 2cn, k2togcn. *(11 sts)*
Row 23: P2cn, 7cr, 2cn.
Row 24: K1cn, 9cr, 1cn.
Row 25: P2togcr, p7cr, p2togcr. *(9 sts)*
Cont in cr, work 2 rows st st.
Knit 3 rows (forms ridge for end of nose).
Work 7 rows st st.
Row 39: K2tog, k5, k2tog. *(7 sts)*
Row 40: Purl.
Row 41: K2tog, k3, k2tog. *(5 sts)*
Work 3 rows st st.
Cast (bind) off.

Tummy

With cr, cast on 1 st.
Row 1: Inc. *(2 sts)*
Row 2 and next 2 alt rows: Purl.
Row 3: Inc into both sts. *(4 sts)*
Row 5: Inc, k2, inc. *(6 sts)*
Row 7: Inc, k4, inc. *(8 sts)*
Work 51 rows st st (measure against body, it should finish under Fox Terrier's muzzle), ending with a p row.
Next row: K2tog, k4, k2tog. *(6 sts)*
Next row: Purl.
Next row: K2tog, k2, k2tog. *(4 sts)*
Next row: Purl.
Cast (bind) off.

Ear

(make 2 the same)

With cn, cast on 5 sts.
Beg with a k row, work 5 rows st st.
Row 6: Knit (forms ridge).
Row 7: Knit.
Row 8: P2tog, p1, p2tog. *(3 sts)*
Row 9: Knit.
Row 10: P3tog and fasten off.

Collar

With gl, cast on 24 sts.
Knit one row.
Cast (bind) off.

To Make Up

Sew in ends, leaving ends from cast on
and cast (bound) off rows for sewing up.
Using mattress or whip stitch, sew up
legs starting at paw. Turn right side out, stuff
each leg, using pipecleaners for rigidity if
necessary. Using whip stitch, sew along top
of leg, leaving an end to sew leg to body.
Using mattress or whip stitch, sew down
centre back and tail. Sew cast on row of
tummy to V at base of back and sew cast
(bound) off row under muzzle. Ease and sew
tummy to fit body. Leave a 2.5cm (1in) gap
between front and back legs on one side.
Turn right side out, stuff body tightly then
sew up gap with mattress stitch. Using whip
stitch, sew legs to body as shown.
Sew up sides of head, sewing muzzle into
square shape. Sew on ears as shown. Crimp
at ridge row and sew tips down.
Using black yarn, embroider the nose using
satin stitch and make two French knots for
eyes. Make moustache by hooking 2 lengths
of cr through each side of nose, as if making
scarf tassel, and cut to desired length.
Sew ends of collar together and slide over
head onto neck.
If legs are floppy, about 2cm (¾in) down
from top edge of leg, sew through leg, body
and opposite leg to make dog more stable.

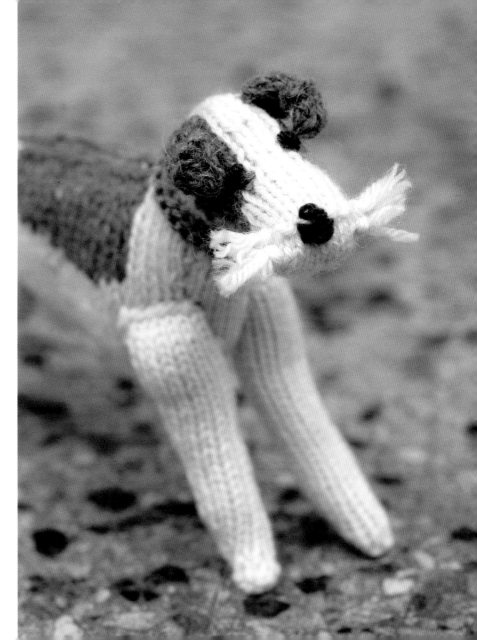

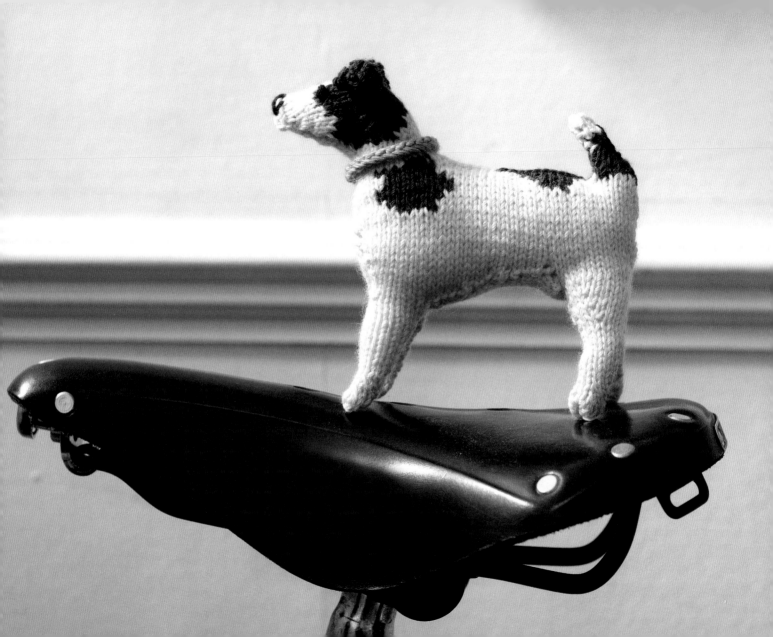

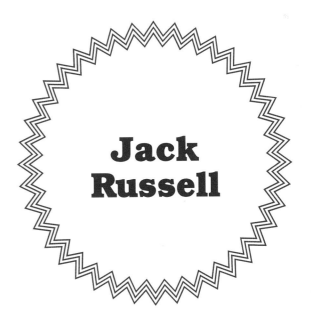

Jack Russell

The Jack Russell is a big dog in a small dog's body. They are sturdy and tough, intelligent and brave with large personalities and they can be willful. Jack Russells are primarily working dogs and enjoy learning tricks, but they do need to be kept occupied and well exercised. Nipper the HMV dog is reputed to be a Jack Russell, but that's debatable. Prince Charles, Goldie Hawn and Serena Williams all own Jack Russells.

Jack Russell

A simple pattern, but you may need to shorten or lengthen the legs to match your Jack Russell.

Measurements
Length: 15cm (6in)
Height to top of head: 14cm (5½in)

Materials
- Pair of 2¾mm (US 2) knitting needles
- 4 spare 2¾mm (US 2) knitting needles or small stitch holders or safety pins
- 20g (¾oz) of Rowan Cashsoft 4ply in Cream 433 (cr)
- 10g (¼oz) of Rowan Cashsoft 4ply in Bark 432 (bk)
- Small amount of Rowan Cashsoft 4 ply in Cherish 453 (ch) for collar
- Tiny amount of Rowan Cashsoft 4ply in Black 422 (bl) for nose and eyes
- 2 pipecleaners for legs

Abbreviations
See page 172.

Right Back Leg
With cr, cast on 9 sts.
Beg with a k row, work 2 rows st st.
Row 3: Inc, k1, k2tog, k1, k2tog, k1, inc. *(9 sts)*
Row 4: Purl.
Rep last 2 rows once more.
Work 4 rows st st.
Row 11: Inc, k7, inc. *(11 sts)*
Work 3 rows st st.**

Row 15: K4, inc, k1, inc, k4. *(13 sts)*
Row 16: Purl.
Row 17: K5, inc, k1, inc, k5. *(15 sts)*
Row 18: Purl.
Row 19: K6, inc, k1, inc, k6. *(17 sts)*
Row 20: Purl.
Row 21: K7, inc, k1, inc, k7. *(19 sts)*
Row 22: Purl.*
Row 23: Cast (bind) off 9 sts, k to end (hold 10 sts on spare needle for Right Side of Body).

Left Back Leg
Work as for Right Back Leg to *.
Row 23: K10, cast (bind) off 9 sts (hold 10 sts on spare needle for Left Side of Body).

Right Front Leg
Work as for Right Back Leg to **.
Row 15: Inc, k9, inc. *(13 sts)*
Row 16: Purl.***
Row 17: Cast (bind) off 6 sts, k to end (hold 7 sts on spare needle for Right Side of Body).

Left Front Leg
Work as for Right Front Leg to ***.
Row 17: K7, cast (bind) off 6 sts (hold 7 sts on spare needle for Left Side of Body).

Right Side of Body
Row 1: With cr, cast on 1 st, with RS facing k7 from spare needle of Right Front Leg, cast on 5 sts. *(13 sts)*
Row 2: Purl.
Row 3: K13, cast on 4 sts. *(17 sts)*
Row 4: Purl.
Row 5: Inc, k16, cast on 3 sts. *(21 sts)*
Row 6: Purl.
Row 7: Inc, k20, with RS facing k10 from spare needle of Right Back Leg, cast on 2 sts. *(34 sts)*
Work 4 rows st st.
Row 12: P25cr, join in bk, p4bk, p5cr.
Row 13: K4cr, k6bk, k24cr.

Row 14: P23cr, p8bk, p3cr.
Row 15: K3cr, k8bk, k23cr.
Row 16: P10cr, p3bk, p11cr, p7bk, p3cr.
Row 17: K4cr, k5bk, k11cr, k5bk, k9cr.
Row 18: P2bk, p7cr, p6bk, p10cr, p5bk, p4cr.
Row 19: K3cr, k6bk, k9cr, k8bk, k2cr, k4bk, k2togbk. *(33 sts)*
Row 20: P2togbk, p4bk (hold 5 sts on spare needle for tail), cast (bind) off 9 sts bk, 7 sts cr, p2cr icos, p3bk, p6cr (hold 11 sts on spare needle for neck).

Left Side of Body

Row 1: With cr, cast on 1 st, with WS facing p7 from spare needle of Left Front Leg, cast on 5 sts. *(13 sts)*
Row 2: Knit.
Row 3: P13, cast on 4 sts. *(17 sts)*

Body

Use the intarsia technique and a separate ball of each colour yarn, twisting the colours firmly over one another at the joins to prevent holes (see page 172).

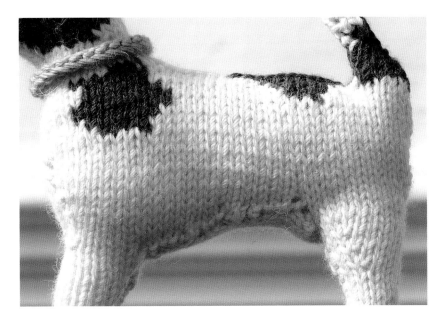

Row 4: Knit.
Row 5: Inc, p16, cast on 3 sts. *(21 sts)*
Row 6: Knit.
Row 7: Inc, p20, with WS facing p10 from spare needle of Left Back Leg, cast on 2 sts. *(34 sts)*
Work 4 rows st st.
Row 12: K24cr, join in bk, k4bk, k6cr.
Row 13: P5cr, p6bk, p23cr.
Row 14: K22cr, k8bk, k4cr.
Row 15: P4cr, p8bk, p22cr.
Row 16: K1bk, k7cr, k4bk, k10cr, k8bk, k4cr.
Row 17: P4cr, p8bk, p9cr, p7bk, p4cr, p2bk.
Row 18: K14bk, k9cr, k6bk, k5cr.
Row 19: P6cr, p4bk, p10cr, p12bk, p2togbk. *(33 sts)*
Row 20: K2togbk, k4bk (hold 5 sts on spare needle for tail), cast (bind) off 7 sts bk and 9 sts cr, k1cr icos, k3bk, k7cr (hold 11 sts on spare needle for neck).

Neck and Head

Row 1: With cr, and with RS facing k11 from spare needle of Right Side of Body then k11 from spare needle of Left Side of Body. *(22 sts)*
Row 2: Purl.
Row 3: K5, k2tog, k8, k2tog, k5. *(20 sts)*
Row 4: Purl.
Row 5: K5, k2tog, k6, k2tog, k5. *(18 sts)*
Row 6: Join in bk, p5bk, p8cr, p5bk.
Row 7: K7bk, k4cr, k4bk, pult (pick up loop below next st on left needle by inserting tip of right needle from back through loop – this stops a hole forming when turning work – then turn, leaving rem 3 sts on left needle unworked).
Cont in bk.
Row 8: Working top of head on centre 12 sts only, p2tog (first st of p2tog is loop picked up at end of last row), p11, pult.
Row 9: K2tog, k11, pult.
Rep last 2 rows once more.
Row 12: P2tog, p11, pult.

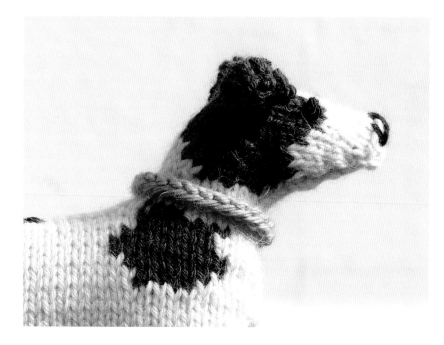

Head

By altering the position of the ears and the embroidery of the nose and eyes, you change your dog's personality.

Row 13: K2tog, k to end. *(18 sts in total)*
Row 14: P8bk, p2cr, p8bk.
Row 15: K8bk, k2cr, k4bk, pult (leave 4 sts unworked on left needle).
Row 16: P2togbk, p3bk, p2cr, p4bk, pult.
Row 17: K2togbk, k3bk, k2cr, k4bk, pult.
Rep last 2 rows once more.
Row 20: P2togbk, p3bk, p2cr, p4bk, pult.
Row 21: K2togbk, k3bk, k2cr, k8bk. *(18 sts in total)*
Row 22: P2cr, p6bk, p2cr, p6bk, p2cr.
Row 23: K2cr, k2togcr, k2bk, k2togbk, k2cr, k2togbk, k2bk, k2togcr, k2cr. *(14 sts)*
Row 24: P4cr, p2bk, p2cr, p2bk, p4cr.
Cont in cr.
Work 2 rows st st.

Row 27: K2tog, k10, k2tog. *(12 sts)*
Row 28: Purl.
Row 29: K2tog, k8, k2tog. *(10 sts)*
Row 30: P2tog, p6, p2tog. *(8 sts)*
Cast (bind) off.

Tail

Row 1: With bk, and with RS facing k3, k2tog from spare needle of Left Side of Body then k2tog, k3 from spare needle of Right Side of Body. *(8 sts)*
Work 3 rows st st.
Row 5: K2. k2tog twice, k2. *(6 sts)*
Row 6: Purl.
Row 7: Join in cr, k2cr, k2bk, k2cr.
Cont in cr.
Work 3 rows st st.
Row 11: K1, k2tog twice, k1. *(4 sts)*
Row 12: P2tog twice. *(2 sts)*
Row 13: K2tog and fasten off.

Tummy

With cr, cast on 8 sts.
Beg with a k row, work 2 rows st st.
Next row: K2tog, k4, k2tog. *(6 sts)*
Next row: P2tog, p2, p2tog. *(4 sts)*
Work 6 rows st st.
Next row: Inc, k2, inc. *(6 sts)*
Next row: Inc, p4, inc. *(8 sts)*
Work 6 rows st st.
Next row: K2tog, k4, k2tog. *(6 sts)*
Work 15 rows st st.
Next row: K2tog, k2, k2tog. *(4 sts)*
Work 5 rows st st.
Next row: Inc, k2, inc. *(6 sts)*
Next row: Inc, p4, inc. *(8 sts)*
Work 8 rows st st.
Next row: K2tog, k4, k2tog. *(6 sts)*
Work 5 rows st st.
Next row: K2tog, k2, k2tog. *(4 sts)*
Work 15 rows st st.
Next row: K2tog twice. *(2 sts)*
Work 5 rows st st.
Next row: K2tog and fasten off.

Ear

(make 2 the same)
With bk, cast on 5 sts.
Beg with a k row, work 2 rows st st.
Knit 6 rows.
Next row: K2tog, k1, k2tog. *(3 sts)*
Knit 2 rows.
Cast (bind) off.

Collar

With ch, cast on 26 sts.
Knit one row.
Cast (bind) off.

To Make Up

Sew in ends, leaving ends from cast on
and cast (bound) off rows for sewing up.
Using mattress or whip stitch, sew up legs
starting at paw. Sew up tail and stuff with
the ends of yarn.
Using mattress or whip stitch, sew along
back of dog and down bottom. At head, fold
in half and sew cast (bound) off edges of
nose together. Using mattress or whip stitch,
sew cast on row of tummy to bottom end of
dog and sew cast (bound) off row to nose.
Ease and sew tummy to fit body, matching
curves to legs. Leave a 2.5cm (1in) gap
between front and back legs on one side.
Turn right side out.
Roll the pipecleaners in some stuffing and
bend them into a U shape. Fold over the
ends and slip into body, one pipecleaner
down front legs and one down back legs.
Stuff and sew up gap with mattress stitch.
Mould into shape.
Sew ears to head at a slight angle as shown
in photograph. Use the end of yarn at the
point of the ear and sew down the ear to
prevent it from flicking up.
Using black yarn, embroider nose in satin
stitch and make two French knots for eyes.
Sew ends of collar together and slide over
head onto neck.

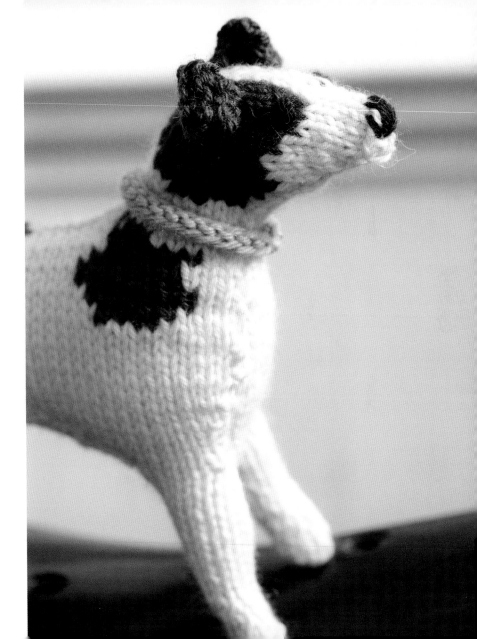

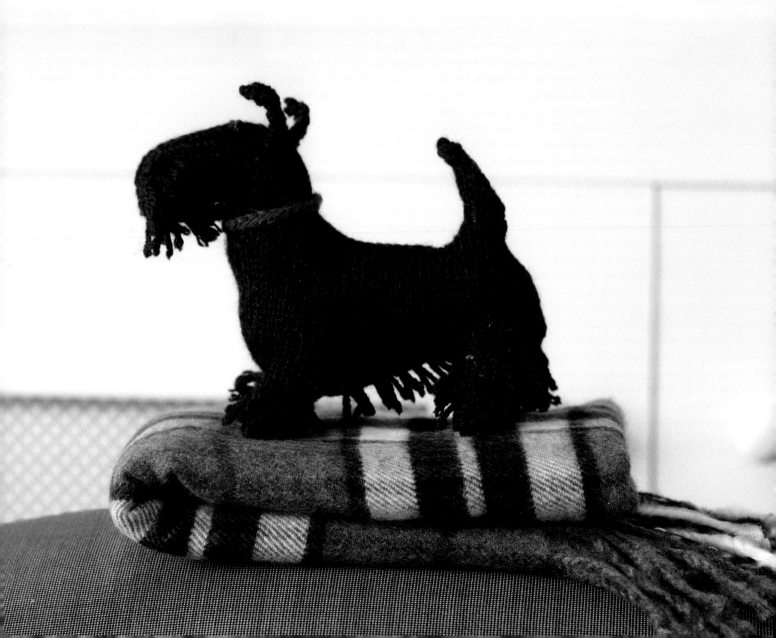

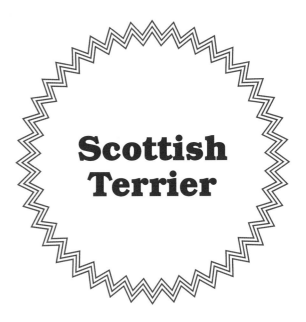

Scottish Terrier

Small and bright-eyed with a distinctive profile, Scotties were bred to hunt badgers. They are typical terriers, inquisitive, but also territorial and they enjoy a fight. As the unofficial mascot for Scotland, this dog is often seen in advertisements and books wearing a tartan collar or a jaunty tam-o-shanter. The Scottie is the only breed of dog that has lived in the White House more than three times. Well-known Scotties include Jock in *Lady and the Tramp* and the Monopoly dog.

Scottish Terrier

To get the tilt of the head, use the method for turning the heel of a sock.

Measurements
Length: 11cm (4½in)
Height to top of head: 13cm (5in)

Materials
- Pair of 2¾mm (US 2) knitting needles
- 4 spare 2¾mm (US 2) knitting needles or small stitch holders or safety pins
- 25g (1oz) of Rowan Cashsoft 4ply in Black 422 (bl)
- Small amount of Rowan Cashsoft 4ply in Poppy 438 (pp) for collar
- Tiny amount of Rowan Pure Wool 4ply in Mocha 417 for nose and eyes

Abbreviations
See page 172.
For loopy stitch technique, see page 173.

Right Back Leg
With bl, cast on 11 sts.
Beg with a k row, work 2 rows st st.
Row 3: K3, k2tog, k1, k2tog, k3. (9 sts)
Row 4: Purl.
Row 5: K1, loopy st 1, k2tog, loopy st 1, k2tog, loopy st 1, k1. (7 sts)
Row 6: Purl.**
Row 7: K1, loopy st 1, k1, loopy st 1, k1, loopy st 1, k1.
Row 8: Purl.
Row 9: Inc, loopy st 1, k1, loopy st 1, k1, loopy st 1, inc. (9 sts)

Row 10: Purl.
Row 11: Inc, loopy st 1, k1, inc, loopy st 1, inc, k1, loopy st 1, inc. (13 sts)
Row 12: Purl.
Row 13: K1, loopy st 1, k3, inc, loopy st 1, inc, k3, loopy st 1, k1. (15 sts)
Row 14: P6, inc, p1, inc, p6.* (17 sts)
Row 15: Cast (bind) off 8 sts, k to end (hold 9 sts on spare needle for Right Side of Body).

Left Back Leg
Work as for Right Back Leg to*.
Row 15: K9, cast (bind) off 8 sts (hold 9 sts on spare needle for Left Side of Body).

Right Front Leg
Work as for Right Back Leg to **.
Row 7: Inc, loopy st 1, k3, loopy st 1, inc. (9 sts)
Row 8: Purl.
Row 9: Inc, loopy st 1, k2, loopy st 1, k2, loopy st 1, inc. (11 sts)
Row 10: Purl.***
Row 11: Cast (bind) off 5 sts, k to end (hold 6 sts on spare needle for Right Side of Body).

Left Front Leg
Work as for Right Front Leg to ***.
Row 11: K6, cast (bind) off 5 sts, k to end (hold 6 sts on spare needle for Left Side of Body).

Right Side of Body
Row 1: With bl, cast on 2 sts, with RS facing k6 from spare needle of Right Front Leg, cast on 5 sts. (13 sts)
Row 2: Purl.
Row 3: Inc, k12, cast on 4 sts. (18 sts)
Row 4: Purl.
Row 5: Inc, k17, cast on 3 sts. (22 sts)
Row 6: Purl.
Row 7: K22, with RS facing k9 from spare needle of Right Back Leg, cast on 2 sts. (33 sts)

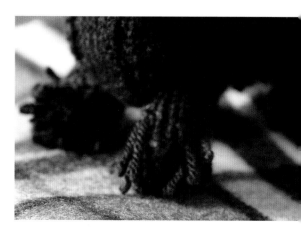

Legs
To give the Scottie its typical hairy look we have used cut loopy stitch.

Work 7 rows st st.

Row 15: K30, k2tog, k1. *(32 sts)*

Row 16: P1, p2tog, p29. *(31 sts)*

Row 17: K28, k2tog, k1. *(30 sts)*

Row 18: P1, p2tog, p27. *(29 sts)*

Row 19: K26, k2tog, k1. *(28 sts)*

Row 20: P6 (hold 6 sts on spare needle for tail), cast (bind) off 12 sts, p to end (hold 10 sts on spare needle for neck).

Left Side of Body

Row 1: With bl, cast on 2 sts, with WS facing p6 from spare needle of Left Front Leg, cast on 5 sts. *(13 sts)*

Row 2: Knit.

Row 3: Inc, p12, cast on 4 sts. *(18 sts)*

Row 4: Knit.

Row 5: Inc, p17, cast on 3 sts. *(22 sts)*

Row 6: Knit.

Row 7: P22, with WS facing p9 from spare needle of Left Back Leg, cast on 2 sts. *(33 sts)*

Work 7 rows st st.

Row 15: P30, p2tog, p1. *(32 sts)*

Row 16: K1, k2tog, k29. *(31 sts)*

Row 17: P28, p2tog, p1. *(30 sts)*

Row 18: K1, k2tog, k27. *(29 sts)*

Row 19: P26, p2tog, p1. *(28 sts)*

Row 20: K6 (hold 6 sts on spare needle for tail), cast (bind) off 12 sts, k to end (hold 10 sts on spare needle for neck).

Neck and Head

Row 1: With bl, and with RS facing k10 from spare needle of Right Side of Body then k10 from spare needle of Left Side of Body. *(20 sts)*

Row 2: Purl.

Row 3: K5, k2tog, k6, k2tog, k5. *(18 sts)*

Row 4: Purl.

Row 5: K5, k2tog, k4, k2tog, k5. *(16 sts)*

Row 6: Purl.

Row 7: K15, pult (pick up loop below next st on left needle by inserting tip of right needle from back through loop – this stops a hole forming when turning work – then turn, leaving rem 1 st on left needle unworked).

Row 8: Working top of head, p2tog (first st of p2tog is loop picked up at end of last row), p13, pult.

Row 9: K2tog, k12, pult.

Row 10: P2tog, p11, pult.

Row 11: K2tog, k10, pult.

Row 12: P2tog, p9, pult.

Row 13: K2tog, k8, pult.

Row 14: P2tog, p7, pult.

Row 15: K2tog, k8, pult.

Row 16: P2tog, p9, pult.

Row 17: K2tog, k10, pult.

Row 18: P2tog, p11, pult.

Row 19: K2tog, k12, pult.

Row 20: P2tog, p13, pult.

Row 21: K2tog, k14. *(16 sts on right needle)*

Row 22: Purl.

Row 23: K3, k2tog, k6, k2tog, k3. *(14 sts)*

Work 3 rows st st.

Body

Be careful not to over-stuff the body because the white stuffing will show if the stitches are over-stretched.

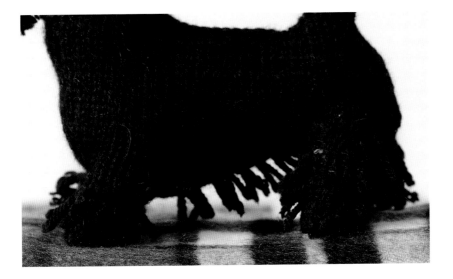

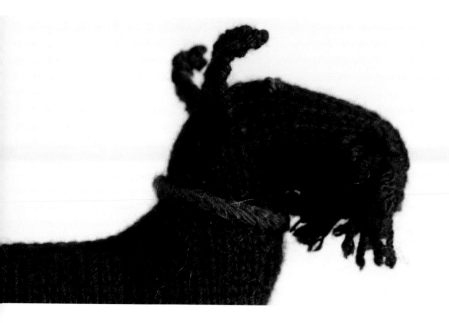

Head

When stuffing the head, make sure it is tilted at this angle. You can add some tassels for eyebrows if you wish.

Row 27: K3, k2tog, k4, k2tog, k3. *(12 sts)*
Row 28: Purl.
Row 29: K1, loopy st 2, k6, loopy st 2, k1.
Row 30: Purl
Row 31: K1, loopy st 2, k2tog, k2, k2tog, loopy st 2, k1. *(10 sts)*
Row 32: Purl.
Cast (bind) off.

Tail

Row 1: With bl, and with RS facing k4, k2tog from spare needle of Left Side of Body then k2tog, k4 from spare needle of Right Side of Body. *(10 sts)*
Row 2: Inc, p2, p2tog twice, p2, inc. *(10 sts)*
Row 3: Knit.
Rep last 2 rows once more.
Row 6: P2tog, p6, p2tog. *(8 sts)*

Row 7: Knit.
Row 8: P2tog, p1, inc into next 2 sts, p1, p2tog. *(8 sts)*
Work 4 rows st st.
Row 13: K2tog, k4, k2tog. *(6 sts)*
Work 2 rows st st.
Row 16: P2tog 3 times. *(3 sts)*
Row 17: K3tog and fasten off.

Tummy

With bl, cast on 6 sts.
Beg with a k row, work 2 rows st st.
Next row: K2tog, k2, k2tog. *(4 sts)*
Next row: P2tog twice. *(2 sts)*
Work 6 rows st st.
Next row: Inc into both sts. *(4 sts)*
Next row: Inc, p2, inc. *(6 sts)*
Work 2 rows st st.
Next row: K1, loopy st 1, k2, loopy st 1, k1.
Next row: Purl.
Next row: K2, loopy st 1, k3.
Next row: Purl.
Next row: K1, loopy st 1, k2, loopy st 1, k1.
Next row: Purl.
Next row: K3, loopy st 1, k2.
Next row: Purl.
Rep last 8 rows once more.
Next row: K1, loopy st 1, k2, loopy st 1, k1.
Next row: Purl.
Next row: K2tog, k2, k2tog. *(4 sts)*
Work 4 rows st st.
Next row: Inc, p2, inc. *(6 sts)*
Work 26 rows st st.
Next row: K2tog, k2, k2tog. *(4 sts)*
Work 5 rows st st.
Next row: Inc, k2, inc. *(6 sts)*
Next row: Purl.
Next row: K2, loopy st 2, k2.
Next row: Purl.
Next row: K1, loopy st 4, k1.
Rep last 2 rows once more.
Next row: Purl.
Next row: K2tog, loopy st 2, k2tog. *(4 sts)*

Next row: Purl.
Cast (bind) off.

Ear

(make 2 the same)
Wth bl, cast on 6 sts.
Knit 4 rows.
Next row: K2tog, k2, k2tog. *(4 sts)*
Knit 4 rows.
Next row: K2tog twice. *(2 sts)*
Knit 2 rows.
Next row: K2tog and fasten off.

Collar

With pp, cast on 26 sts.
Knit one row
Cast (bind) off.

To Make Up

Sew in ends, leaving ends from cast on
and cast (bound) off rows for sewing up.
Using mattress or whip stitch, sew up legs
starting at paw. Stuff all four legs.
Using mattress or whip stitch, sew down
centre back, around tail and down bottom.
At head, fold in half and sew cast (bound) off
edges of nose together. Sew cast on row of
tummy to V at base of back and sew cast
(bound) off row under chin. Ease and sew
tummy to fit body, matching curves to legs.
Leave a 2.5cm (1in) gap between front and
back legs on one side. Turn right side out.
Stuff head and body, mould to match
photograph (the head needs to be as
boxy as possible), then sew up gap using
mattress stitch.
Sew ears to head as shown in photograph.
Using mocha yarn, make two French knots
for eyes.
Cut loops of loopy stitch and trim to length
as necessary.
Sew ends of collar together and slide over
head onto neck.

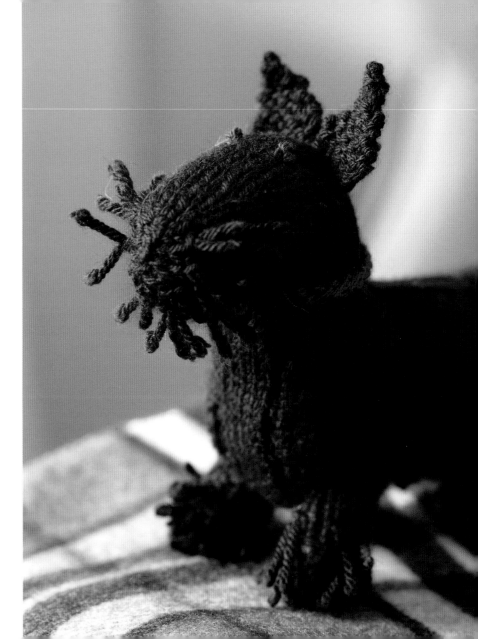

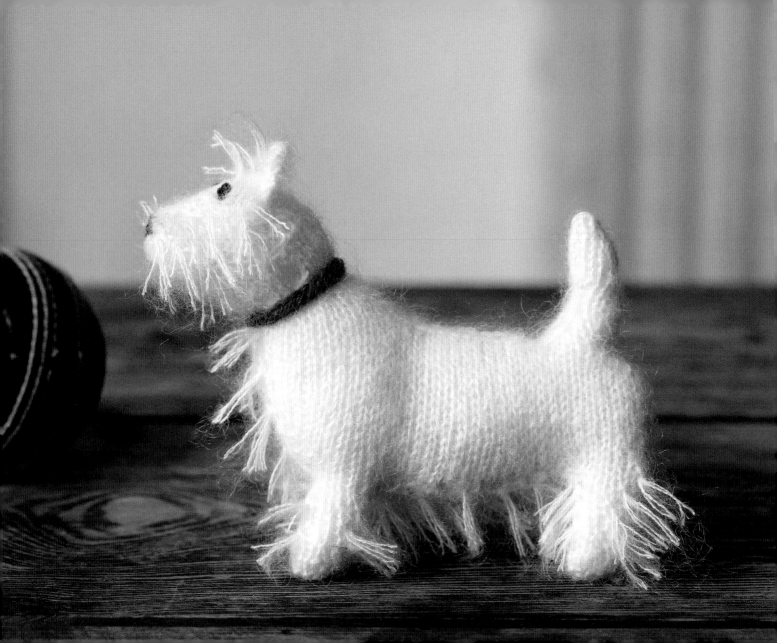

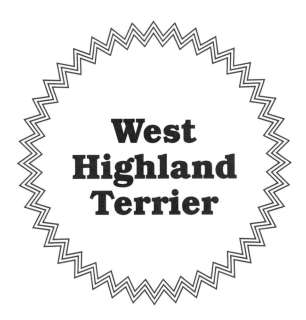

West Highland Terrier

Irrepressibly perky, the Westie is easily identified by its white coat that was developed in Argyll by Colonel Edward Donald Malcolm after his red terrier was mistaken for a fox and shot. As well as being the emblem for Black & White Whisky and Cesar dog food, Westies are the rather surprising pet of choice of the founder of Pakistan, Mohammad Ali Jinnah.

West Highland Terrier

Delicate and quite simple to make in a furry yarn that is used doubled for all the knitting.

Measurements

Length: 15cm (6in)
Height to top of head: 12cm (4¾in)

Materials

- Pair of 2¾mm (US 2) knitting needles
- 4 spare 2¾mm (US 2) knitting needles or small stitch holders or safety pins
- 20g (¾oz) of Rowan Kildsilk Haze in Cream 634 (cr) used DOUBLE throughout
- Small amount of Rowan Pure Wool 4Ply in Hessian 416 (he) for collar
- Tiny amount of Rowan Pure Wool 4ply in Black 404 for nose and eyes

Abbreviations

See page 172.
For loopy stitch technique, see page 173.

Tail

It's easier to sew up the tail from the right side as it's quite thin.

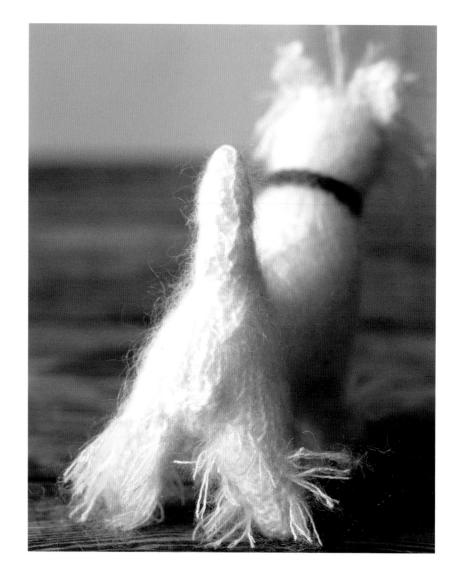

Right Back Leg

Left Back Leg

Right Front Leg

Left Front Leg

Right Side Of Body

Left Side Of Body

For all these pieces follow the pattern for the Scottish Terrier (see pages 48–53), but work all parts in cr (yarn used double).

Neck And Head

Row 1: With cr, and with RS facing k10 from spare needle of Right Side of Body then k10 from spare needle of Left Side of Body. *(20 sts)*

Row 2: Purl.

Row 3: K4, k2tog, k8, k2tog, k4. *(18 sts)*

Row 4: Purl.

Row 5: K15, pult (pick up loop below next st on left needle by inserting tip of right needle from back through loop – this stops a hole forming when turning work – then turn, leaving rem 3 sts on left needle unworked).

Row 6: Working top of head on centre 12 sts only, p2tog (first st of p2tog is loop picked up at end of last row), p11, pult.

Row 7: K2tog, k11, pult.

Rep last 2 rows once more.

Row 10: P2tog, p11, pult.

Row 11: K2tog, k to end. *(18 sts on right needle)*

Row 12: Purl.

Row 13: K14, pult (leave 4 sts on left needle).

Row 14: P2tog, p9, pult.

Row 15: K2tog, k9, pult.

Rep last 2 rows once more.

Row 18: P2tog, p9, pult.

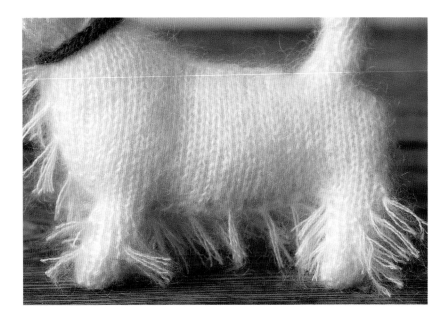

Row 19: K2tog, k2, loopy st 4, k7. *(18 sts on right needle)*

Row 20: P4, p2tog, p2, p2tog, p2, p2tog, p4. *(15 sts)*

Row 21: K2tog, k2, loopy st 3, k1, loopy st 3, k2, k2tog. *(13 sts)*

Row 22: Purl.

Row 23: Knit.

Row 24: Purl.

Row 25: K1, loopy st 3, k2tog, k1, k2tog, loopy st 3, k1. *(11 sts)*

Row 26: Purl.

Row 27: K1, loopy st 2, k2tog, k1, k2tog, loopy st 2, k1. *(9 sts)*

Row 28: Purl.

Row 29: K1, loopy st 2, k3, loopy st 2, k1.

Cast (bind) off.

Body

Cut the loops of the loopy stitch and trim them to the desired length.

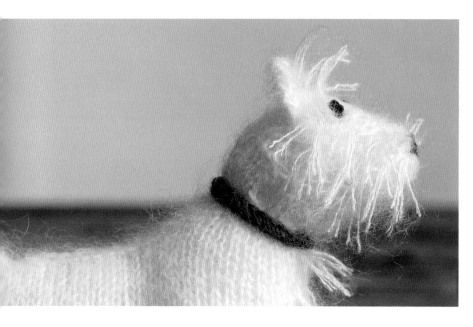

Head

You can add more loopy stitch for a hairier face.

Tail

Row 1: With cr, and with RS facing k4, k2tog from spare needle of Left Side of Body then k2tog, k4 from spare needle of Right Side of Body. *(10 sts)*
Row 2: Inc, p2, p2tog twice, p2, inc. *(10 sts)*
Row 3: Knit.
Rep last 2 rows once more.
Row 6: P2tog, p6, p2tog. *(8 sts)*
Row 7: Knit.
Row 8: P2tog, p1, inc into next 2 sts, p1, p2tog. *(8 sts)*
Work 4 rows st st.
Row 13: K2tog, k4, k2tog. *(6 sts)*
Work 2 rows st st.
Row 16: P2tog 3 times. *(3 sts)*
Row 17: K3tog and fasten off.

Tummy

With cr, cast on 6 sts.
Beg with a k row, work 2 rows st st.
Next row: K2tog, k2, k2tog. *(4 sts)*
Next row: P2tog twice. *(2 sts)*
Work 8 rows st st.
Next row: Inc into both sts. *(4 sts)*
Next row: Inc, p2, inc. *(6 sts)*
Work 2 rows st st.
Next row: K1, loopy st 1, k2, loopy st 1, k1.
Next row: Purl.
Next row: K2, loopy st 1, k3.
Next row: Purl.
Next row: K1, loopy st 1, k2, loopy st 1, k1.
Next row: Purl.
Next row: K3, loopy st 1, k2.
Next row: Purl.
Rep last 8 rows twice more.
Next row: K2tog, k2, k2tog. *(4 sts)*
Work 4 rows st st.
Next row: Inc, p2, inc. *(6 sts)*
Work 2 rows st st.
Next row: K1, loopy st 1, k2, loopy st 1, k1.
Work 3 rows st st.
Rep last 4 rows 3 times more.
Work 3 rows st st.
Next row: K2tog, k2, k2tog. *(4 sts)*
Work 5 rows st st.
Next row: K1, loopy st 2, k1.
Next row: Purl.
Next row: K1, loopy st 2, k1.
Next row: P2tog twice. *(2 sts)*
Next row: K2tog and fasten off.

Ear

(make 2 the same)
With cr, cast on 5 sts.
Knit 4 rows.
Next row: K2tog, k1, k2tog. *(3 sts)*
Knit 2 rows.
Next row: K3tog and fasten off.

Collar

With he, cast on 24 sts.
Knit one row.
Cast (bind) off.

To Make Up

Sew in ends, leaving ends from cast on
and cast (bound) off rows for sewing up.
Using mattress or whip stitch, sew up legs
starting at paw. Stuff all four legs.
Using mattress or whip stitch, sew down
centre back, around tail and down bottom.
At head, fold in half and sew cast (bound) off
edges of nose together. Sew cast on row of
tummy to bottom end of dog and sew cast
(bound) off row to nose.
Ease and sew tummy to fit body, matching
curves to legs. Leave a 2.5cm (1in) gap
between front and back legs on one side.
Turn right side out. Stuff the head and body,
shape to match photograph, then sew up
gap using mattress stitch.
Sew ears to head as shown in photograph.
Using black yarn, embroider the nose
using satin stitch and make two French
knots for eyes. Cut loops of loopy stitch
and trim as necessary.
Sew ends of collar together and slide over
head onto neck.

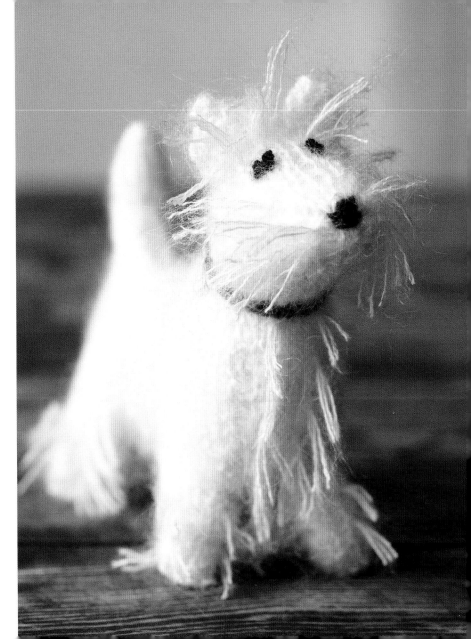

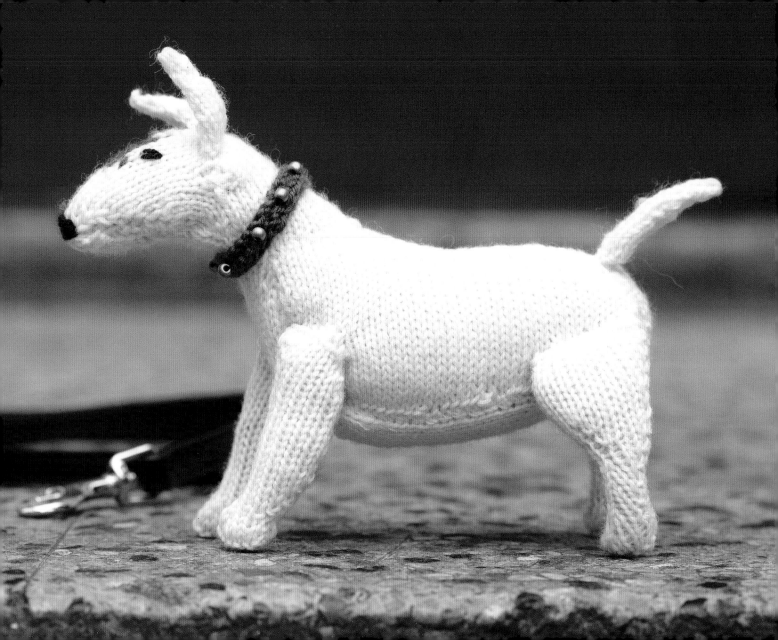

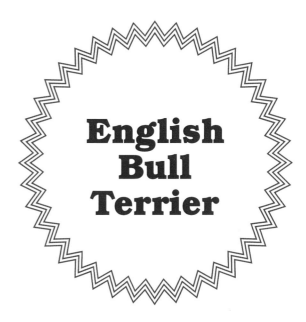

English Bull Terrier

Extraordinary looking with a Roman nose, tiny triangular eyes and an extremely muscular body, the Bull Terrier is the gladiator of the canine world. They are affectionate and make excellent guard dogs, but need firm handling and rigorous training. It's not advisable to have two of the same gender, they are very possessive of their food and cats may not be safe. Bull Terrier heroes include Bodger from *The Incredible Journey* and of course Bill Sykes' dog, Bullseye, in *Oliver Twist*.

English Bull Terrier

Sew stud-like metal beads to the collar to make your Bull Terrier look extra butch.

Measurements
Length: 19cm (7½in)
Height to top of head: 13cm (5in)

Materials
- Pair of 2¾mm (US 2) knitting needles
- 30g (1⅛oz) of Rowan Pure Wool 4ply in Snow 412 (sn)
- 5g (⅛oz) of Rowan Pure Wool 4ply in Mocha 417 (mo)
- Small amount of Rowan Pure Wool 4ply in Hessian 416 (he) for collar
- Tiny amount of Rowan Pure Wool 4ply in Black 404 (bl) and in Powder 443 (po) for embroidery detail
- 9 small metal beads (optional)
- Beading needle and thread (optional)

Abbreviations
See page 172.

Back Leg
(make 2 the same)
With sn, cast on 16 sts.
Beg with a k row, work 2 rows st st.
Row 3: K5, k2tog 3 times, k5. *(13 sts)*
Row 4: P2tog, p2, p2tog, p1, p2tog, p2, p2tog. *(9 sts)*
Work 2 rows st st.
Row 7: Inc, k1, k2tog, k1, k2tog, k1, inc. *(9 sts)*
Row 8: Purl.
Row 9: Inc, k7, inc. *(11 sts)*
Row 10: Purl.
Row 11: Inc, k2, k2tog, k1, k2tog, k2, inc. *(11 sts)*
Row 12: Purl.
Row 13: Inc, k2, k2tog, k1, k2tog, k2, inc. *(11 sts)*
Row 14: Purl.
Row 15: Inc, k2tog, inc, k3, inc, k2tog, inc. *(13 sts)*
Row 16: Purl.
Row 17: K5, inc, k1, inc, k5. *(15 sts)*
Row 18: Purl.
Row 19: K6, inc, k1, inc, k6. *(17 sts)*
Row 20: Purl.
Row 21: Inc, k15, inc. *(19 sts)*
Row 22: Purl.
Row 23: Inc, k17, inc. *(21 sts)*
Row 24: Purl.
Row 25: Inc, k19, inc. *(23 sts)*
Row 26: Purl.
Cast (bind) off.

Front Leg
(make 2 the same)
With sn, cast on 14 sts.
Beg with a k row, work 2 rows st st.
Row 3: K5, k2tog twice, k5. *(12 sts)*
Row 4: P2tog, p2, p2tog, p2tog, p2, p2tog. *(8 sts)*
Work 2 rows st st.
Row 7: Inc, k6, inc. *(10 sts)*
Row 8: Purl.

Work 2 rows st st.
Row 11: Inc, k8, inc. *(12 sts)*
Row 12: Purl.
Row 13: Inc, k10, inc. *(14 sts)*
Row 14: Purl.
Work 12 rows st st.
Row 27: K2tog, k4, inc into next 2 sts, k4, k2tog. *(14 sts)*
Row 28: Purl.
Row 29: K2tog, k4, inc into next 2 sts, k4, k2tog. *(14 sts)*
Row 30: Purl.
Cast (bind) off.

Right Side of Body
With sn, cast on 12 sts.
Row 1: K12, cast on 6 sts. *(18 sts)*
Row 2: Purl.
Row 3: K18, cast on 6 sts. *(24 sts)*
Row 4: P23, inc. *(25 sts)*
Row 5: K25, cast on 8 sts. *(33 sts)*
Row 6: Purl.
Work 3 rows st st.
Row 10: P32, inc. *(34 sts)*
Work 3 rows st st.
Row 14: P33, inc. *(35 sts)*
Row 15: K33, k2tog. *(34 sts)*
Row 16: P32, p2tog. *(33 sts)*
Row 17: Knit.
Row 18: P31, p2tog. *(32 sts)*
Row 19: Knit.
Row 20: P30, p2tog. *(31 sts)*
Row 21: Knit.
Row 22: Cast (bind) off 18 sts, p to end. *(13 sts)*
Row 23: K11, k2tog. *(12 sts)*
Row 24: Purl.
Cast (bind) off.

Left Side of Body
With sn, cast on 12 sts.
Row 1: P12, cast on 6 sts. *(18 sts)*
Row 2: Knit.
Row 3: P18, cast on 6 sts. *(24 sts)*

Row 4: K23, inc. *(25 sts)*
Row 5: P25, cast on 8 sts. *(33 sts)*
Row 6: Knit.
Row 7: Purl.
Row 8: Knit.
Row 9: Purl.
Row 10: K32, inc. *(34 sts)*
Row 11: Purl.
Row 12: Knit.
Row 13: Purl.
Row 14: K33, inc. *(35 sts)*
Row 15: P33, p2tog. *(34 sts)*
Row 16: K32, k2tog. *(33 sts)*
Row 17: Purl.
Row 18: K31, k2tog. *(32 sts)*
Row 19: Purl.

Row 20: K30, k2tog. *(31 sts)*
Row 21: Purl.
Row 22: Cast (bind) off 18 sts, k to end.
(13 sts)
Row 23: P11, p2tog. *(12 sts)*
Row 24: Knit.
Cast (bind) off.

Neck and Head

Row 1: With sn, and with RS facing pick up and k10 from cast (bound) off row of Right Side of Body then k10 from cast (bound) off row of Left Side of Body. *(20 sts)*
Row 2: Purl.
Row 3: Inc, k8, k2tog, k8, inc. *(21 sts)*
Row 4: Purl.
Row 5: Inc, k7, k2tog, k1, k2tog, k7, inc. *(21 sts)*
Row 6: Purl.
Rep last 2 rows 3 times more. *(21 sts)*
Row 13: K16, pult (pick up loop below next st on left needle by inserting tip of right needle from back through loop – this stops a hole forming when turning work – then turn, leaving rem 5 sts on left needle unworked).
Row 14: Working top of head on centre 11 sts only, p2tog (first st of p2tog is loop picked up at end of last row), p10, pult.
Row 15: K2tog, k10, pult.
Row 16: P2tog, p10, pult.
Row 17: K2tog, k10, pult.
Row 18: P2tog, p10, pult.
Row 19: K2tog, k to end.
Row 20: Purl.
Row 21: K2togsn, k3sn, join in mo, k5mo, k9sn, k2togsn. *(19 sts)*
Row 22: P9sn, p5mo, p5sn.
Row 23: K2togsn, k4sn, k5mo, k6sn, k2togsn. *(17 sts)*
Row 24: P7sn, p5mo, p5sn. *(17 sts)*
Row 25: K5sn, k5mo, k7sn. *(17 sts)*
Row 26: P7sn, p5mo, p5sn. *(17 sts)*
Row 27: K2togsn, k3sn, k5mo, k5sn, k2togsn. *(15 sts)*

Body

Sew on the back legs at a slight angle to the well-stuffed body.

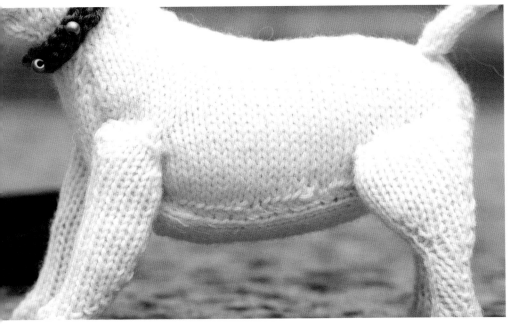

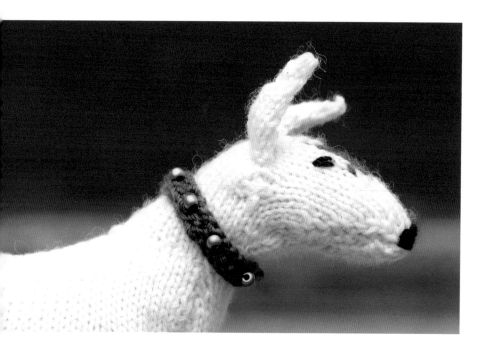

Head

To give the Bull Terrier its distinctive nose, stuff the head well and mould it into shape.

Row 28: P6sn, p4mo, p5sn.
Row 29: K5sn, k4mo, k6sn.
Row 30: Cont in sn, purl.
Row 31: K2tog, k11, k2tog. *(13 sts)*
Row 32: Purl.
Row 33: K2tog, k9, k2tog. *(11 sts)*
Row 34: Purl.
Row 35: K2tog, k7, k2tog. *(9 sts)*
Row 36: Purl.
Row 37: K2tog, k5, k2tog. *(7 sts)*
Row 38: Purl.
Row 39: K2tog, k3, k2tog. *(5 sts)*
Row 40: Purl.
Row 41: K2tog, k1, k2tog. *(3 sts)*
Cast (bind) off.

Tummy

With sn, cast on 1 st.
Row 1: Inc. *(2 sts)*
Row 2: Inc into both sts. *(4 sts)*
Row 3: Inc, k2, inc. *(6 sts)*
Row 4: Inc, p4, inc. *(8 sts)*
Row 5: Inc, k6, inc. *(10 sts)*
Row 6: Inc, p8, inc. *(12 sts)*
Row 7: Inc, k10, inc. *(14 sts)*
Row 8: Purl.
Work 50 rows st st (measure against dog, it should reach bottom of dog's chest, adjust rows if necessary), ending with a p row.
Next row: K2tog, k10, k2tog. *(12 sts)*
Work 5 rows st st.
Next row: K2tog, k8, k2tog. *(10 sts)*
Work 13 rows st st.
Next row: K2tog, k6, k2tog. *(8 sts)*
Work 7 rows st st.
Next row: K2tog, k4, k2tog. *(6 sts)*
Work 7 rows st st.
Cast (bind) off.

Tail

With sn, cast on 8 sts.
Beg with a k row, work 8 rows st st.
Row 9: K2tog, k4, k2tog. *(6 sts)*
Work 4 rows st st.
Row 14: P2tog, p2, p2tog. *(4 sts)*
Work 4 rows st st.
Row 19: K2tog twice. *(2 sts)*
Row 20: P2tog and fasten off.

Ear

(make 2 the same)
With sn, cast on 8 sts.
Beg with a k row, work 4 rows st st.
Row 5: K2tog, k4, k2tog. *(6 sts)*
Work 4 rows st st.
Row 10: P2tog, p2, p2tog. *(4 sts)*
Work 4 rows st st.
Row 15: K2tog twice. *(2 sts)*
Row 16: P2tog and fasten off.

Collar

With he, cast on 26 sts.
Knit 2 rows.
Cast (bind) off.

To Make Up

Sew in ends, leaving ends from cast on
and cast (bound) off rows for sewing up.
Using mattress or whip stitch, sew up legs
starting at paw. Stuff each leg. Using whip
stitch, sew along top of leg, leaving an end
to sew leg to body.
Using mattress stitch, sew up tail and leave
the end open.
Using mattress or whip stitch, sew down
centre back. Sew cast on row of tummy to
bottom of dog and sew cast (bound) off row
to nose. Ease and sew tummy to fit body.
Leave a 2.5cm (1in) gap between front and
back legs on one side. Turn right side out,
stuff then sew up gap with mattress stitch.
Sew legs to body as shown in photograph,
with all seams at back.
Sew on the tail where the back meets the
bottom so that tail sticks out.
With powder yarn, embroider inside of ears
with satin stitch and sew on as shown in
photograph.
Using black yarn, embroider the nose
using satin stitch and make two French
knots for eyes.
Sew ends of collar together. Using beading
needle and thread, sew on metal beads.
Alternatively, you can get a similar effect by
embroidering French knots. Slide collar over
head onto neck.

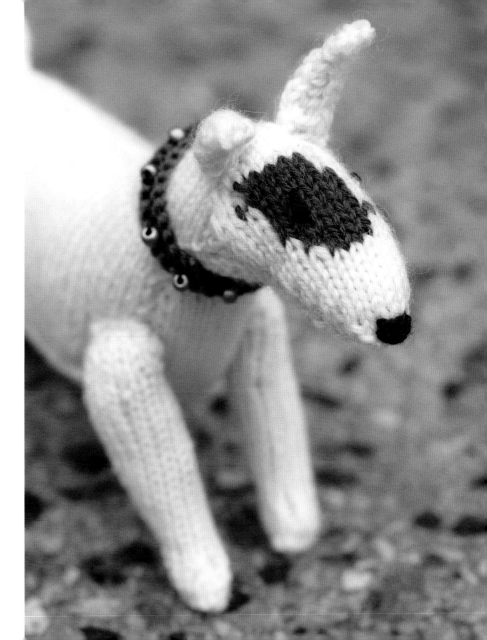

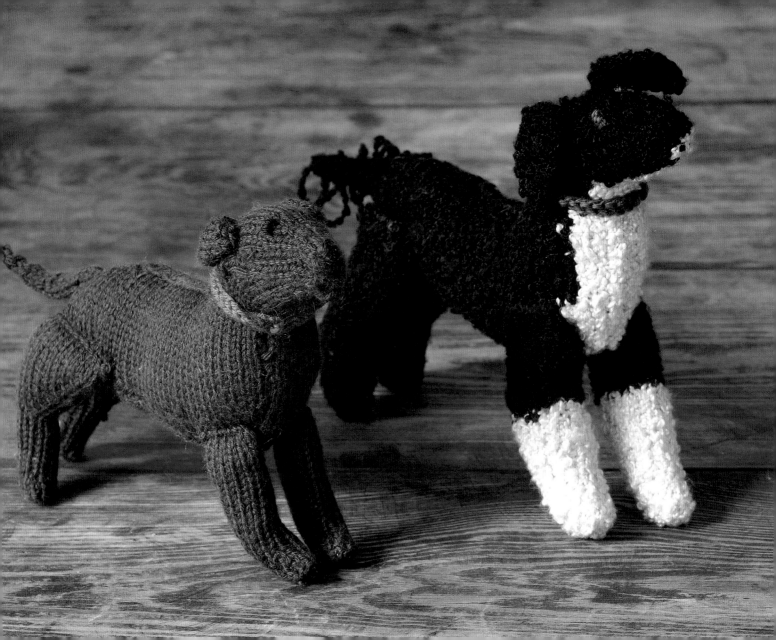

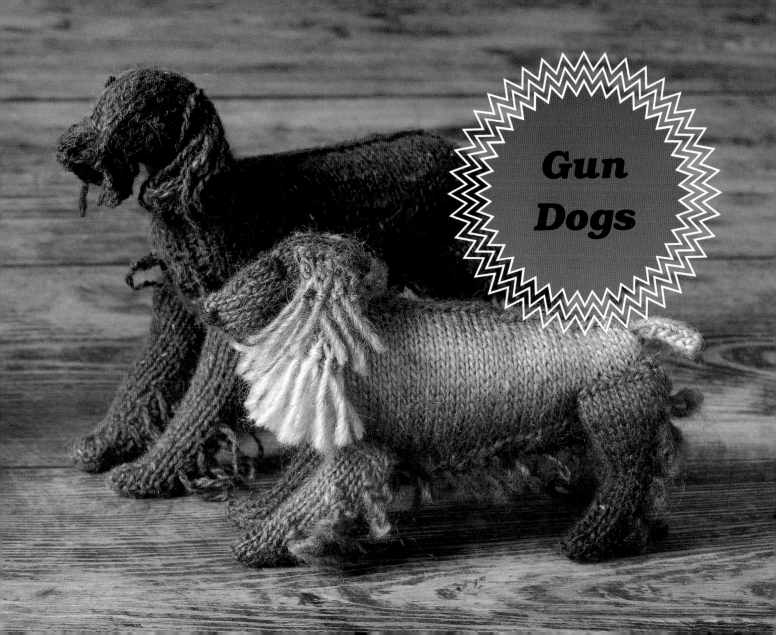

Gun Dogs

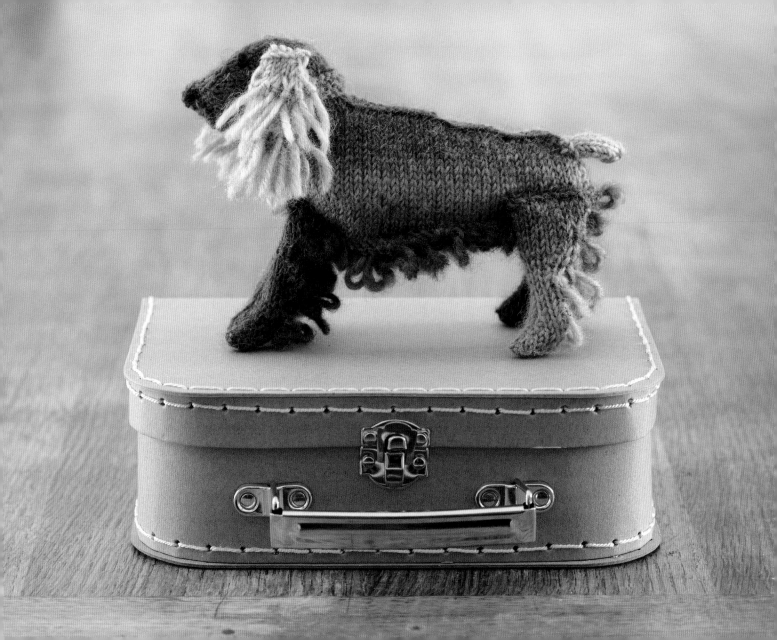

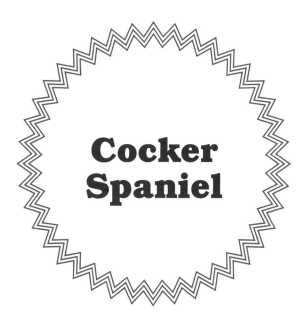

Cocker Spaniel

Loyal and affectionate with a doe-eyed, appealing look, Cocker Spaniels are gun dogs, but have become popular family pets. Elizabeth Barratt Browning famously adored Flush, her constant companion and bedfellow. She even wrote him a poem; not really one of her best works, but probably better than *Millie's Book*, the eponymous memoirs of Barbara Bush's spaniel.

Cocker Spaniel

This is fairly simple as it is knitted in variegated yarn, so you don't need to do any intarsia.

Measurements

Length: 17cm (6¾in)
Height to top of head: 13cm (5in)

Materials

- Pair of 2¾mm (US 2) knitting needles
- 2 spare 2¾mm (US 2) knitting needles
- 40g (1½oz) of Rowan Tapestry SH177 in Lead Mine (le)
- Small amount of Rowan Cashsoft 4ply in Bluebottle 449 (bl) for collar
- Tiny amount of Rowan Pure Wool 4ply in Black 404 for nose and eyes
- Pipecleaners for legs

Abbreviations

See page 172.
For loopy stitch technique, see page 173.

Back Leg

(make 2 the same)
With le, cast on 11 sts.
Beg with a k row, work 2 rows st st.
Row 3: Inc, k2, k2tog, k1, k2tog, k2, inc. *(11 sts)*
Row 4: Purl.
Rep last 2 rows once more.
Row 7: K3, k2tog, k1, k2tog, k3. *(9 sts)*
Work 5 rows st st, working 2-finger loopy st on 2nd and 2nd last st on first and every alt p row for rest of leg.

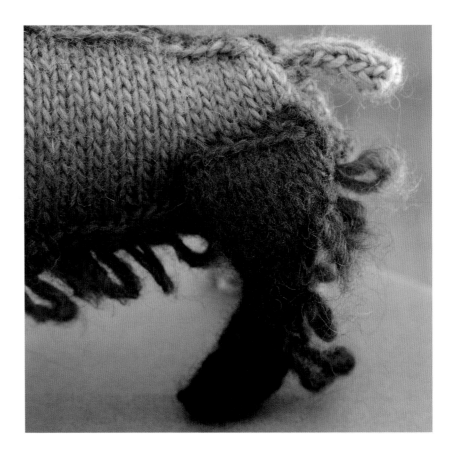

Row 13: Inc, k1, inc, k3, inc, k1, inc. *(13 sts)*
Row 14: Purl.
Row 15: K2tog, [k1, inc] 4 times, k1, k2tog. *(15 sts)*
Row 16: Purl.
Row 17: Inc, k13, inc. *(17 sts)*
Row 18: Purl.
Row 19: Inc, k15, inc. *(19 sts)*

Legs

The legs have uncut loopy stitch to give them that feathered look.

Row 21: Purl.
Row 22: Inc, k17, inc. *(21 sts)*
Row 23: Purl.
Cast (bind) off.

Front Leg

(make 2 the same)
With le, cast on 9 sts.
Beg with a k row, work 2 rows st st.
Row 3: Inc, k1, k2tog, k1, k2tog, k1, inc. *(9 sts)*
Row 4: Purl.
Row 5: Inc, k1, k2tog, k1, k2tog, k1, inc. *(9 sts)*
Work 2 rows st st.

Body

As Cocker Spaniels are different heights, you can adjust the position of the legs on the body when sewing them on.

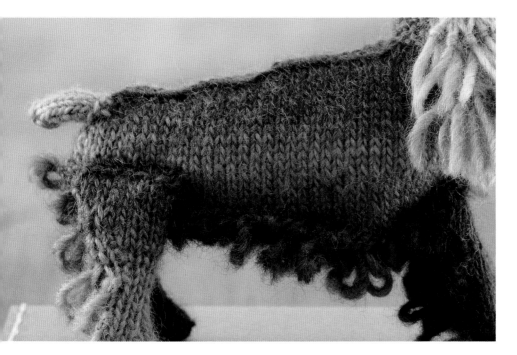

Row 8: Purl, working 2-finger loopy st on 2nd and 2nd last st on this and every alt p row for rest of leg.
Row 9: Inc, k7, inc. *(11 sts)*
Work 7 rows st st.
Row 17: Inc, k9, inc. *(13 sts)*
Work 3 rows st st.
Cast (bind) off.

Right Side of Body

With le, cast on 12 sts.
Row 1: K12, cast on 5 sts. *(17 sts)*
Row 2: P16, inc. *(18 sts)*
Row 3: K18, cast on 3 sts. *(21 sts)*
Row 4: P20, inc. *(22 sts)*
Row 5: K22, cast on 11 sts. *(33 sts)*
Row 6: Inc, p31, inc. *(35 sts)*
Row 7: Knit.
Row 8: P34, inc. *(36 sts)*
Row 9: Knit.
Row 10: P35, inc. *(37 sts)*
Row 11: Knit.
Row 12: P2tog, p35. *(36 sts)*
Row 13: K34, k2tog. *(35 sts)*
Row 14: P2tog, p33. *(34 sts)*
Row 15: K32, k2tog. *(33 sts)*
Row 16: Cast (bind) off 6 sts, p to last 2 sts, p2tog. *(26 sts)*
Row 17: K24, k2tog. *(25 sts)*
Row 18: Cast (bind) off 4 sts, p to end. *(21 sts)*
Row 19: K19, k2tog. *(20 sts)*
Row 20: Cast (bind) off 12 sts (hold 8 sts on spare needle for right neck).

Left Side of Body

With le, cast on 12 sts.
Row 1: Knit.
Row 2: P12, cast on 5 sts. *(17 sts)*
Row 3: K16, inc. *(18 sts)*
Row 4: P18, cast on 3 sts. *(21 sts)*
Row 5: K20, inc. *(22 sts)*
Row 6: P22, cast on 11 sts. *(33 sts)*
Row 7: Inc, k31, inc. *(35 sts)*

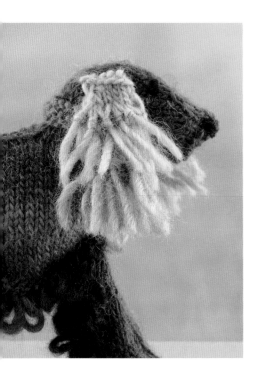

Head

Try to use matching sections of the yarn for the ears as the colour variation is quite extreme.

Row 8: Purl.
Row 9: K34, inc. *(36 sts)*
Row 10: Purl.
Row 11: K35, inc. *(37 sts)*
Row 12: Purl.
Row 13: K2tog, k35. *(36 sts)*
Row 14: P34, p2tog. *(35 sts)*
Row 15: K2tog, k33. *(34 sts)*
Row 16: P32, p2tog. *(33 sts)*
Row 17: Cast (bind) off 6 sts, k to last 2 sts, k2tog. *(26 sts)*
Row 18: P24, p2tog. *(25 sts)*
Row 19: Cast (bind) off 4 sts, k to end. *(21 sts)*
Row 20: P19, p2tog. *(20 sts)*
Row 21: Cast (bind) off 12 sts (hold 8 sts on spare needle for left neck).

Head

With le, and with RS facing k8 from spare needle of Right Side of Body then k8 from spare needle of Left Side of Body. *(16 sts)*
Row 1: Purl.
Work 2 rows st st.
Row 4: K12, pult (pick up loop below next st on left needle by inserting tip of right needle from back through loop – this stops a hole forming when turning work – then turn, leaving rem 4 sts on left needle unworked).
Row 5: Working top of head on centre 8 sts only, p2tog (first st of p2tog is loop picked up at end of last row), p7, pult.
Row 6: K2tog, k7, pult.
Row 7: P2tog, p7, pult.
Row 8: K2tog, k7, pult.
Row 9: P2tog, p7, pult.
Row 10: K2tog, k11. *(16 sts in total)*
Row 11: Purl.
Row 12: K5, k2tog 3 times, k5. *(13 sts)*
Row 13: Purl.
Work 2 rows st st.
Row 16: Inc, k3, k2tog, k1, k2tog, k3, inc. *(13 sts)*
Row 17: Purl.

Row 18: Inc, k3, k2tog, k1, k2tog, k3, inc. *(13 sts)*
Row 19: Purl.
Row 20: Cast (bind) off 4 sts, k to end. *(9 sts)*
Row 21: Cast (bind) off 4 sts, p to end. *(5 sts)*
Row 22: K2tog, k1, k2tog. *(3 sts)*
Row 23: P2tog, p1. *(2 sts)*
Row 24: K2tog and fasten off.

Tummy

With le, cast on 4 sts.
Beg with a k row, work 2 rows st st.
Row 3: Inc, k2, inc. *(6 sts)*
Row 4: Purl, working 2-finger loopy st on 2nd and 2nd last st of this and all other p rows until otherwise stated.
Row 5: Inc, k4, inc. *(8 sts)*
Row 6: Purl.
Row 7: Inc, k6, inc. *(10 sts)*
Row 8: Purl.
Work 40 rows st st.
Next row: K2tog, k6, k2tog. *(8 sts)*
Work 3 rows st st.
Next row: K2tog, k4, k2tog. *(6 sts)*
Next row: Purl.
Next row: Knit.
Next row: Purl; this is the last loopy st row.
Work 7 rows st st.
Cast (bind) off.

Tail

With le, cast on 6 sts.
Beg with a k row, work 8 rows st st.
Cast (bind) off.

Ear

(make 2 the same)
With le, cast on 8 sts.
Row 1: Knit.
Row 2: Purl, working 3-finger loopy st on every st.
Beg with a k row, work 5 rows st st.
Row 8: Purl, working 2-finger loopy st on every st.

Beg with a k row, work 2 rows st st.
Row 11: K2tog, k4, k2tog. *(6 sts)*
Row 12: Purl.
Cast (bind) off.

Collar

With bl, cast on 24 sts.
Knit 2 rows.
Cast (bind) off.

To Make Up

Sew in ends, leaving ends from cast on
and cast (bound) off rows for sewing up.
Using mattress or whip stitch, sew up legs
starting at paw. Turn right side out, stuff
each leg, using pipecleaners for rigidity if
necessary. Using whip stitch, sew along top
of leg, leaving an end to sew leg to body.
Sew cast on row of tummy to V at base of
back and sew cast (bound) off row under
chin. Ease and sew tummy to fit body. Leave
a 2.5cm (1in) gap between front and back
legs on one side. Turn right side out, stuff
then sew up gap with mattress stitch.
Using whip stitch, sew legs to body as
shown in photograph, with back legs
at an angle.
Sew up two sides of head and sew on ears
and tail as shown in photograph. Using
black yarn, embroider the nose using satin
stitch and make two French knots for eyes.
Cut loops of loopy stitch on ears and fluff
out yarn.
Sew ends of collar together and slide over
head onto neck.
If legs are floppy, about 2cm (¾in) down
from top edge of leg, sew through leg, body
and opposite leg to make dog more stable.

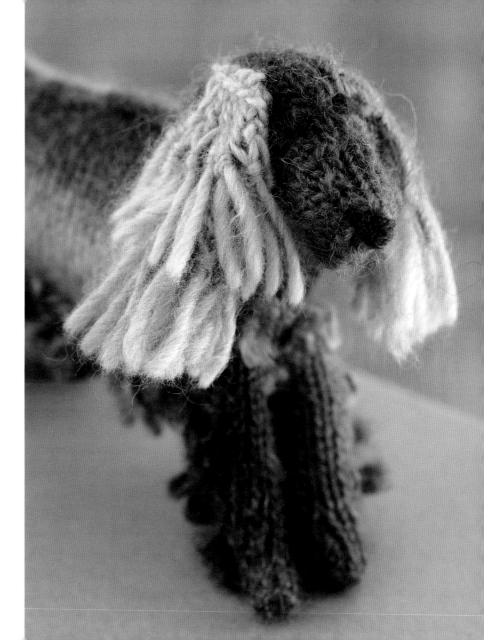

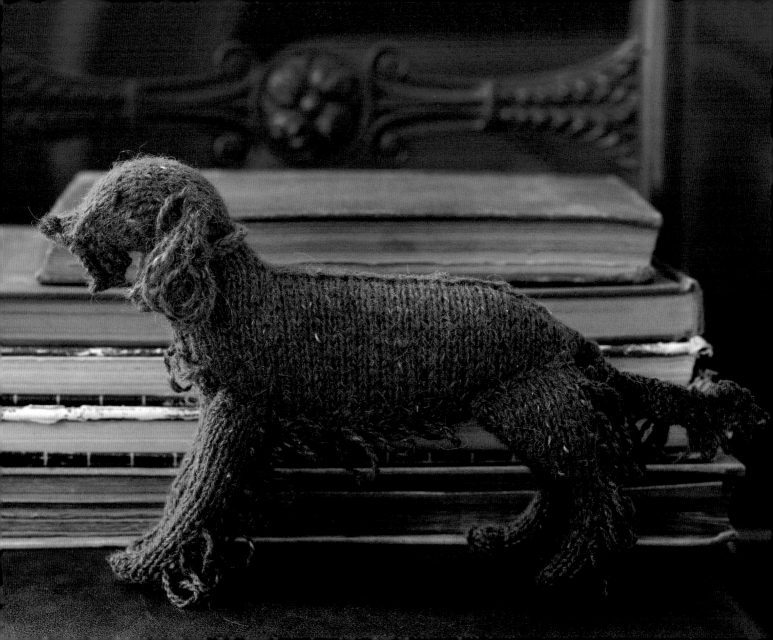

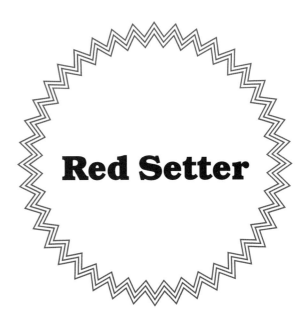

Red Setter

Also known as an Irish Setter, the Red Setter
has a long, rich auburn coat; yarn dyes mean ours
has a rather more unconventional tandoori tone.
A majestic and useful gun dog, Setters are sleek,
poised and affectionate. They have the reputation of
not being the most intellectual of breeds, but this is
the fault of over-breeding and they are in fact highly
trainable. Constantly on the go, the Red Setter
needs long walks, stick-throwing and entertaining,
and in return is loving towards humans.

Red Setter

Straightforward to make, this dog uses a small amount of loopy stitch. Also note the trademark jowls in garter stitch.

Measurements
Length: 21cm (8in)
Height to top of head: 15cm (6in)

Materials
- Pair of 2¾mm (US 2) knitting needles
- 2 spare 2¾mm (US 2) knitting needles
- 35g (1¼oz) of Rowan Felted Tweed in Ginger 154 (gn)
- Small amount of Rowan Pure Wool 4ply in Glade 421 (gl) for collar
- Tiny amount of Rowan Pure Wool 4ply in Mocha 417 for nose and eyes
- Pipecleaners for legs (optional)

Abbreviations
See page 172.
For loopy stitch technique, see page 173.

Back Leg
(make 2 the same)
With gn, cast on 9 sts.
Beg with a k row, work 2 rows st st.
Row 3: Inc, k1, k2tog, k1, k2tog, k1, inc. *(9 sts)*
Work 15 rows st st, working 2-finger loopy st on 2nd and 2nd last st on row 10 and every alt p row for rest of leg.
Row 19: K2tog, inc into next 2 sts, k1, inc into next 2 sts, k2tog. *(11 sts)*

Row 20 and every alt row: Purl.
Row 21: K2tog, inc, k1, inc, k1, inc, k1, inc, k2tog. *(13 sts)*
Row 23: K5, inc, k1, inc, k5. *(15 sts)*
Row 25: K6, inc, k1, inc, k6. *(17 sts)*
Row 27: K7, inc, k1, inc, k7. *(19 sts)*
Row 29: K8, inc, k1, inc, k8. *(21 sts)*
Row 31: K9, inc, k1, inc, k9. *(23 sts)*
Row 33: K10, inc, k1, inc, k10. *(25 sts)*
Row 35: Knit.
Cast (bind) off.

Front Leg
(make 2 the same)
With gn, cast on 9 sts.
Beg with a k row, work 2 rows st st.
Row 3: Inc, k1, k2tog, k1, k2tog, k1, inc. *(9 sts)*
Row 4: Purl.
Rep last 2 rows once more.
Work 2 rows st st.
Row 9: Inc, k7, inc. *(11 sts)*
Work 11 rows st st, working 2-finger loopy st on 2nd and 2nd last st on next and every alt p row for rest of leg.
Row 21: Inc, k9, inc. *(13 sts)*
Work 7 rows st st.
Row 29: Inc, k11, inc. *(15 sts)*
Work 4 rows st st.
Cast (bind) off.

Right Side of Body
With gn, cast on 8 sts.
Row 1: K8, cast on 8 sts. *(16 sts)*
Row 2: P15, inc. *(17 sts)*
Row 3: K17, cast on 6 sts. *(23 sts)*
Row 4: P22, inc. *(24 sts)*
Row 5: K24, cast on 6 sts. *(30 sts)*
Row 6: P29, inc. *(31 sts)*
Row 7: K31, cast on 6 sts. *(37 sts)*
Row 8: P36, inc. *(38 sts)*
Work 7 rows st st.
Row 16: P2tog, p36. *(37 sts)*
Row 17: K35, k2tog. *(36 sts)*
Row 18: P2tog, p34. *(35 sts)*

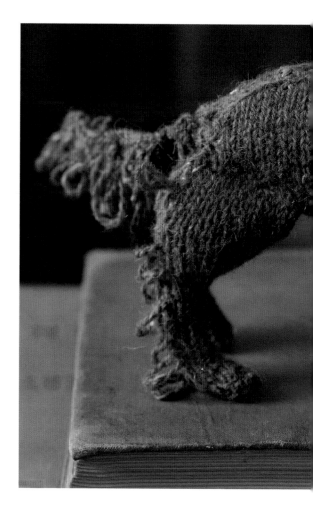

Legs
The legs have uncut loopy stitch to give them that feathered look.

Row 19: K33, k2tog. *(34 sts)*
Row 20: Cast (bind) off 5 sts, p to end. *(29 sts)*
Row 21: K8, (hold 8 sts on spare needle for right neck), cast (bind) off rem 21 sts.

Left Side of Body

With gn, cast on 8 sts.
Row 1: Knit.
Row 2: P8, cast on 8 sts. *(16 sts)*
Row 3: K15, inc. *(17 sts)*
Row 4: P17, cast on 6 sts. *(23 sts)*
Row 5: K22, inc. *(24 sts)*
Row 6: P24, cast on 6 sts. *(30 sts)*
Row 7: K29, inc. *(31 sts)*
Row 8: P31, cast on 6 sts. *(37 sts)*
Row 9: K36, inc. *(38 sts)*
Work 7 rows st st.
Row 17: K2tog, k36. *(37 sts)*
Row 18: P35, p2tog. *(36 sts)*
Row 19: K2tog, k34. *(35 sts)*
Row 20: P33, p2tog. *(34 sts)*
Row 21: Cast (bind) off 5 sts, k to end. *(29 sts)*
Row 22: P8, (hold 8 sts on spare needle for left neck), cast (bind) off rem 21 sts.

Neck and Head

Row 1: With gn, and with RS facing k8 from spare needle of Right Side of Body then k8 from spare needle of Left Side of Body. *(16 sts)*
Row 2: Purl.
Row 3: Inc, k5, k2tog twice, k5, inc. *(16 sts)*
Row 4: Purl.
Row 5: Inc, k5, k2tog twice, k5, inc. *(16 sts)*
Row 6: Purl.
Row 7: Inc, k14, inc. *(18 sts)*
Row 8: Inc, p16, inc. *(20sts)*
Row 9: K15, pult (pick up loop below next st on left needle by inserting tip of right needle from back through loop – this stops a hole forming when turning work – then turn, leaving rem 5 sts on left needle unworked).

Row 10: Working top of head on centre 10 sts only, p2tog (first st of p2tog is loop picked up at end of last row), p9, pult.
Row 11: K2tog, k9, pult.
Row 12: P2tog, p9, pult.
Rep last 2 rows twice more.
Row 17: K2tog, k to end. *(20 sts)*
Row 18: Purl.
Row 19: K15, pult.
Row 20: Working top of head on centre 10 sts only, p2tog (first st of p2tog is loop picked up at end of last row), p9, pult.
Row 21: K2tog, k9, pult.
Row 22: P2tog, p9, pult.

Body
Sew on the back legs at a slight backward angle to the body.

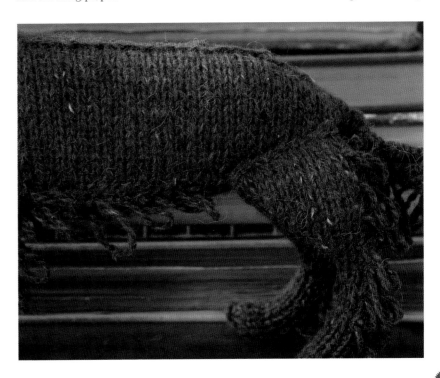

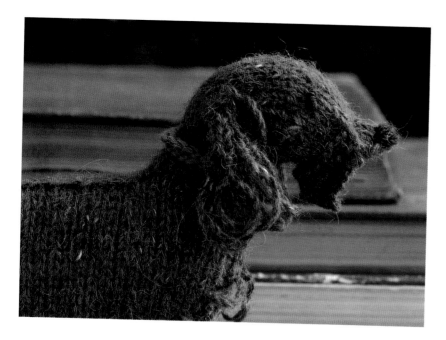

Head

Be careful with ear placement, Red Setters' ears are set fairly low on their head.

Rep last 2 rows once more.
Row 25: K2tog, knit to end. *(20 sts on right needle)*
Row 26: Purl.
Row 27: K1, k2tog twice, k10, k2tog twice, k1. *(16 sts)*
Row 28: Purl.
Row 29: Inc, k14, inc. *(18 sts)*
Start garter stitch jowls
Row 30: K7, p4, k7.
Row 31: Inc, k16, inc. *(20 sts)*
Row 32: K8, p4, k8.
Row 33: Knit.
Row 34: Purl.
Row 35: Cast (bind) off 8 sts, k4 icos, cast (bind) off 8 sts.
Row 36: Rejoin yarn, cast (bind) off 4 sts.

Tummy

With gn, cast on l st.
Row 1: Inc. *(2 sts)*
Row 2: Inc into both sts. *(4 sts)*
Row 3: Purl.
Row 4: Inc, k2, inc. *(6 sts)*
Row 5: Purl.
Row 6: Inc, k4, inc. *(8 sts)*
Row 7: Purl.
Row 8: Inc, k6, inc. *(10 sts)*
Row 9: Purl.
Work 11 rows st st.
Rows 21–57: Work 37 rows st st, starting with p row, working 2-finger loopy st on 2nd and 2nd last st on this and every alt p row.
Row 58: K2tog, k6, k2tog. *(8 sts)*
Work 2 rows st st.
Row 61: Purl, working 2-finger loopy st on 2nd and 2nd last st.
Row 62: K2tog, k4, k2tog. *(6 sts)*
Work 2 rows st st.
Row 65: As row 61.
Work 14 rows st st, without loopy st, until tummy reaches to start of jowls.
Cast (bind) off.

Tail

With gn, cast on 28 sts.
Row 1: Knit.
Row 2: Purl, working 2-finger loopy st on first 6 alt sts and 3-finger loopy st on foll 8 alt sts.
Cast (bind) off.

Ear

(make 2 the same)
With gn, cast on 6 sts.
Beg with a k row, work 5 rows st st.
Row 6: Purl, working 3-finger loopy st on every st.
Work 2 rows st st.
Row 9: K2tog, k2, k2tog. *(4 sts)*
Work 3 rows st st.
Cast (bind) off.

Collar

With gl, cast on 24 sts.
Knit 1 row.
Cast (bind) off.

To Make Up

Sew in ends, leaving ends from cast on
and cast (bound) off rows for sewing up.
Using mattress or whip stitch, sew up legs
starting at paw. Stuff each leg, using
pipecleaners for rigidity if necessary.
Sew along top of leg, leaving an end to sew
leg to body.
Using mattress or whip stitch, sew body
along back and around bottom. Sew cast
on row of tummy to bottom and sew cast
(bound) off row under where jowls begin.
Ease and sew tummy to fit body. Leave a
2.5cm (1in) gap between front and back legs
on one side. Turn right side out, stuff then
sew up gap with mattress stitch.
Sew down sides of head leaving jowls
hanging free.
Sew on tail where curve of bottom starts,
with loops on the underside and longest
loops closest to body. Thread yarn from cast
on end through tail to body and pull up
slightly to make tail curve.
Sew ears to head as shown in photograph.
Using mocha yarn, embroider the nose
using satin stitch and make two French
knots for eyes.
Sew ends of collar together and slide over
head onto neck.
About 2cm (¾in) down from top edge of leg,
sew through leg, body and opposite leg to
make dog more stable.

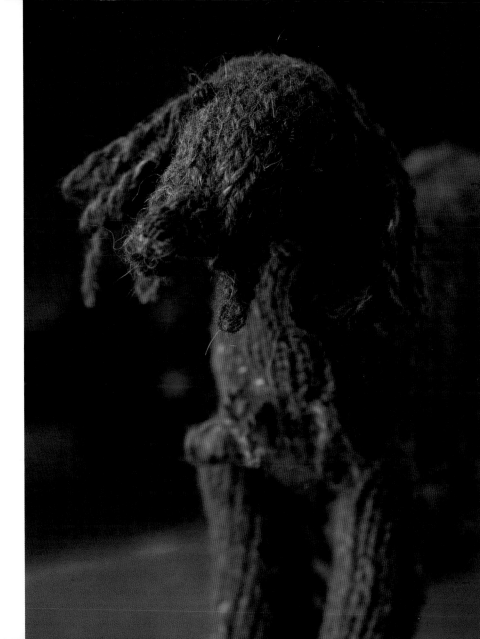

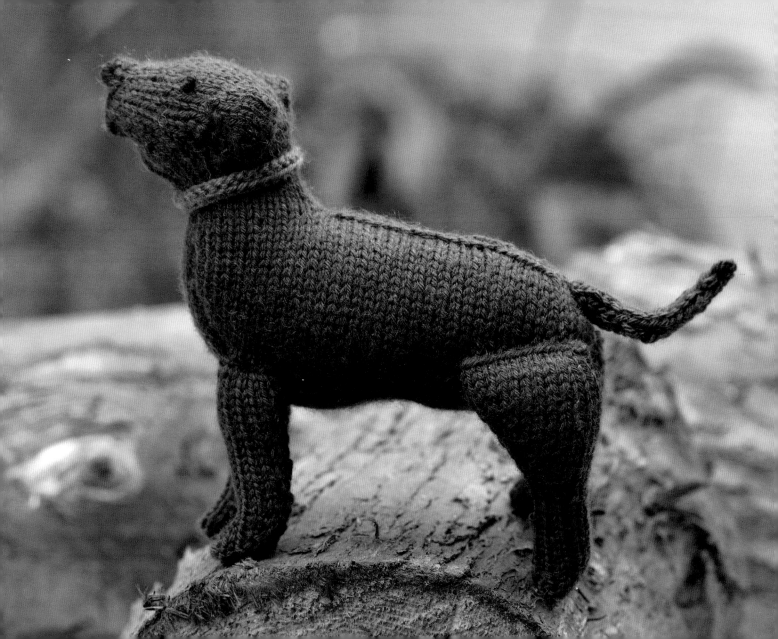

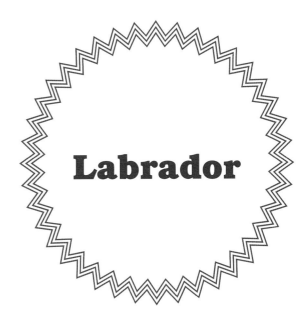

Labrador

The Labrador retriever is the world's most popular dog, loved for their mellow and friendly temperament. They are gentle with children, so gentle that the Labrador can carry an egg in its mouth without breaking it. A really useful dog, Labradors are often used for guiding the blind and for retrieving game. Vladimir Putin has a black Labrador called Koni. Buddy, the Clinton's chocolate Labrador, was tragically run over before he had time to write his White House memoirs.

Labrador

One of the simpler dogs to knit, ours is chocolate but you can choose your own colour.

Measurements

Length: 15cm (6in)
Height to top of head: 13cm (5in)

Materials

- Pair of 2¾mm (US 2) knitting needles
- 2 spare 2¾mm (US 2) knitting needles
- Pair of 2¾mm (US 2) double-pointed knitting needles
- 30g (1⅛oz) of Rowan Cashsoft 4ply in Bark 432 (ba)
- Small amount of Rowan Pure Wool 4ply in Framboise 456 (fr) for collar
- Tiny amount of Rowan Pure Wool 4ply in Black 404 for nose and eyes
- Pipecleaners for legs

Abbreviations

See page 172.

Back Leg

(make 2 the same)
With 2¾mm (US 2) knitting needles and ba, cast on 9 sts.
Beg with a k row, work 2 rows st st.
Row 3: Inc, k1, k2tog, k1, k2tog, k1, inc. *(9 sts)*
Work 11 rows st st.
Row 15: K2tog, inc into next 2 sts, k1, inc into next 2 sts, k2tog. *(11 sts)*
Row 16 and every alt row: Purl.

Row 17: K2tog, inc, k1, inc, k1, inc, k1, inc, k2tog. *(13 sts)*
Row 19: K5, inc, k1, inc, k5. *(15 sts)*
Row 21: K6, inc, k1, inc, k6. *(17 sts)*
Row 23: K7, inc, k1, inc, k7. *(19 sts)*
Row 25: K8, inc, k1, inc, k8. *(21 sts)*
Row 27: K9, inc, k1, inc, k9. *(23 sts)*
Row 29: K10, inc, k1, inc, k10. *(25 sts)*
Row 31: Knit.
Cast (bind) off.

Front Leg

(make 2 the same)
With 2¾mm (US 2) knitting needles and ba, cast on 9 sts.
Beg with a k row, work 2 rows st st.
Row 3: Inc, k1, k2tog, k1, k2tog, k1, inc. *(9 sts)*
Row 4: Purl.
Rep last 2 rows once more.
Work 2 rows st st.
Row 9: Inc, k7, inc. *(11 sts)*
Work 7 rows st st.
Row 17: Inc, k9, inc. *(13 sts)*
Work 9 rows st st.
Row 27: Inc, k11, inc. *(15 sts)*
Work 3 rows st st.
Cast (bind) off.

Right Side of Body

With 2¾mm (US 2) knitting needles and ba, cast on 8 sts.
Row 1: K8, cast on 8 sts. *(16 sts)*
Row 2: P15, inc. *(17 sts)*
Row 3: K17, cast on 5 sts. *(22 sts)*
Row 4: P21, inc. *(23 sts)*
Row 5: K23, cast on 11 sts. *(34 sts)*
Row 6: P33, inc. *(35 sts)*
Row 7: K35.
Row 8: P34, inc. *(36 sts)*
Work 7 rows st st.
Row 16: P2tog, p34. *(35 sts)*
Row 17: K33, k2tog. *(34 sts)*
Row 18: P2tog, p32. *(33 sts)*
Row 19: K31, k2tog. *(32 sts)*

Body

For a Golden Labrador you could use Rowan Cashsoft 4ply in Savannah 439.

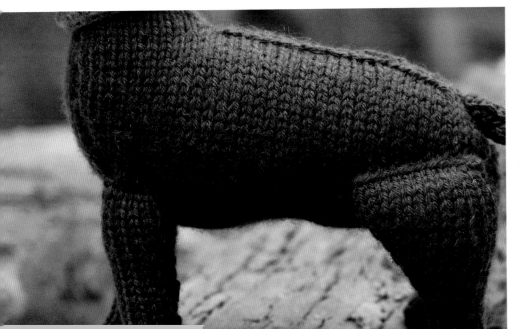

Row 20: Cast (bind) off 5 sts, p to end. *(27 sts)*
Row 21: K11 (hold 11 sts on spare needle for right neck), cast (bind) off rem 16 sts.

Left Side of Body
With 2¾mm (US 2) knitting needles and ba, cast on 8 sts.
Row 1: Knit.
Row 2: P8, cast on 8 sts. *(16 sts)*
Row 3: K15, inc. *(17 sts)*
Row 4: P17, cast on 5 sts. *(22 sts)*
Row 5: K21, inc. *(23 sts)*
Row 6: P23, cast on 11 sts. *(34 sts)*
Row 7: K33, inc. *(35 sts)*

Row 8: P35.
Row 9: K34, inc. *(36 sts)*
Work 7 rows st st.
Row 17: K2tog, k34. *(35 sts)*
Row 18: P33, p2tog. *(34 sts)*
Row 19: K2tog, k32. *(33 sts)*
Row 20: P31, p2tog. *(32 sts)*
Row 21: Cast (bind) off 5 sts, k to end. *(27 sts)*
Row 22: P11, (hold 11 sts on spare needle for left neck), cast (bind) off rem 16 sts.

Neck and Head
Row 1: With 2¾mm (US 2) knitting needles and ba, and with RS facing k11 from spare needle of Right Side of Body then k11 from spare needle of Left Side of Body. *(22 sts)*
Row 2: Purl.
Row 3: Inc, k20, inc. *(24 sts)*
Row 4: Purl.
Row 5: Inc, k22, inc. *(26 sts)*
Row 6: Purl.
Row 7: K20, pult (pick up loop below next st on left needle by inserting tip of right needle from back through loop – this stops a hole forming when turning work – then turn, leaving rem 6 sts on left needle unworked).
Row 8: Working top of head on centre 14 sts only, p2tog (first st of p2tog is loop picked up at end of last row), p13, pult.
Row 9: K2tog, k13, pult.
Row 10: P2tog, p13, pult.
Row 11: K2tog, k13, pult.
Row 12: P2tog, p13, pult.
Row 13: K2tog, k to end. *(26 sts)*
Row 14: Purl.
Row 15: K20, pult.
Row 16: Working top of head on these 14 sts only, p2tog (first st of p2tog is loop picked up at end of last row), p13, pult.
Row 17: K2tog, k13, pult.
Row 18: P2tog, p13, pult.
Row 19: K2tog, k to end. *(26 sts)*
Row 20: Purl.

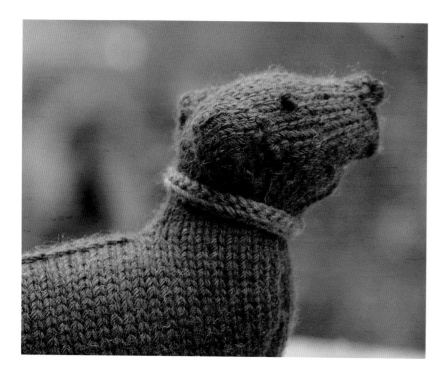

Head

The labrador's ears are set very wide apart.

Row 21: [K1, k2tog] 8 times, k2. *(18 sts)*
Row 22: Purl.
Row 23: K6, [k2tog] 3 times, k6. *(15 sts)*
Row 24: Purl.
Row 25: K2tog, k11, k2tog. *(13 sts)*
Row 26: Purl.
Row 27: Cast (bind) off 4 sts, k to end. *(9 sts)*
Row 28: Cast (bind) off 4 sts, p to end. *(5 sts)*
Cast (bind) off.

Tummy

With 2¾mm (US 2) knitting needles and ba, cast on 1 st.
Row 1: Inc. *(2 sts)*
Row 2: Inc into both sts. *(4 sts)*
Row 3: Inc, k2, inc. *(6 sts)*
Row 4: Inc, p4, inc. *(8 sts)*
Row 5: Inc, k6, inc. *(10 sts)*
Work 59 rows st st, until knitting reaches halfway up chest, ending with a p row.
Next row: K2tog, k6, k2tog. *(8 sts)*
Work 5 rows st st.
Next row: K2tog, k4, k2tog. *(6 sts)*
Work 5 rows st st.
Next row: K2tog, k2, k2tog. *(4 sts)*
Work 7 rows st st.
Next row: K2tog twice. *(2 sts)*
Next row: P2tog and fasten off.

Tail

With 2¾mm (US 2) double-pointed knitting needles and ba, cast on 6 sts.
Work in i-cord as folls:
Knit 10 rows.
Next row: K2tog, k2, k2tog. *(4 sts)*
Knit 5 rows.
Next row: K2tog twice. *(2 sts)*
Knit 1 row.
Next row: K2tog and fasten off.

Ear

(make 2 the same)
With 2¾mm (US 2) knitting needles and ba, cast on 7 sts.
Beg with a k row, work 6 rows st st.
Row 7: K2tog, k3, k2tog. *(5 sts)*
Row 8: P2tog, p1, p2tog. *(3 sts)*
Row 9: K2tog, k1. *(2 sts)*
Row 10: P2tog and fasten off.

Collar

With 2¾mm (US 2) knitting needles and fr.
cast on 26 sts.
Knit 2 rows.
Cast (bind) off.

To Make Up

Sew in ends, leaving ends from cast on
and cast (bound) off rows for sewing up.
Using mattress or whip stitch, sew up legs
starting at paw. Turn right side out, stuff
each leg, using pipecleaners for rigidity if
necessary. Sew along top of leg, leaving an
end to sew leg to body.
Using mattress or whip stitch, sew down
centre back. Sew cast on row of tummy to V
at base of back and sew cast (bound) off row
under chin. Ease and sew tummy to fit body.
Leave a 2.5cm (1in) gap between front and
back legs on one side. Turn right side out,
stuff then sew up gap with mattress stitch.
Using whip stitch, sew legs to body as
shown in photograph, with back legs at
an angle.
Sew up two sides of head, sew on ears and
catch down the tips with one stitch. Sew
on tail as shown in photograph.
Using black yarn, embroider the nose
using satin stitch and make two French
knots for eyes.
Sew ends of collar together and slide over
head onto neck.
If legs are floppy, about 2cm (¾in) down
from top edge of leg, sew through leg, body
and opposite leg to make dog more stable.

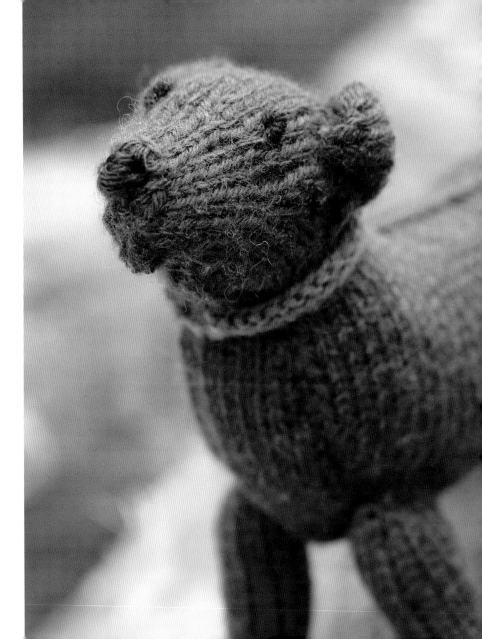

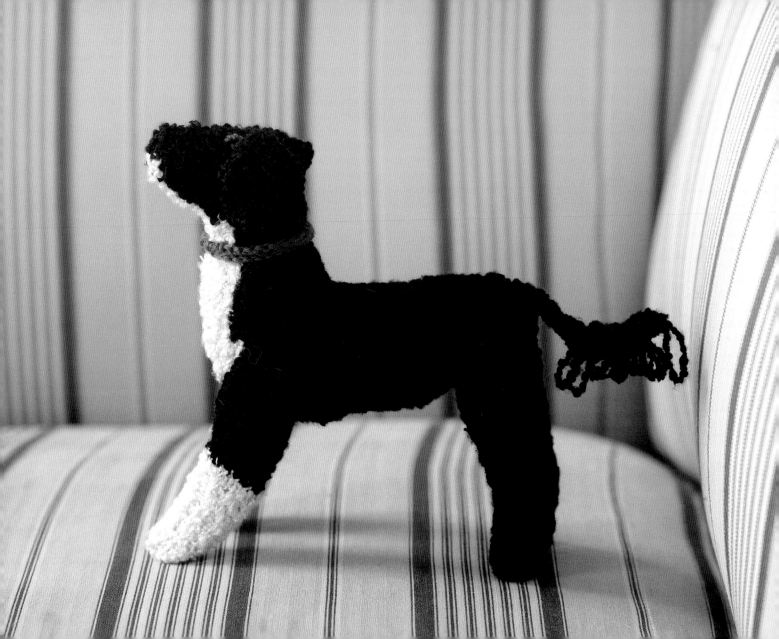

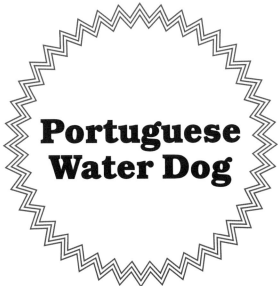

Portuguese Water Dog

It's fair to say that nobody had paid much attention to the Portuguese Water Dog until the arrival of Bo Obama at the White House. PWDs have been around since the 12th century, but in the 1960s were listed in the Guinness Book of Records as the rarest breed of pedigree dog. Originally bred to help fishermen, they herded the catch, retrieved anything that fell in the water and carried messages from ship to shore. Bo, the Obama's PWD, was given to them by Ted Kennedy, whose own PWD, Splash, was another of the numerous dogs to have written his memoirs of life in Washington.

Portuguese Water Dog

This is knitted in bouclé yarn to create the PWD's distinctive curly coat.

Measurements
Length: 16cm (6¼in)
Height to top of head: 15cm (6in)

Materials
- Pair of 2¾mm (US 2) knitting needles
- 2 spare 2¾mm (US 2) knitting needles
- 30g (1⅛oz) of Halcyon Yarn Gemstone Silk Bouclé in Black 101 (bl)
- 10g (¼oz) of Halcyon Yarn Stardust in Natural 000 (na)
- Small amount of Rowan Pure Wool 4ply in Hessian 416 (he) for collar and eyes
- 3 pipecleaners (optional for legs, essential for tail)

Abbreviations
See page 172.
For loopy stitch technique, see page 173.

Back Leg
(make 2 the same)
With bl, cast on 9 sts.
Beg with a k row, work 2 rows st st.
Row 3: Inc, k1, k2tog, k1, k2tog, k1, inc. *(9 sts)*
Row 4: Purl.
Rep last 2 rows once more.*
Work 6 rows st st.
Row 13: K2tog, k1, inc, k1, inc, k1, k2tog. *(9 sts)*

Work 3 rows st st.
Row 17: K3, inc, k1, inc, k3. *(11 sts)*
Work 3 rows st st.
Row 21: K4, inc, k1, inc, k4. *(13 sts)*
Work 3 rows st st.
Row 25: K5, inc, k1, inc, k5. *(15 sts)*
Work 5 rows st st.
Row 31: K5, k2tog, k1, k2tog, k5. *(13 sts)*
Row 32: P4, p2tog, p1, p2tog, p4. *(11 sts)*
Cast (bind) off.

Right Front Leg
With na, cast on 9 sts.
Follow instructions for Back Leg to *.
Work 8 rows st st.
Row 15: Inc, k7, inc. *(11 sts)*
Row 16: Purl.**
Row 17: K8na, join in bl, k3bl.
Row 18: P4bl, p7na.
Cont in bl.
Work 14 rows st st.
Cast (bind) off.

Left Front Leg
As for Right Front Leg to **.
Row 17: Join in bl, k3bl, k8na.
Row 18: P7na, p4bl.
Cont in bl.
Work 14 rows st st.
Cast (bind) off.

Right Side of Body
With bl, cast on 9 sts.
Row 1: Knit.
Row 2: P8, inc. *(10 sts)*
Row 3: Join in na, k1na, k9bl, cast on 5 sts bl. *(15 sts)*
Row 4: P14bl, incna. *(16 sts)*
Row 5: K2na, k14bl, cast on 2 sts bl. *(18 sts)*
Row 6: P15bl, p3na.
Row 7: K3na, k15bl, cast on 2 sts bl. *(20 sts)*
Row 8: P17bl, p2na, incna. *(21 sts)*
Row 9: K4na, k17bl, cast on 5 sts bl. *(26 sts)*
Row 10: P22bl, p4na.

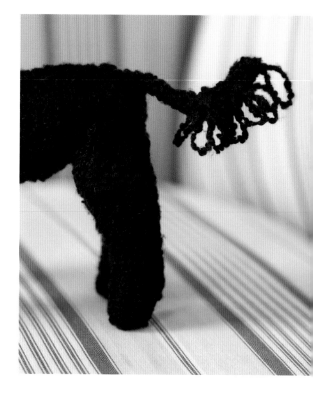

Tail
The loopy stitch should hang down on the underside of the tail.

Row 11: K4na, k22bl.
Rep last 2 rows once more.
Row 14: P23bl, p3na.
Row 15: K3na, k23bl.
Rep last 2 rows twice more.
Row 20: P1bl, p2togbl, p20bl, p3na. *(25 sts)*
Row 21: K3na, k19bl, k2togbl, k1bl. *(24 sts)*
Row 22: Cast (bind) off 4 sts, p17bl icos, p3na.
Row 23: K3na, k6bl (hold 9 sts on spare needle for right neck), cast (bind) off rem 11 sts bl.

Left Side of Body

With bl, cast on 9 sts.
Row 1: Purl.
Row 2: K8, inc. *(10 sts)*
Row 3: Join in na, p1na, p9bl, cast on 5 sts bl. *(15 sts)*

Body

PWDs have different markings, ours is based on Bo Obama.

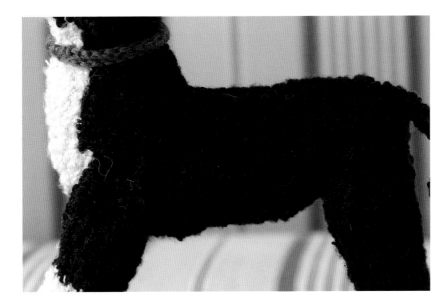

Row 4: K14bl, incna. *(16 sts)*
Row 5: P2na, p14bl, cast on 2 sts bl. *(18 sts)*
Row 6: K15bl, k3na.
Row 7: P3na, p15bl, cast on 2 sts bl. *(20 sts)*
Row 8: K17bl, k2na, incna. *(21 sts)*
Row 9: K4na, k17bl, cast on 5 sts bl. *(26 sts)*
Row 10: K22bl, k4na.
Row 11: P4na, p22bl.
Rep last 2 rows once more.
Row 14: K23bl, k3na.
Row 15: P3na, p23bl.
Rep last 2 rows twice more.
Row 20: K1bl, k2togbl, k20bl, k3na. *(25 sts)*
Row 21: P3na, p19bl, p2togbl, p1bl. *(24 sts)*
Row 22: Cast (bind) off 4 sts, k17bl icos, k3na.
Row 23: P3na, p6bl (hold 9 sts on spare needle for left neck), cast (bind) off rem 11 sts bl.

Neck and Head

Row 1: With na and bl, and with RS facing k3na, k6bl spare needle of Right Side of Body then k6bl, k3na from spare needle of Left Side of Body. *(18 sts)*
Row 2: P3na, p12bl, p3na.
Row 3: K2na, k2bl, k2togbl, k6bl, k2togbl, k2bl, k2na. *(16 sts)*
Row 4: P2na, p12bl, p2na.
Row 5: K2na, k12bl, k2na.
Rep last 2 rows once more.
Row 8: P2na, p12bl, p2na.
Row 9: K1na, k12bl, pult (pick up loop below next st on left needle by inserting tip of right needle from back through loop – this stops a hole forming when turning work – then turn, leaving rem 3 sts on left needle unworked).
Row 10: Working top of head on centre 10 sts only, p2tog (first st of p2tog is loop picked up at end of last row), p9bl, pult.
Row 11: K2togbl, k9bl, pult.
Row 12: P2togbl, p9bl, pult.
Rep last 2 rows once more.
Row 15: K2togbl, k11bl, k1na. *(16 sts in total)*

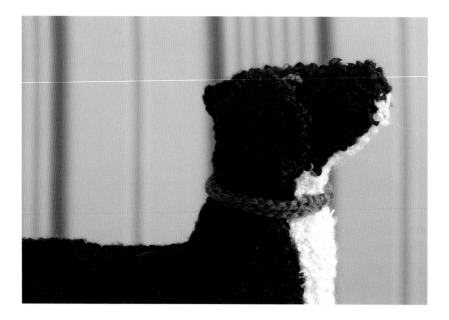

Head

Stuff the head carefully and mould it into shape.

Row 16: P1na, p14bl, p1na.
Row 17: K1na, k14bl, k1na.
Row 18: P1na, p14bl, p1na.
Row 19: K1na, k11bl, pult (leave 4 sts on left needle).
Row 20: P2togbl, p7bl, pult.
Row 21: K2tog, k7bl, pult.
Rep last 2 rows once more.
Row 24: P2togbl, p7bl, pult.
Row 25: K2togbl, k10bl, k1na. *(16 sts in total)*
Row 26: P1na, p2bl, p2togbl, p2bl, p2togbl, p2bl, p2togbl, p2bl, p1na. *(13 sts)*
Row 27: K1na, k11bl, k1na.
Row 28: P1na, p11bl, p1na.
Row 29: K1na, k11bl, k1na.
Row 30: P1na, p2bl, p2togbl, p3bl, p2togbl, p2bl, p1na. *(11 sts)*
Row 31: K1na, k9bl, k1na.

Row 32: P1na, p9bl, p1na.
Row 33: K1na, k9bl, k1na.
Row 34: P2togna, p7bl, p2togna. *(9 sts)*
Row 35: Cast (bind) off 1 st na, 7 sts bl, 1st na.

Tail

With bl, cast on 3 sts.
Beg with a k row, work 11 rows st st.
Row 12: Inc, p1, inc. *(5 sts)*
Row 13: K1, loopy st 1, k1, loopy st 1, k1.
Row 14: Purl.
Rep last 2 rows 3 times more.
Row 21: K2tog, loopy st 1, k2tog. *(3 sts)*
Row 22: P3tog and fasten off.

Ear

(make 2 the same)
With bl, cast on 6 sts.
Beg with a k row, work 2 rows st st.
Knit 10 rows.
Next row: K2tog, k2, k2tog. *(4 sts)*
Next row: Knit.
Cast (bind) off.

Collar

With he, cast on 26 sts.
Knit one row.
Cast (bind) off.

To Make Up

Sew in ends, leaving ends from cast on and cast (bound) off rows for sewing up. Using mattress or whip stitch, sew up legs starting at paw. Stuff each leg; pipecleaners are useful for rigidity. Using whip stitch, sew along top of leg, leaving an end to sew leg to body.
Cut a pipecleaner 2.5cm (1in) longer than tail, fold over one end of pipecleaner (tip of tail), roll the pipecleaner in stuffing, place on inside of tail and carefully sew up tail from the outside using mattress stitch. There should be about 1cm (½in) of pipecleaner sticking out, which is pushed

into the body when sewing on the tail.
At head, fold in half and sew cast (bound)
off edges of nose together.

Using mattress or whip stitch, sew down
centre back, around bottom and along
tummy to under the chin. Leave a 2.5cm
(1in) gap between front and back legs for
stuffing. Turn right side out, stuff then
sew up gap with mattress stitch.

Using whip stitch, sew legs to body as
shown in photograph.

Sew on tail where curve of dog's bottom
starts, with loops on the underside.

Sew ears to head as shown in photograph.
Fold over the ear and mould to shape.

Using hessian yarn, make two French
knots for eyes.

Sew ends of collar together and slide
over head onto neck.

About 2cm (¾in) down from top edge of leg,
sew through leg, body and opposite leg to
make dog more stable.

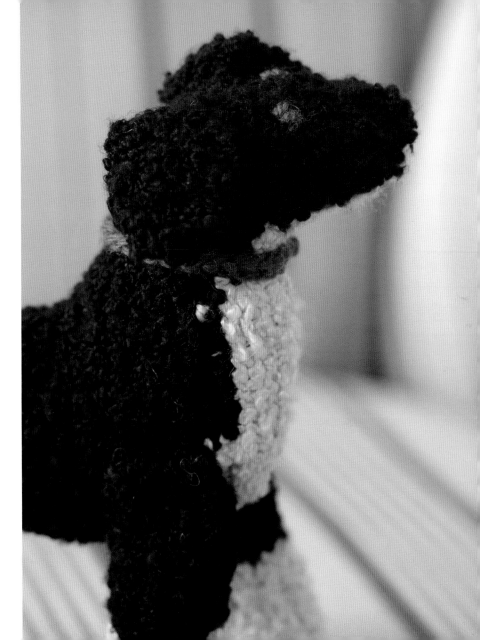

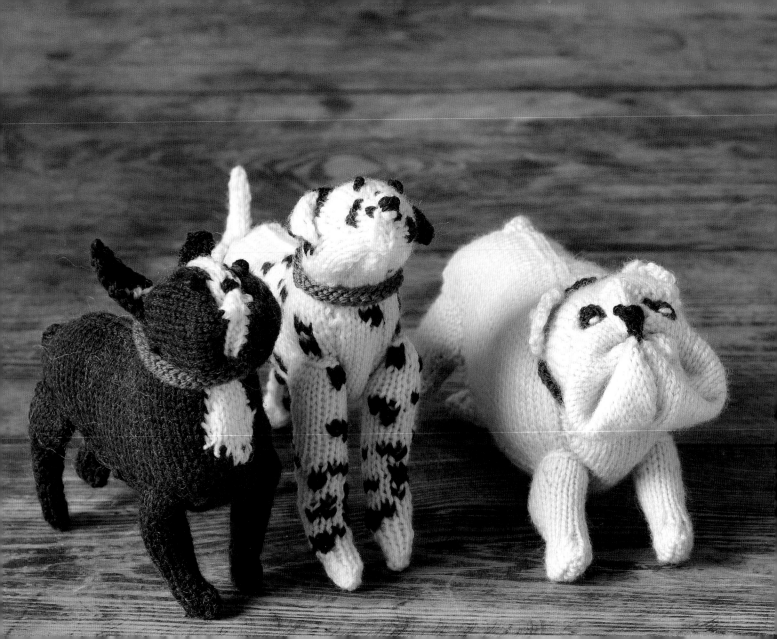

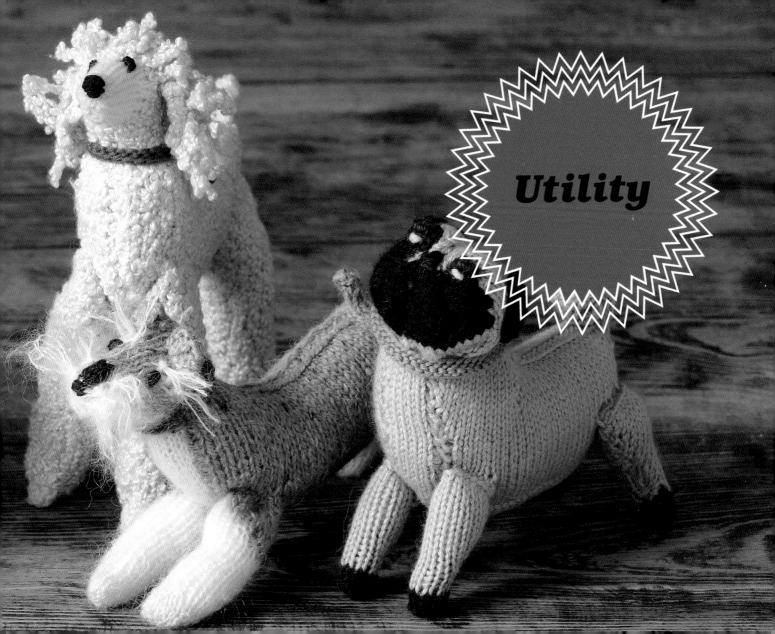

Utility

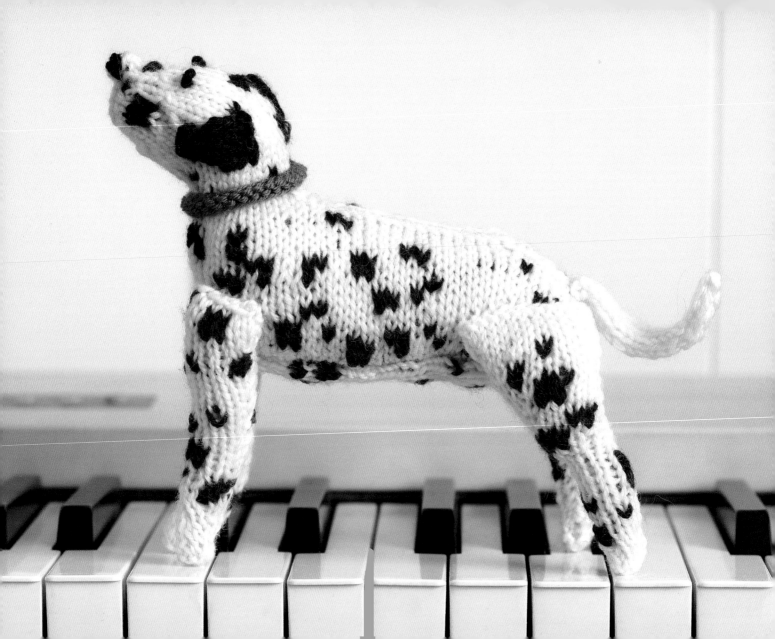

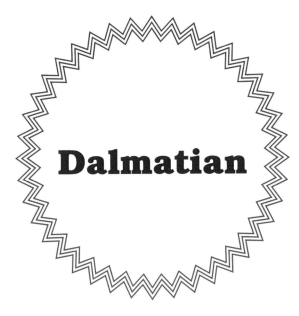

Dalmatian

With their traffic-stopping elegance and distinctive markings, the Dalmatian is a uniquely handsome beast. Probably originating in Croatia, they first came to England during the 18th century. Strong and muscular, they worked as coach dogs running alongside carriages and have retained a close affinity with horses. They were immortalized by Dodie Smith in the novel *The Hundred and One Dalmatians* and also the Walt Disney film. A well-known Dalmatian is Pongo, hero of the above-mentioned book and film.

Dalmatian

This is a more complex pattern to knit, all the spots need to be worked in intarsia or Fair Isle.

Measurements
Length: 15cm (6in)
Height to top of head: 14cm (5½in)

Materials
- Pair of 2¾mm (US 2) knitting needles
- 2 spare 2¾mm (US 2) knitting needles
- Pair of 2¾mm (US 2) double-pointed knitting needles
- 25g (1oz) of Rowan Pure Wool 4ply in Snow 412 (sn)
- 10g (¼oz) of Rowan Pure Wool 4ply in Black 404 (bl)
- Small amount of Rowan Pure Wool 4ply in Glade 421 (gl) for collar
- Pipecleaners for legs

Abbreviations
See page 172.
If there are no more than 4 stitches between colours you can use the Fair Isle technique, otherwise use intarsia (see page 172).

Back Leg
(make 2 the same)
With 2¾mm (US 2) knitting needles and sn, cast on 9 sts.
Beg with a k row, work 2 rows st st.
Row 3: Inc, k1, k2tog, k1, k2tog, k1, inc. *(9 sts)*
Row 4: Purl.
Row 5: K4sn, join in bl, k2bl, k3sn.

Row 6: P3sn, p2bl, p4sn.
Row 7: K2sn, k1bl, k6sn.
Row 8: P9sn.
Row 9: K4sn, k2bl, k3sn.
Row 10: P2sn, p2bl, p3sn, p2bl.
Row 11: K2bl, k7sn.
Row 12: P8sn, p1bl.
Row 13: K9sn.
Row 14: P9sn.
Row 15: With sn, k2tog, inc into next 2 sts, k1, inc into next 2 sts, k2tog. *(11 sts)*
Row 16: P4sn, p3bl, p4sn.
Row 17: K2togsn, incsn, k1sn, incbl, k1bl, incbl, k1sn, incsn, k2togsn. *(13 sts)*
Row 18: P10sn, p1bl, p2sn.
Row 19: K2sn, k2bl, k1sn, incsn, k1sn, incsn, k5sn. *(15 sts)*
Row 20: P15sn.
Row 21: With sn, k6, inc, k1, inc, k6. *(17 sts)*
Row 22: P11sn, p2bl, p4sn.
Row 23: K4sn, k2bl, k1sn, incsn, k1sn, incsn, k7sn. *(19 sts)*
Row 24: P4sn, p2bl, p5sn, p1bl, p7sn.
Row 25: K7sn, k1bl, incsn, k1sn, incsn, k2sn, k2bl, k4sn. *(21 sts)*
Row 26: P21sn.
Row 27: K5sn, k1bl, k3sn, incsn, k1sn, incsn, k1sn, k2bl, k6sn. *(23 sts)*
Row 28: P4sn, p1bl, p18sn.
Row 29: K10sn, incsn, k1sn, incsn, k4sn, k2bl, k4sn. *(25 sts)*
Row 30: P4sn, p2bl, p19sn.
Row 31: K25sn.
Cast (bind) off.

Front Leg
(make 2 the same)
With 2¾mm (US 2) knitting needles and sn, cast on 9 sts.
Beg with a k row, work 2 rows st st.
Row 3: Inc, k1, k2tog, k1, k2tog, k1, inc. *(9 sts)*
Row 4: Purl.
Row 5: Inc, k1, k2tog, k1, k2tog, k1, inc. *(9 sts)*
Row 6: P2sn, join in bl, p2bl, p5sn.

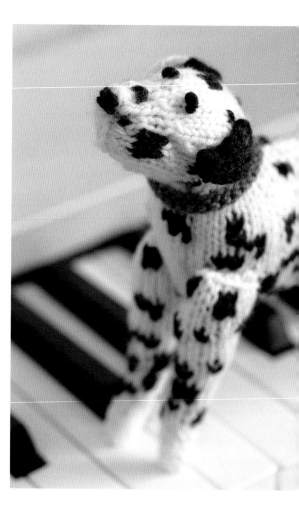

Legs
If you make a mistake with the spots, don't worry as it will not show.

Row 7: K5sn, k2bl, k2sn.
Row 8: P4sn, p1bl, p2sn, p2bl.
Row 9: Incbl, k1bl, k6sn, incsn. *(11 sts)*
Row 10: P6sn, p1bl, p4sn.
Row 11: K6sn, k2bl, k3sn.
Row 12: P3sn, p2bl, p6sn.
Row 13: K3sn, k1bl, k7sn.
Row 14: P11sn.
Row 15: K7sn, k1bl, k3sn.
Row 16: P2bl, p2sn, p2bl, p5sn.
Row 17: With sn, inc, k9, inc. *(13 sts)*
Row 18: P9sn, p1bl, p3sn.
Row 19: K13sn.
Row 20: P13sn.
Row 21: K6sn, k1bl, k6sn.
Row 22: P5sn, p2bl, p6sn.
Row 23: K13sn.
Row 24: P8sn, p1bl, p2sn, p2bl.
Row 25: K2bl, k11sn.
Row 26: P13sn.
Row 27: With sn, inc, k11, inc. *(15 sts)*
Row 28: P10sn, p2bl, p3sn.
Row 29: K3sn, k2bl, k2sn, k2bl, k6sn.
Row 30: P6sn, p2bl, p7sn.
Cast (bind) off.

Right Side of Body

With 2¾mm (US 2) knitting needles and sn, cast on 8 sts.
Row 1: K8sn, cast on 8 sts sn. *(16 sts)*
Row 2: P15sn, inc. *(17 sts)*
Row 3: K17sn, cast on 5 sts sn. *(22 sts)*
Row 4: P7sn, join in bl, p2bl, p8sn, p1bl, p3sn, incsn. *(23 sts)*
Row 5: K4sn, k2bl, k2sn, k2bl, k4sn, k2bl, k7sn, cast on 11 sts sn. *(34 sts)*
Row 6: P15sn, p1bl, p5sn, p1bl, p2sn, p2bl, p7sn, incsn. *(35 sts)*
Row 7: K18sn, k2bl, k2sn, k1bl, k2sn, k2bl, k8sn.
Row 8: P13sn, p2bl, p2sn, p2bl, p3sn, p1bl, p8sn, p2bl, p1sn, incsn. *(36 sts)*
Row 9: K36sn.
Row 10: P6sn, p1bl, p11sn, p1bl, p17sn.

Row 11: K3sn, k2bl, k11sn, k2bl, k10sn, k2bl, k6sn.
Row 12: P9sn, p1bl, p2sn, p1bl, p8sn, p1bl, p10sn, p1bl, p3sn.
Row 13: K13sn, k1bl, k4sn, k2bl, k2sn, k2bl, k2sn, k2bl, k8sn.
Row 14: P7sn, p1bl, p8sn, p2bl, p13sn, p2bl, p3sn.
Row 15: K8sn, k2bl, k1sn, k1bl, k18sn, k1bl, k5sn.
Row 16: P2togsn, p2sn, p2bl, p25sn, p2bl, p3sn. *(35 sts)*
Row 17: With sn, k33, k2tog. *(34 sts)*
Row 18: P2togsn, p4sn, p1bl, p13sn, p2bl, p12sn. *(33 sts)*
Row 19: K12sn, k2bl, k17sn, k2tog. *(32 sts)*
Row 20: Cast (bind) off 5 sts sn, p to end. *(27 sts)*
Row 21: K11sn (hold 11 sts on spare needle for right neck), cast (bind) off rem 16 sts sn.

Left Side of Body

With 2¾mm (US 2) knitting needles and sn, cast on 8 sts.
Row 1: Knit.
Row 2: P8sn, cast on 8 sts sn. *(16 sts)*
Row 3: K15sn, inc. *(17 sts)*
Row 4: P17sn, cast on 5 sts sn. *(22 sts)*
Row 5: K7sn, join in bl, k2bl, k8sn, k1bl, k3sn, incsn. *(23 sts)*
Row 6: P4sn, p2bl, p2sn, p2bl, p4sn, p2bl, p7sn, cast on 11 sts sn. *(34 sts)*
Row 7: K15sn, k1bl, k5sn, k1bl, k2sn, k2bl, k7sn, incsn. *(35 sts)*
Row 8: P18sn, p2bl, p2sn, p1bl, p2sn, p2bl, p8sn.
Row 9: K13sn, k2bl, k2sn, k2bl, k3sn, k1bl, k8sn, k2bl, k1sn, incsn. *(36 sts)*
Row 10: P36sn.
Row 11: K6sn, k1bl, k11sn, k1bl, k17sn.
Row 12: P3sn, p2bl, p11sn, p2bl, p10sn, p2bl, p6sn.
Row 13: K9sn, k1bl, k2sn, k1bl, k8sn, k1bl, k10sn, k1bl, k3sn.

Row 14: P13sn, p1bl, p4sn, p2bl, p2sn, p2bl, p2sn, p2bl, p8sn.
Row 15: K7sn, k1bl, k8sn, k2bl, k13sn, k2bl, k3sn.
Row 16: P8sn, p2bl, p1sn, p1bl, p18sn, p1bl, p5sn.
Row 17: K2togsn, k2sn, k2bl, k25sn, k2bl, k3sn. *(35 sts)*
Row 18: With sn, p33, p2tog. *(34 sts)*
Row 19: K2togsn, k4sn, k1bl, k13sn, k2bl, k12sn. *(33 sts)*
Row 20: P12sn, p2bl, p17sn, p2togsn. *(32 sts)*
Row 21: Cast (bind) off 5 sts sn, k to end. *(27 sts)*
Row 22: P11sn (hold 11 sts sts on spare needle for left neck), cast (bind) off rem 16 sts sn.

Neck and Head

Row 1: With sn, and with RS facing k11 from spare needle of Right Side of Body then k11 from spare needle of Left Side of Body. *(22 sts)*
Row 2: Join in bl, p2bl, p6sn, p2bl, p6sn, p1bl, p5sn. *(22 sts)*
Row 3: Incsn, k3sn, k2bl, k2sn, k2bl, k3sn, k1bl, k6sn, k1bl, incsn. *(24 sts)*
Row 4: P24sn.
Row 5: Incsn, k3sn, k1bl, k11sn, k2bl, k5sn, incsn. *(26 sts)*
Row 6: P4sn, p1bl, p2sn, p2bl, p4sn, p2bl, p4sn, p2bl, p5sn.
Row 7: K11sn, k2bl, k4sn, k2bl,1sn, pult (pick up loop below next st on left needle by inserting tip of right needle from back through loop – this stops a hole forming when turning work – then turn, leaving rem 6 sts on left needle unworked).
Row 8: Working top of head on centre 14 sts only, p2togsn (first st of p2tog is loop picked up at end of last row), p13sn, pult.
Row 9: With sn, k2tog, k13, pult.
Row 10: With sn, p2tog, p13, pult.

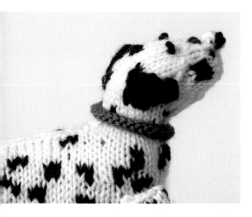

Head

For the Fair Isle technique use a separate ball of each colour yarn, twisting the colours firmly over one another at the joins to prevent holes (see page 172).

Row 11: With sn, k2tog, k13, pult.
Row 12: With sn, p2tog, p13, pult.
Row 13: K2togsn, k9sn, k1bl, 9sn. *(26 sts)*
Row 14: P12sn, p2bl, p3sn, p2bl, p7sn.
Row 15: K7sn, k2bl, k3sn, k2bl, k6sn, pult (pick up loop below next st on left needle by inserting tip of right needle from back through loop – this stops a hole forming when turning work) then turn – leaving rem 6 sts on left needle unworked).
Row 16: Working top of head on centre 14 sts only, p2togsn (first st is loop picked up at end of last row), p13sn, pult.
Row 17: With sn, k2tog, k13, pult.
Row 18: With sn, p2tog, p13, pult.
Row 19: With sn, k2tog, k to end. *(26 sts)*
Row 20: P26sn.
Row 21: K2tog, [k1, k2tog] 8 times. *(17 sts)*
Row 22: P3sn, p2bl, p6sn, p2bl, p4sn.
Row 23: K4sn, k2bl, k2togsn, k1sn, k2togsn, k1sn, k2bl, k3sn. *(15 sts)*
Row 24: P7sn, p1bl, p7sn.
Row 25: With sn, k2tog, k11, k2tog. *(13 sts)*
Row 26: P4sn, p1bl, p3sn, p1bl, p4sn.
Row 27: With sn, cast (bind) off 4 sts, k to end. *(9 sts)*
Row 28: With sn, cast (bind) off 4 sts, p to end. *(5 sts)*
Row 29: With sn, cast (bind) off.

Tummy

With 2¾mm (US 2) knitting needles and sn, cast on 1 st.
Row 1: Inc. *(2 sts)*
Row 2: Inc into both sts. *(4 sts)*
Row 3: Inc, p2, inc. *(6 sts)*
Row 4: Inc, k4, inc. *(8 sts)*
Row 5: Inc, p6, inc. *(10 sts)*
Work 3 rows st st.
Row 9: K4sn, join in bl, k2bl, k4sn.
Row 10: P4sn, p2bl, p4sn.
Row 11: K6sn, k1bl, k3sn.
Row 12: P10sn.
Row 13: K2sn, k2bl, k6sn.

Row 14: P6sn, p2bl, p2sn.
Work 4 rows st st.
Row 19: K4sn, k1bl, k5sn.
Row 20: P3sn, p2bl, p5sn.
Row 21: K5sn, k2bl, k3sn.
Row 22: P7sn, p1bl, p2sn
With sn, work 4 rows st st.
Row 27: K4sn, k2bl, k4sn.
Row 28: P4sn, p2bl, p4sn.
With sn, work 10 rows st st.
Row 39: K1sn, k1bl, k8sn.
With sn, work 2 rows st st.
Row 42: P7sn, p2bl, p1sn.
Row 43: K4sn, k1bl, k5sn.
Row 44: P4sn, p2bl, p4sn.
Row 45: K2sn, k1bl, k7sn.
Row 46: With sn, purl.
Row 47: K7sn, k2bl, k1sn.
Row 48: P1sn, p2bl, p7sn.
With sn, work 4 rows st st.
Row 53: K6sn, k1bl, k3sn.
With sn, work 9 rows st st.
Row 63: K2sn, k2bl, k6sn.
Row 64: P5sn, p2bl, p3sn.
Row 65: K2tog, k2sn, k2bl, k2sn, k2togsn. *(8 sts)*
Cont in sn.
Work 5 rows st st.
Row 71: K2tog, k4, k2tog. *(6 sts)*
Work 5 rows st st.
Row 77: K2tog, k2, k2tog. *(4 sts)*
Work 3 rows st st.
Row 81: K2tog twice. *(2 sts)*
Row 82: P2tog and fasten off.

Tail

With 2¾mm (US 2) double-pointed knitting needles and sn, cast on 6 sts.
Work in i-cord as folls:
Knit 10 rows.
Next row: K2tog, k2, k2tog. *(4 sts)*
Knit 5 rows.
Next row: K2tog twice. *(2 sts)*
Next row: K2tog and fasten off.

Ear 1

With 2¾mm (US 2) knitting needles and bl, cast on 7 sts.

Beg with a k row, work 6 rows st st.

Row 7: K2tog, k3, k2tog. *(5 sts)*
Row 8: P2tog, p1, p2tog. *(3 sts)*
Row 9: K2tog, k1. *(2 sts)*
Row 10: P2tog and fasten off.

Ear 2

With 2¾mm (US 2) knitting needles and bl, cast on 7 sts.

Beg with a k row, work 2 rows st st.

Row 3: K2bl, join in sn, k5sn.
Row 4: P5sn, p2bl.
Row 5: K7sn.
Row 6: P7sn.
Row 7: K2togsn, k3sn, k2togsn. *(5 sts)*
Row 8: P2togsn, p1sn, p2togsn. *(3 sts)*
Row 9: K2togsn, k1sn. *(2 sts)*
Row 10: P2togsn and fasten off.

Collar

With 2¾mm (US 2) knitting needles and gl, cast on 26 sts.

Knit one row.

Cast (bind) off.

To Make Up

Sew in ends, leaving ends from cast on and cast (bound) off rows for sewing up. Using mattress or whip stitch, sew up legs starting at paw. Turn right side out, stuff each leg, using pipecleaners for rigidity if necessary. Using whip stitch, sew along top of leg, leaving an end to sew leg to body. Using mattress or whip stitch, sew down centre back. Sew cast on row of tummy to V at base of back and sew cast (bound) off row under chin. Ease and sew tummy to fit body. Leave a 2.5cm (1in) gap between front and back legs on one side. Turn right side out, stuff body tightly, then sew up gap with mattress stitch.

Using whip stitch, sew legs to body as shown in photograph, with back legs at an angle.

Sew up two sides of head, sew on ears and catch down the tips with one stitch. Sew on tail as shown in photograph.

Using black yarn, embroider the nose using satin stitch and make two French knots for eyes.

Sew ends of collar together and slide over head onto neck.

If legs are floppy, about 2cm (¾in) down from top edge of leg, sew through leg, body and opposite leg to make dog more stable.

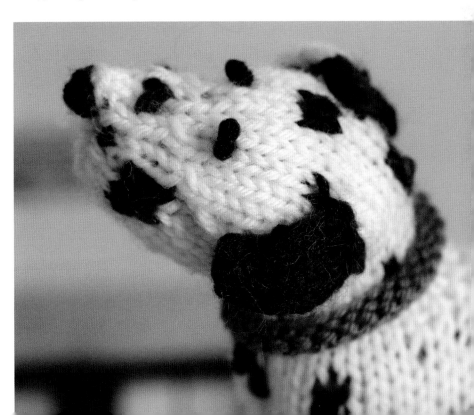

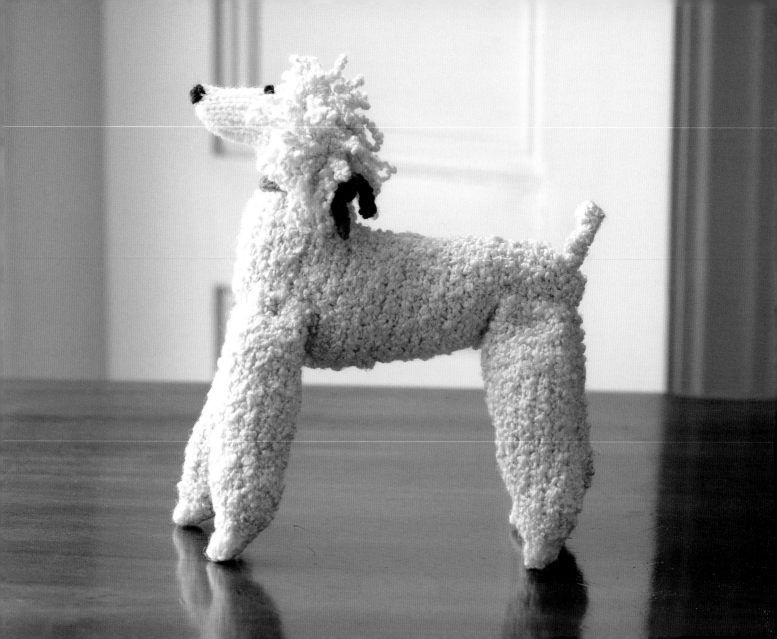

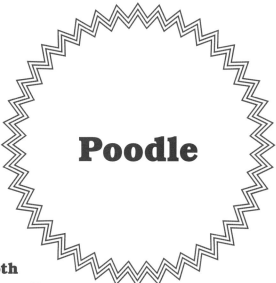

Poodle

The epitome of French chic, the Poodle is both elegant and highly intelligent. They are a versatile breed and would suit most owners: Toy Poodles for apartment dwellers who prefer to carry their dogs; Miniature Poodles for families; and Standard Poodles for people who like to be noticed. Poodle crosses are popular as they produce hypoallergenic dogs with comical names, such as the Cockapoo and Labradoodle. Winston Churchill and Marilyn Monroe were Poodle owners. Growing up we both owned Poodles called: Pastis, Pernod, Puddle, Pin, Bognor, Friday, Twinkle Toes, Sadie (a very bad-tempered dog) and Jonah.

Poodle

The pattern describes the white dog shown. For a black poodle, use black 4ply and bouclé yarns.

Measurements
Length: 17cm (6½in)
Height to top of head: 18cm (7in)

Materials
- Pair of 2¾mm (US 2) knitting needles
- 2 spare 2¾mm (US 2) knitting needles
- 5g (⅛oz) of Rowan Pure Wool 4ply in Snow 412 (sn) or Black 404
- 30g (1⅛oz) of Halcyon Yarn Stardust in Natural 000 (na) or Halcyon Yarn Gemstone Silk Bouclé in Black 101
- Small amount of Rowan Pure Wool 4ply in Raspberry 428 (ra) for collar
- Tiny amount of Rowan Pure Wool 4ply in Black 404 or Mocha 417 for nose and eyes

Abbreviations
See page 172.
For loopy stitch technique, see page 173.

Legs
The poodle's shapely legs will require firm stuffing: use a chopstick to push stuffing right down into the toes.

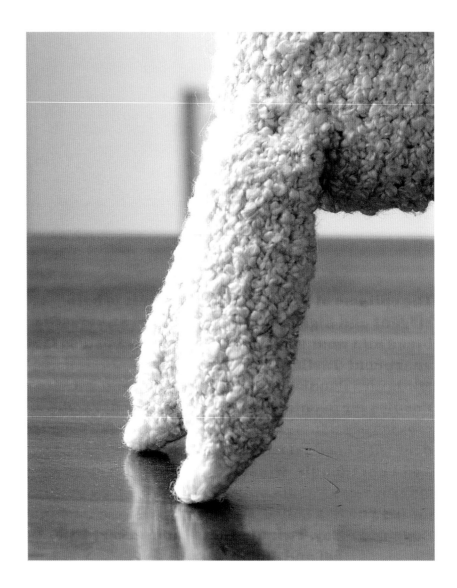

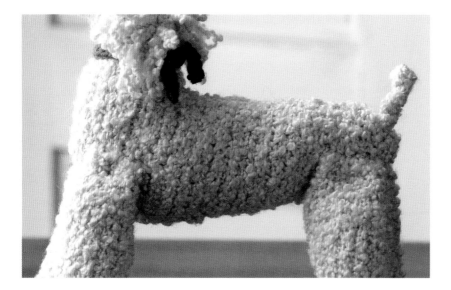

Body

A bouclé yarn offers an effective way to create the poodle's distinctive curly coat without having to use a complicated stitch pattern.

Back Leg

(make 2 the same)
With sn, cast on 8 sts.
Beg with a k row, work 2 rows st st.
Row 3: Inc, k1, k2tog twice, k1, inc. *(8 sts)*
Row 4: P1, p2tog, p2, p2tog, p1. *(6 sts)*
Change to na.
Row 5: Inc, k1, inc into next 2 sts, k1, inc. *(10 sts)*
Row 6: Purl.
Row 7: Inc, k8, inc. *(12 sts)* **
Work 5 rows st st.
Row 13: K2tog, k3, inc into next 2 sts, k3, k2tog. *(12 sts)*
Work 9 rows st st.
Row 23: K5, inc into next 2 sts, k5. *(14 sts)*
Work 3 rows st st.
Row 27: K6, inc into next 2 sts, k6. *(16 sts)*
Work 5 rows st st.
Row 33: K6, k2tog twice, k6. *(14 sts)*

Row 34: Purl.
Row 35: K5, k2tog twice, k5. *(12 sts)*
Row 36: Purl.
Cast (bind) off.

Front Leg

(make 2 the same)
Work as for Back Leg to **.
Work 9 rows st st.
Row 17: Inc, k3, k2tog twice, k3, inc. *(12 sts)*
Work 17 rows st st.
Row 35: K4, k2tog twice, k4. *(10 sts)*
Row 36: Purl.
Cast (bind) off.

Right Side of Body

With na, cast on 9 sts.
Row 1: Knit.
Row 2: P8, inc. *(10 sts)*
Row 3: K10, cast on 5 sts. *(15 sts)*
Row 4: P14, inc. *(16 sts)*
Work 2 rows st st.
Row 7: K16, cast on 2 sts. *(18 sts)*
Row 8: P17, inc. *(19 sts)*
Row 9: K19, cast on 2 sts. *(21 sts)*
Row 10: Purl.
Row 11: K21, cast on 5 sts. *(26 sts)*
Work 9 rows st st.
Row 21: K24, k2tog. *(25 sts)*
Row 22: Cast (bind) off 4 sts, p to end. *(21 sts)*
Row 23: K9 (hold 9 sts on spare needle for right neck), cast (bind) off rem 12 sts.

Left Side of Body

With na, cast on 9 sts
Row 1: Purl.
Row 2: K8, inc. *(10 sts)*
Row 3: P10, cast on 5 sts. *(15 sts)*
Row 4: K14, inc. *(16 sts)*
Work 2 rows st st.
Row 7: P16, cast on 2 sts. *(18 sts)*
Row 8: K17, inc. *(19 sts)*
Row 9: P19, cast on 2 sts. *(21 sts)*
Row 10: Knit.

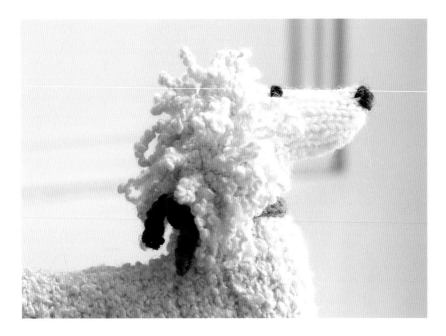

Head

Loopy stitch makes for a full and flamboyant topknot. If you wish, you can cut the loops and trim the ends for a classic poodle coiffure.

Row 11: P21, cast on 5 sts. *(26 sts)*
Work 9 rows st st.
Row 21: P24, p2tog. *(25 sts)*
Row 22: Cast (bind) off 4 sts, k to end. *(21 sts)*
Row 23: P9 (hold 9 sts on spare needle for left neck), cast (bind) off rem 12 sts.

Neck and Head

Row 1: With na, and with RS facing k9 from spare needle of Right Side of Body then k9 from spare needle of Left Side of Body. *(18 sts)*
Row 2: Purl.
Row 3: K2tog, k14, k2tog. *(16 sts)*
Row 4: Purl.
Row 5: K4, k2tog, k4, k2tog, k4. *(14 sts)*
Work 5 rows st st.

Row 11: K11, pult (pick up loop below next st on left needle by inserting tip of right needle from back through loop – this stops a hole forming when turning work – then turn. leaving rem 3 sts on left needle unworked).
Row 12: Working top of head on centre 8 sts only, p2tog (first st of p2tog is loop picked up at end of last row), p7, pult.
Row 13: K2tog, k6, pult.
Row 14: P2tog, p5, pult.
Row 15: K2tog, loopy st 5, pult.
Row 16: P2tog, loopy st 5, pult.
Row 17: K2tog, loopy st 5, pult.
Row 18: P2tog, loopy st 5, pult.
Row 19: K2tog, loopy st 5, k to end. *(14 sts)*
Change to sn.
Work 3 rows st st.
Row 23: K3, k2tog, k4, k2tog, k3. *(12 sts)*
Work 6 rows st st.
Row 30: P2tog, p8, p2tog. *(10 sts)*
Row 31: K2tog, k6, k2tog. *(8 sts)*
Cast (bind) off.

Tail

With na, cast on 2 sts.
Work 4 rows st st.
Next row: K2tog.
To work bobble for tail, k into the front and back of the st twice. *(4 sts)*
Work 4 rows st st.
Next row: Slip 2nd, 3rd and 4th sts over 1st st.
Thread yarn through rem st and fasten off.
Using the end of yarn, sew through the edges of the circle to form a bobble.

Ear

(make 2 the same)
With na, cast on 6 sts.
Row 1: Knit.
Row 2: K1, loopy st 4, k1.
Rep last 2 rows 3 times more.
Row 9: K2tog, k2, k2tog. *(4 sts)*
Cast (bind) off.

Collar

With ra, cast on 50 sts.
Knit one row.
Cast (bind) off.

To Make Up

Sew in ends, leaving ends from cast on
and cast (bound) off rows for sewing up.
Using mattress or whip stitch, sew up legs
starting at paw. Turn right side out and stuff
each leg. Using mattress stitch, sew along
top of leg, leaving an end to sew leg to body.
Tidy up the tail, making a good bobble, and
strengthen the stalk of the tail with a row of
whip stitch.
Using mattress or whip stitch, sew down
centre back, around tail, down bottom and
along tummy. Leave a 2.5cm (1in) gap
between front and back legs for stuffing. At
head, fold in half and sew cast (bound) off
edges of nose together.
Cont sewing head and two sides of body
together, leaving a 2.5cm (1in) gap in tummy
for stuffing. Turn right side out, stuff then
sew up gap with mattress stitch.
Using whip stitch, sew legs to body as
shown in photograph.
About 1cm (½in) down from top edge of leg,
sew through the leg, body and opposite leg
to make the dog more stable.
Sew on the tail.
Sew ears to head as shown in photograph,
just under the loopy st on the topknot.
Using black yarn (mocha yarn for black
poodle), embroider the nose using satin
stitch and make two French knots for eyes.
Tie collar around neck using a knot.

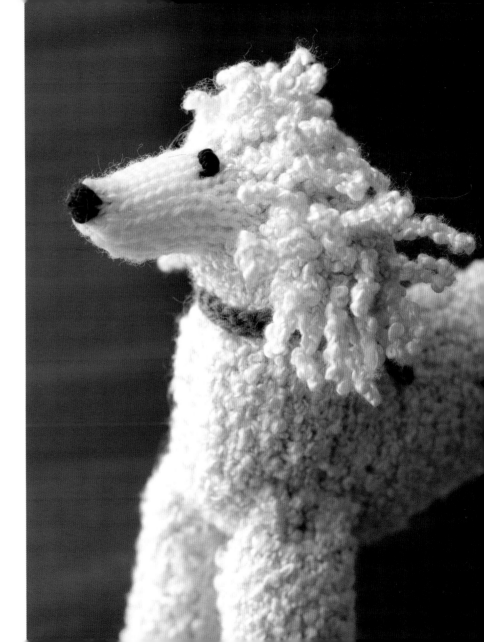

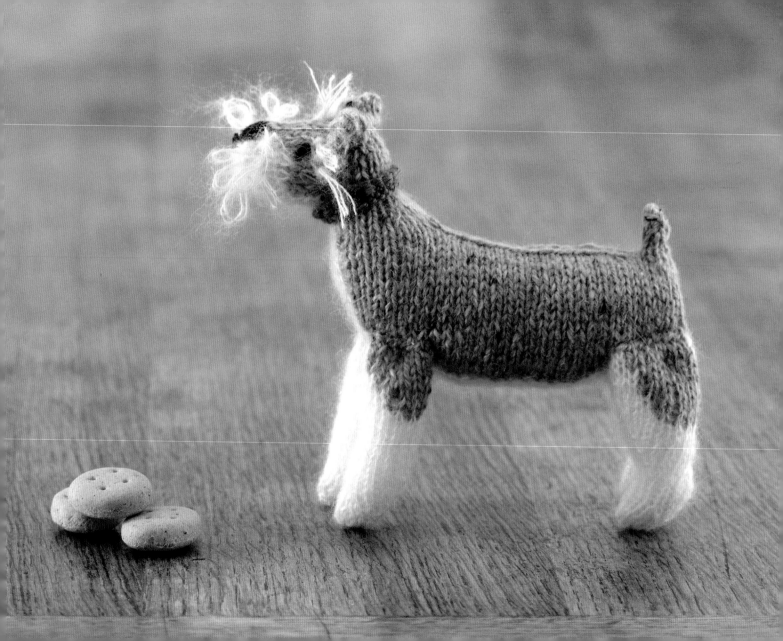

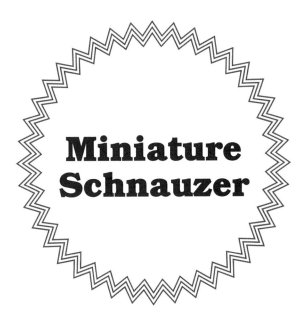

Miniature Schnauzer

Originating in Germany - *schnauze* means muzzle in German - Miniature Schnauzers are very popular pets, being friendly, intelligent and easy to please. With their splendidly bewhiskered faces they have a comical look that they live up to, as they are extrovert and humorous. Unsuccessful presidential candidate, Bob Dole, had a Miniature Schnauzer called Leader who published *Follow the Leader*, a book about his life in Washington.

Miniature Schnauzer

Neat and easy to knit with a small amount of intarsia and some loopy stitch on the head.

Measurements
Length: 15cm (6in)
Height to top of head: 13cm (5in)

Materials
- Pair of 2¾mm (US 2) knitting needles
- 2 spare 2¾mm (US 2) knitting needles
- 2 small stitch holders or safety pins
- 10g (¼oz) of Rowan Kidsilk Haze in Cream 634 (cr)
- 15g (½oz) of Rowan Felted Tweed in Scree 165 (sc)
- Small amount of Rowan Cashsoft 4ply in Fennel 436 (fe) for collar
- Tiny amount of Rowan Pure Wool 4ply in Black 404 for nose and eyes

Abbreviations
See page 172.
For loopy stitch technique, see page 173.

Right Back Leg
With cr, cast on 11 sts.
Beg with a k row, work 2 rows st st.
Row 3: Inc, k2, k2tog, k1, k2tog, k2, inc. *(11 sts)*
Row 4: Purl.
Rep last 2 rows once more.
Work 2 rows st st.**

Row 9: K2tog, k2, inc, k1, inc, k2, k2tog. *(11 sts)*
Row 10: Purl.
Rep last 2 rows once more.
Row 13: K4, inc, k1, inc, k4. *(13 sts)*
Row 14: Purl.
Row 15: K5, inc, k1, inc, k5. *(15 sts)*
Row 16: Purl.*
Row 17: K12cr, join in sc, k3sc.
Row 18: P4sc, p11cr.
Row 19: K6cr, inccr, k1cr, inccr, k1cr, k5sc. *(17 sts)*
Row 20: P5sc, p12cr.
Row 21: K12cr, k5sc.
Row 22: P6sc, p11cr.
Row 23: K7cr, inccr, k1cr, inccr, k1cr, k6sc. *(19 sts)*
Row 24: P6sc, p13cr.
Row 25: K12cr, k7sc.
Row 26: P7sc, p12cr.
Cast (bind) off 12 sts cr, 7 sts sc.

Left Back Leg
Work as for Right Back Leg to *.
Row 17: Join in sc, k3sc, k12cr.
Row 18: P11cr, p4sc.
Row 19: K5sc, k1cr, inccr, k1cr, inccr, k6cr. *(17 sts)*
Row 20: P12cr, p5sc.
Row 21: K5sc, k12cr.
Row 22: P11cr, p6sc.
Row 23: K6sc, k1cr, inccr, k1cr, inccr, k7cr. *(19 sts)*
Row 24: P13cr, p6sc.
Row 25: K7sc, k12cr.
Row 26: P12cr, p7sc.
Cast (bind) off 7 sts sc, 12 sts cr.

Right Front Leg
As for Right Back Leg to **.
Row 9: Knit.
Row 10: Purl.
Row 11: Inc, k9, inc. *(13 sts)*
Work 7 rows st st.***

Row 19: K10cr, join in sc, k3sc.
Row 20: P4sc, p9cr.
Row 21: K9cr, k4sc.
Row 22: P5sc, p8cr.
Row 23: K8cr, k5sc.
Row 24: P6sc, p7cr.
Row 25: K7cr, k6sc.
Row 26: P6sc, p7cr.
Cast (bind) off 7 sts cr, 6 sts sc.

Left Front Leg

As for Right Front Leg to ***.
Row 19: Join in sc, k3sc, k10cr.
Row 20: P9cr, p4sc.
Row 21: K4sc, k9cr.
Row 22: P8cr, p5sc.
Row 23: K5sc, k8cr.
Row 24: P7cr, p6sc.
Row 25: K6sc, k7cr.
Row 26: P7cr, p6sc.
Cast (bind) off 6 sts sc, 7 sts cr.

Body

Use the intarsia technique and a separate ball of each colour yarn, twisting the colours firmly over one another at the joins to prevent holes (see page 172).

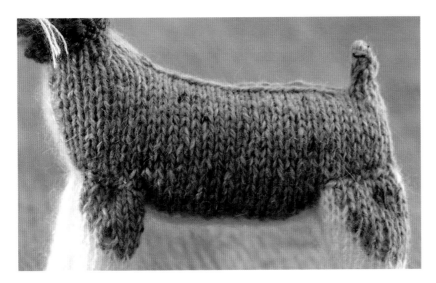

Right Side of Body

With sc, cast on 14 sts.
Row 1: K14, cast on 6 sts. *(20 sts)*
Row 2: Purl.
Row 3: Inc, k19, cast on 4 sts. *(25 sts)*
Row 4: Purl.
Row 5: K25, cast on 6 sts. *(31 sts)*
Work 10 rows st st.
Row 16: P1, p2tog, p28. *(30 sts)*
Row 17: K27, k2tog, k1. *(29 sts)*
Row 18: P3, (put these 3 sts on holder for tail), cast (bind) off 17 sts, p to end (hold 9 sts on spare needle for right neck).

Left Side of Body

With sc, cast on 14 sts.
Row 1: P14, cast on 6 sts. *(20 sts)*
Row 2: Knit.
Row 3: Inc, p19, cast on 4 sts. *(25 sts)*
Row 4: Knit.
Row 5: P25, cast on 6 sts. *(31 sts)*
Work 10 rows st st.
Row 16: K1, k2tog, k28. *(30 sts)*
Row 17: P27, p2tog, p1. *(29 sts)*
Row 18: K3, (put these 3 sts on holder for tail), cast (bind) off 17 sts, k to end (hold 9 sts on spare needle for left neck).

Neck and Head

Row 1: With sc, and with RS facing k9 from spare needle of Right Side of Body then k9 from spare needle of Left Side of Body. *(18 sts)*
Row 2: Purl.
Row 3: K4, k2tog, k6, k2tog, k4. *(16 sts)*
Row 4: Purl.
Row 5: K4, k2tog, k4, k2tog, k4. *(14 sts)*
Row 6: Purl.
Row 7: K4, k2tog, k2, k2tog, k4. *(12 sts)*
Row 8: Purl.
Row 9: K11, pult (pick up loop below next st on left needle by inserting tip of right needle from back through loop – this stops a hole forming when turning work – then turn, leaving rem 1 st on left needle unworked).

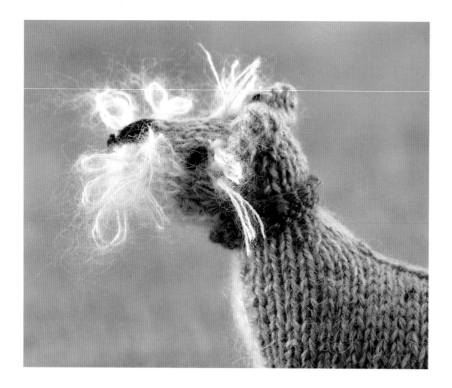

Head

The loopy stitch eyebrows and whiskers set the positions for the embroidered eyes and nose.

Row 10: Working top of head, p2tog (first st of p2tog is loop picked up at end of last row), p9, pult.
Row 11: K2tog, k8, pult.
Row 12: P2tog, p7, pult.
Row 13: K2tog, k6, pult.
Row 14: P2tog, p5, pult.
Row 15: K2tog, k4, pult.
Row 16: P2tog, p3, pult.
Row 17: K2tog, k4, pult.
Row 18: P2tog, p5, pult.
Row 19: K2tog, k6, pult.
Row 20: P2tog, p7, pult.

Row 21 (eyebrow row): K2tog at the same time making loopy st 1cr, loopy st 2cr, k2sc, loopy st 3cr, k1sc, pult.
Row 22: P2tog, p9, pult.
Row 23: K2tog, k10. *(12 sts on right needle)*
Row 24: P3cr, p6sc, p3cr.
Row 25: K2cr, k2togcr, k4sc, k2togcr, k2cr. *(10 sts)*
Row 26: P4cr, p2sc, p4cr.
Row 27: K1cr, loopy st 3cr, k2bl, loopy st 3cr, k1cr.
Row 28: P4cr, p2bl, p4cr.
Row 29: K1cr, loopy st 3cr, k2bl, loopy st 3cr, k1cr.
Cast (bind) off 4 sts cr, 2 sts bl, 4 sts cr.

Tail

Row 1: With sc, and with RS facing knit 3 sts from holder from Left Side of Body and 3 sts from holder from Right Side of Body. *(6 sts)*
Beg with a p row, work 2 rows st st.
Row 4: P1, p2tog twice, p1. *(4 sts)*
Cast (bind) off.

Tummy

With cr, cast on 6 sts.
Beg with a k row, work 70 rows st st (measure against the chest and alter length if necessary).
Cast (bind) off.

Ear

(make 2 the same)
With sc, cast on 4 sts.
Beg with a k row, work 2 rows st st.
Garter st (knit) 6 rows.
Next row: K2tog twice.
Next row: K2tog and fasten off.

Collar

With fe, cast on 26 sts.
Knit one row.
Cast (bind) off.

To Make Up

Sew in ends, leaving ends from cast on and cast (bound) off rows for sewing up. Using mattress or whip stitch, sew up legs starting at paw. Turn right side out and stuff each leg. Using mattress stitch, sew along top of leg, leaving an end to sew leg to body.

Using mattress or whip stitch, sew down centre back, around tail and down bottom. At head, fold in half and sew cast (bound) off edges of nose together.

Using mattress or whip stitch, sew cast on row of tummy to bottom end of dog and sew cast (bound) off row to nose. Ease and sew tummy to fit body. Leave a 2.5cm (1in) gap between front and back legs on one side. Turn right side out, stuff then sew up gap with mattress stitch.

Using whip stitch, sew legs to body as shown in photograph.

About 2cm (¾in) down from top edge of leg, sew through leg, body and opposite leg to make dog more stable.

Sew ears to head as shown in photograph and catch down the tip of ear just above the eyebrow.

Using black yarn, embroider the nose using satin stitch and make two French knots for eyes.

At the eyebrows cut the loops on the loopy st, do not cut the loopy st on the cheeks. Sew ends of collar together and slide over head onto neck.

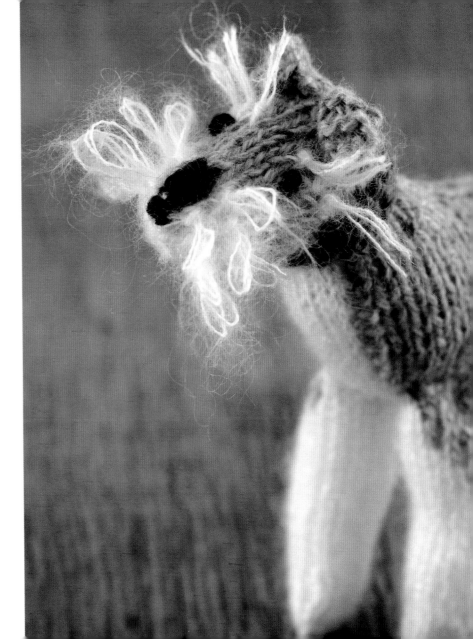

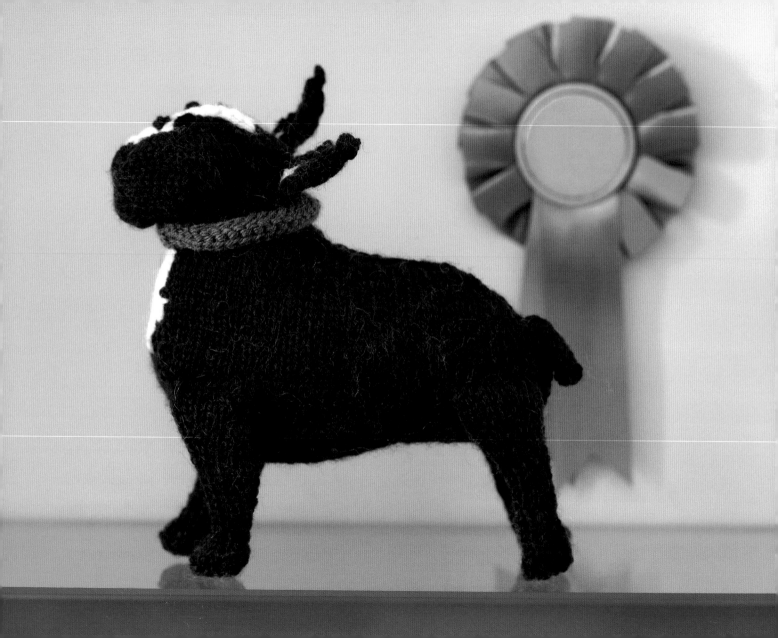

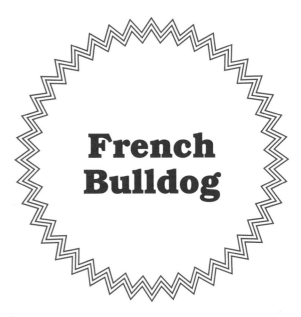

French Bulldog

Intelligent and companionable, French Bulldogs do need a decent amount of exercise, but they are basically lap dogs. As with many dog breeds their origins are debatable, but one theory is that English laceworkers brought them to northern France. These dogs are short and muscular with trademark bat ears and an expressive gaze. Toulouse Lautrec had French Bulldogs, as does Martha Stewart. The famous El Bulli restaurant, often described as the best restaurant in the world, is named after the original owners' French Bulldog.

French Bulldog

Mostly one colour,
so there's only a tiny
bit of intarsia knitting
to tackle.

Measurements
Length: 12cm (4¾in)
Height to top of head: 13cm (5in)

Materials
- Pair of 2¾mm (US 2) knitting needles
- 2 spare 2¾mm (US 2) knitting needles
- 30g (1⅛oz) of Rowan Pure Wool 4ply in Black 404 (bl)
- 20g (¾oz) of Rowan Pure Wool 4ply in Snow 412 (sn)
- Small amount of Rowan Pure Wool 4ply in Framboise 456 (fr) for collar
- Tiny amount of Rowan Pure Wool 4ply in Hessian 416 for eyes
- Pipecleaners for legs

Abbreviations
See page 172.

Back Leg
(make 2 the same)
With bl, cast on 12 sts.
Beg with a k row, work 2 rows st st.
Row 3: K3, k2tog 3 times, k3. *(9 sts)*
Row 4: P2tog, p5, p2tog. *(7 sts)*
Work 2 rows st st.
Row 7: Inc, k2tog, k1, k2tog, inc. *(7 sts)*
Row 8: Purl.
Row 9: Inc, k5, inc. *(9 sts)*
Row 10: Purl.

Row 11: Inc, k1, k2tog, k1, k2tog, k1, inc. *(9 sts)*
Row 12: Purl.
Row 13: Inc, k1, k2tog, k1, k2tog, k1, inc. *(9 sts)*
Row 14: Purl.
Row 15: Inc, k1, inc, k3, inc, k1, inc. *(13 sts)*
Row 16: Purl.
Row 17: K5, inc, k1, inc, k5. *(15 sts)*
Row 18: Purl.
Row 19: K6, inc, k1, inc, k6. *(17 sts)*
Row 20: Purl.
Row 21: Inc, k15, inc. *(19 sts)*
Cast (bind) off.

Front Leg
(make 2 the same)
With bl, cast on 12 sts.
Beg with a k row, work 2 rows st st.
Row 3: K3, k2tog 3 times, k3. *(9 sts)*
Row 4: P2tog, p5, p2tog. *(7 sts)*
Row 5: Knit.
Row 6: Purl.
Row 7: Inc, k5, inc. *(9 sts)*
Row 8: Purl.
Row 9: Inc, k7, inc. *(11 sts)*
Row 10: Purl.
Row 11: Inc, k9, inc. *(13 sts)*
Row 12: Purl.
Work 4 rows st st.
Row 17: K2tog, k2, inc, k3, inc, k2, k2tog. *(13 sts)*
Row 18: Purl.
Row 19: K2tog, k2, inc, k3, inc, k2, k2tog. *(13 sts)*
Row 20: Purl.
Row 21: Inc, k11, inc. *(15 sts)*
Row 22: Purl.
Cast (bind) off.

Right Side of Body
With bl, cast on 12 sts.
Row 1: Knit.
Row 2: Purl.

Row 3: K12, cast on 4 sts. *(16 sts)*
Row 4: Purl.
Row 5: Inc, k15, cast on 4 sts. *(21 sts)*
Row 6: Purl.
Row 7: K21, cast on 6 sts. *(27 sts)*
Row 8: Purl.
Row 9: Inc, k26, cast on 6 sts. *(34 sts)*
Row 10: Purl.
Work 4 rows st st.
Row 15: Inc, k33. *(35 sts)*
Row 16: Purl.
Row 17: K to last 2 sts, k2tog. *(34 sts)*
Row 18: P2tog, p to end. *(33 sts)*
Rep last 2 rows twice more. *(29 sts)*
Row 23: Knit.
Row 24: Cast (bind) off 14 sts, p to end.
(15 sts)
Row 25: K13, k2tog (hold 14 sts on spare
needle for right neck).

Left Side of Body
With bl, cast on 12 sts.
Row 1: Knit.
Row 2: Purl, cast on 4 sts. *(16 sts)*
Row 3: Knit.
Row 4: Inc, p15, cast on 4 sts. *(21 sts)*
Row 5: Knit.
Row 6: P21, cast on 6 sts. *(27 sts)*
Row 7: Knit.
Row 8: Inc, p26, cast on 6 sts. *(34 sts)*
Row 9: Knit.
Work 4 rows st st.
Row 14: Inc, p33. *(35 sts)*
Row 15: Knit.
Row 16: P to last 2 sts, p2tog. *(34 sts)*
Row 17: K2tog, k to end. *(33 sts)*
Rep last 2 rows twice more. *(29 sts)*
Row 22: Purl.
Row 23: Cast (bind) off 14 sts, k to end.
(15 sts)
Row 24: P13, p2tog.
Row 25: K14 (hold 14 sts on spare needle
for left neck).

Head
With bl, return to 14 sts from Right Side of
Body, cast (bind) off first 4 sts, k rem sts from
spare needle of Right Side of Body, then k14
from spare needle of Left Side of Body.
Row 1: Cast (bind) off 4 sts, p to end. *(20 sts)*
Row 2: K16, pult (pick up loop below next st
on left needle by inserting tip of right needle
from back through loop – this stops a hole
forming when turning work – then turn,
leaving rem 4 sts on left needle unworked).
Row 3: Working top of head on centre
12 sts only, p2tog (first st of p2tog is loop
picked up at end of last row), p11, pult.

Body
Use the intarsia technique
and a separate ball of each
colour yarn, twisting the colours
firmly over one another at the joins
to prevent holes (see page 172).

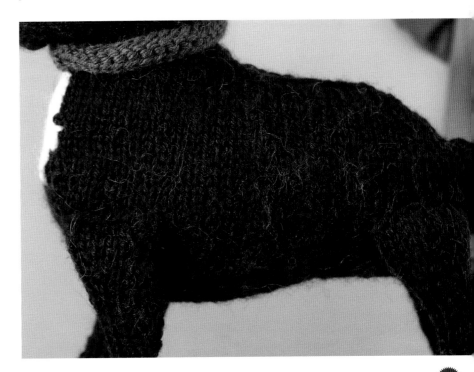

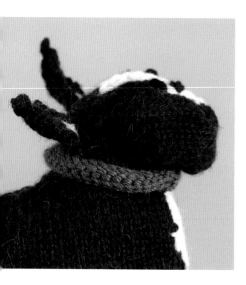

Head

The eyes are French knots wrapped with brown yarn to create the appealing expression.

Row 4: K2tog, k11, pult.
Row 5: P2tog, p11, pult.
Row 6: K2tog, k11, pult.
Row 7: P2tog, p11, pult.
Row 8: K2tog, k to end.
Row 9: Purl. *(20 sts)*

Head is worked in 3 sections from here

Right section
Next row: K7, turn, working on these 7 sts only (leave rem 13 sts on needle).
Next row: Purl.
Working st st, inc at outside edge of every row until you have 15 sts, ending with a p row.
Work 4 rows st st straight (even).
Cont in st st, work 2tog at outside edge of every row until you have 11 sts.
Next row: Join in and cont in sn, cast (bind) off 5 sts, k to end. *(6 sts)*
Next row: P4, p2tog. *(5 sts)*
Cast (bind) off.

Centre section
Rejoin bl and working on centre 6 sts, k2bl, join in sn, k2sn, k2bl.
Work 5 rows st st starting with a p row, (p2bl, p2sn, p2bl), keeping colours correct.
Next row: K1bl, k4sn, k1bl.
Next row: P1bl, p4sn, p1bl.
Next row: K6sn.
Next row: P2togsn, p2sn, p2togsn. *(4 sts)*
Next row: K2tog twice sn. *(2 sts)*
Next row: P2togsn and fasten off.

Left section
Rejoin bl and work on final 7 sts.
Beg with a k row, work 2 rows st st.
Cont in st st, inc at outside edge of every row until you have 15 sts, ending with a p row.
Work 4 rows st st straight (even).
Cont in st st, work 2tog at outside edge on every row until you have 11 sts.
Next row: Knit.
Next row: Join in and cont in sn, cast (bind) off 5 sts, k to end. *(6 sts)*
Next row: K4, k2tog. *(5 sts)*
Cast (bind) off.

Tummy

With bl, cast on 1 st.
Row 1: Inc. *(2 sts)*
Row 2: Purl.
Row 3: Inc into both sts. *(4 sts)*
Row 4: Purl.
Row 5: Inc, k2, inc. *(6 sts)*
Row 6: Purl.
Row 7: Inc, k4, inc. *(8 sts)*
Row 8: Purl.
Row 9: Inc, k6, inc. *(10 sts)*
Row 10: Purl.
Row 11: Inc, k8, inc. *(12 sts)*
Row 12: Purl.
Cont in st st to fit all along tummy (approx 42 rows) to bottom of chest, ending with a p row.
Next row: K2tog, k8, k2tog. *(10 sts)*
Work 5 rows st st.
Next row: K2togbl, k2bl, join in sn, k2sn, k2bl, k2togbl. *(8 sts)*
Next row: P2bl, p4sn, p2bl.
Next row: K1bl, k6sn, k1bl.
Next row: Cont in sn, purl.
Next row: Knit.
Next row: Purl.
Next row: K2tog, k4, k2tog. *(6 sts)*
Work 3 rows st st.
Next row: K2tog, k2, k2tog. *(4 sts)*
Work 3 rows st st.
Next row: K2tog twice. *(2 sts)*
Next row: P2tog and fasten off.

Tail

With bl, cast on 6 sts.
Beg with a k row, work 5 rows st st.
Row 6: P2tog, p2, p2tog. *(4 sts)*
Row 7: P2tog twice. *(2 sts)*
Row 8: P2tog and fasten off.

Ear

(make 2 the same)
With bl, cast on 7 sts.
Beg with a k row, work 6 rows st st.

Row 7: K2tog, k3, k2tog. *(5 sts)*
Row 8: Purl.
Row 9: K2tog, k1, k2tog. *(3 sts)*
Row 10: Purl.
Row 11: K2tog, k1.
Row 12: P2tog and fasten off.

Collar

With fr, cast on 40 sts.
Knit one row.
Cast (bind) off.

To Make Up

Sew in ends, leaving ends from cast on
and cast (bound) off rows for sewing up.
Using whip stitch, sew up legs starting at
paw. Stuff each leg; pipecleaners are useful
for rigidity. Using mattress stitch, sew along
top of leg, leaving an end to sew leg to body.
Using mattress stitch, sew central to side
seams on head. Fold nose back on itself as
in photograph and sew tip of nose to centre
of middle head section with black yarn and
satin stitch.

Using mattress or whip stitch, sew down
centre back. Sew cast on row of tummy to V
at base of back and sew cast (bound) off row
under chin. Ease and sew tummy to fit body.
Leave a 2.5cm (1in) gap between front and
back legs on one side. Turn right side out.
Stuff body tightly, head less so then sew
up gap with mattress stitch. Sew cheeks to
neck and under chin. Sew chin up under
nose for extra jowl effect.

Sew on ears and tail (folded in half) as
shown. Embroider inside ears with sn and
satin stitch. Using black yarn, make French
knots for eyes and sew round French knots
in hessian to make iris. Sew ends of collar
together and slide over head onto neck.
If legs are floppy, about 2cm (¾in) down
from top edge of leg, sew through leg, body
and opposite leg to make dog more stable.

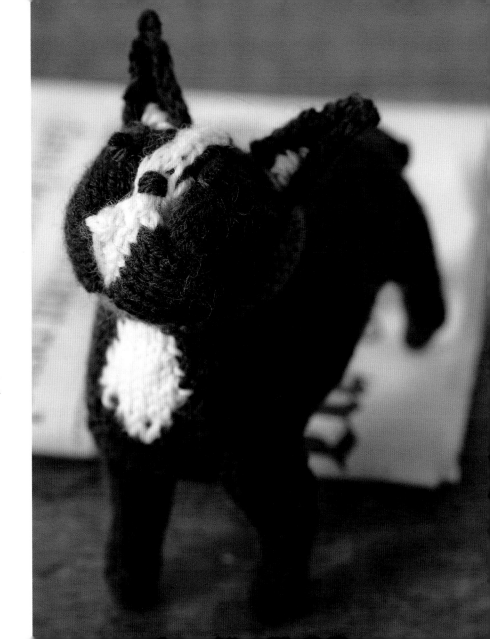

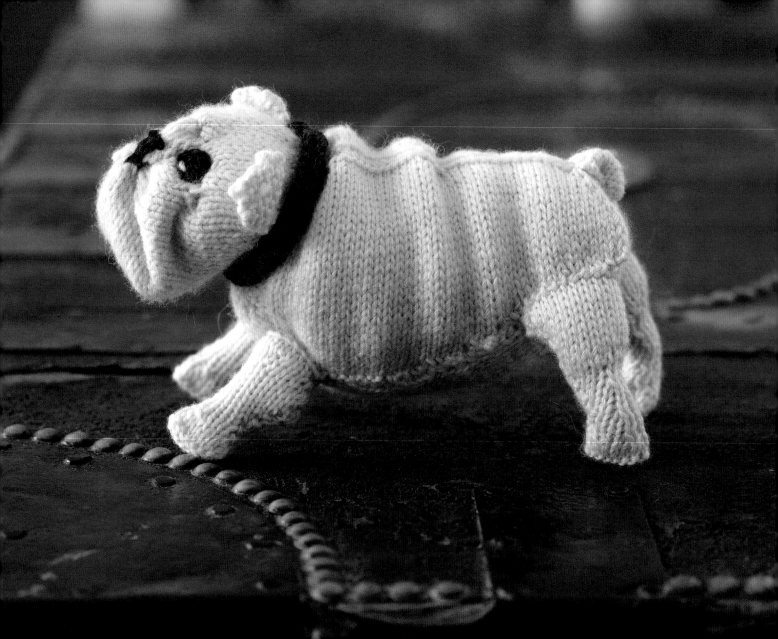

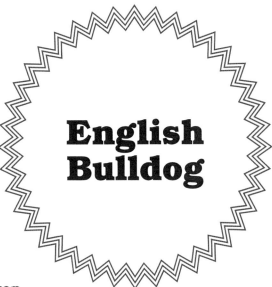

English Bulldog

Loyal, friendly and particularly fond of children, the English Bulldog is an instantly recognizable breed that is not as miserable as the face implies. Although prone to drooling and snoring, the English Bulldog has a devoted following. It has become a mascot for England and is closely associated with Winston Churchill, who never owned one but did rather resemble one. Originally bred for bullbaiting, the Bulldog is mentioned in Shakespeare's *Henry VI*. Famous Bulldogs are Spike in *Tom and Jerry* and Bulldog Drummond, the popular and hair-raisingly non-PC detective of the 1920s.

Bulldog

The stuffing is crucial;
don't over-stuff your
Bulldog as he needs
to be slightly wrinkly.

Measurements
Length: 18cm (7in)
Height to top of head: 11cm (4½in)

Materials
- Pair of 2¾mm (US 2) knitting needles
- 30g (1⅛oz) of Rowan Cashsoft 4ply in Cream 443 (cr)
- Small amount of Rowan Pure Wool 4ply in Mocha 417 (mo) for collar
- Tiny amounts of Rowan Pure Wool 4ply in Black 404 and in Snow 412 for nose and eyes

Abbreviations
See page 172.

Front Leg
(make 2 the same)
With cr, cast on 16 sts.
Beg with a k row, work 2 rows st st.
Row 3: K5, k2tog 3 times, k5. *(13 sts)*
Row 4: P2tog, p2, p2tog, p1, p2tog, p2, p2tog. *(9 sts)*
Row 5: Knit.
Row 6: Purl.
Row 7: Inc, k7, inc. *(11 sts)*
Row 8: Purl.
Row 9: Inc, k9, inc. *(13 sts)*
Row 10: Purl.
Row 11: Inc, k11, inc. *(15 sts)*

Row 12: Purl.
Row 13: Inc, k13, inc. *(17 sts)*
Row 14: Purl.
Row 15: K2tog, k4, inc, k3, inc, k4, k2tog. *(17 sts)*
Row 16: Purl.
Row 17: K2tog, k3, inc, k5, inc, k3, k2tog. *(17 sts)*
Row 18: Purl.
Cast (bind) off.

Back Leg
(make 2 the same)
With cr, cast on 16 sts.
Beg with a k row, work 2 rows st st.
Row 3: K5, k2tog 3 times, k5. *(13 sts)*
Row 4: P2tog, p2, p2tog, p1, p2tog, p2, p2tog. *(9 sts)*
Work 2 rows st st.
Row 7: Inc, k1, k2tog, k1, k2tog, k1, inc. *(9 sts)*
Row 8: Purl.
Row 9: Inc, k7, inc. *(11 sts)*
Row 10: Purl.
Row 11: Inc, k2, k2tog, k1, k2tog, k2, inc. *(11 sts)*
Row 12: Purl.
Row 13: Inc, k2, k2tog, k1, k2tog, k2, inc. *(11 sts)*
Row 14: Purl.
Row 15: K4, inc, k1, inc, k4. *(13 sts)*
Row 16: Purl.
Row 17: K5, inc, k1, inc, k5. *(15 sts)*
Row 18: Purl.
Row 19: K6, inc, k1, inc, k6. *(17 sts)*
Row 20: Purl.
Row 21: Inc, k15, inc. *(19 sts)*
Row 22: Purl.
Row 23: Inc, k17, inc. *(21 sts)*
Row 24: Purl.
Row 25: Inc, k19, inc. *(23 sts)*
Cast (bind) off.

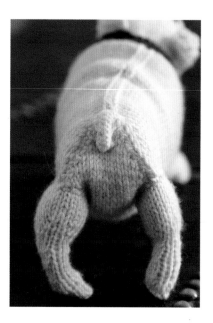

Legs
Sew on the legs along the seam where the tummy meets the body.

Body

Squash the body lengthways between your hands to give your Bulldog the concertina look.

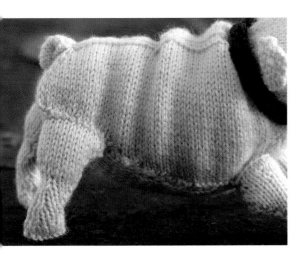

Right Side of Body

With cr, cast on 16 sts.
Row 1: K16, cast on 4 sts. *(20 sts)*
Row 2: Purl.
Row 3: K20, cast on 3 sts. *(23 sts)*
Row 4: Purl.
Row 5: Inc, k22, cast on 3 sts. *(27 sts)*
Row 6: Purl.
Row 7: K27, cast on 6 sts. *(33 sts)*
Row 8: Purl.
Row 9: Inc, k32, cast on 6 sts. *(40 sts)*
Row 10: Purl.
Work 4 rows st st.
Row 15: Inc, k to end. *(41 sts)*
Row 16: Purl.
Row 17: K to last 2 sts, k2tog. *(40 sts)*
Row 18: Purl.
Rep last 2 rows 3 times more. *(37 sts)*
Row 25: Knit.
Row 26: Cast (bind) off 16 sts, p to end. *(21 sts)*
Row 27: K19, k2tog. *(20 sts)*
Cast (bind) off.

Left Side of Body

With cr, cast on 16 sts.
Row 1: Knit.
Row 2: P16, cast on 4 sts. *(20 sts)*
Row 3: Knit.
Row 4: P20, cast on 3 sts. *(23 sts)*
Row 5: Knit.
Row 6: Inc, p 22, cast on 3 sts. *(27 sts)*
Row 7: Knit.
Row 8: P27, cast on 6 sts. *(33 sts)*
Row 9: Knit.
Row 10: Inc, p32, cast on 6 sts. *(40 sts)*
Row 11: Knit.
Work 4 rows st st.
Row 16: Inc, p39. *(41 sts)*
Row 17: Knit.
Row 18: P to last 2 sts, p2tog. *(40 sts)*
Row 19: Knit.
Rep last 2 rows 3 times more. *(37 sts)*
Row 26: Purl.

Row 27: Cast (bind) off 16 sts, k to end. *(21 sts)*
Row 28: P19, p2tog. *(20 sts)*
Cast (bind) off.

Head

Using mattress stitch, sew up back seam. Starting 2cm (¾in) from edge, pick up and knit 20 sts from Right Side of Body and 20 sts from Left Side of Body. *(40 sts)*
Next row: Purl.
Next row: K30, pult (pick up loop below next st on left needle by inserting tip of right needle from back through loop – this stops a hole forming when turning work – then turn, leaving rem 10 sts on left needle unworked).
Next row: Working back of neck on centre 20 sts only, p2tog (first st of p2tog is loop picked up at end of last row), p19, pult.
Next row: K2tog, k19, pult.
Next row: P2tog, p19, pult.
Next row: K2tog, k to end of row.
Next row: Purl.
Cast (bind) off 4 sts at beg of next 2 rows. *(32 sts)*
Head is worked in 3 sections from here
Right section
Next row: K11, turn, working on these 11 sts only (leave rem 21 sts on needle).
Next row: Purl.
Working st st, inc on outside edge of every row until you have 24 sts, ending with a k row. Work 4 rows st st straight (even).
Cont in st st, work 2tog on outside edge of every row until you have 16 sts.
Next row: Purl.
Next row: Cast (bind) off 10 sts, k to end. *(6 sts)*
Cast (bind) off.
Centre section
Rejoin yarn and working on centre 10 sts and beg with a k row, work 10 rows st st.
Next row: K2tog, k6, k2tog. *(8 sts)*
Next row: Purl.
Next row: K2tog, k4, k2tog. *(6 sts)*

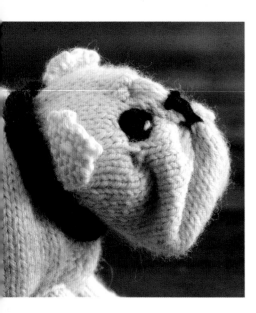

Head

Try not to be alarmed by the look of the head before folding the nose. You will need to mould the stuffing carefully to get the Bulldog look.

Next row: Purl.
Next row: K2tog, k2, k2tog. *(4 sts)*
Next row: Purl.
Next row: K2tog twice. *(2 sts)*
Next row: Purl.
Next row: K2tog and fasten off.

Left section
Rejoin yarn and work on final 11 sts.
Beg with a k row, work 2 rows st st.
Cont in st st, inc on outside edge of every row until you have 24 sts, ending with a k row.
Work 4 rows st st straight (even).
Cont in st st, work 2tog on outside edge of every row until you have 16 sts.
Cast (bind) off 10 sts, p to end. *(6 sts)*
Cast (bind) off.

Tummy

With cr, cast on 1 st.
Row 1: Inc. *(2 sts)*
Row 2: Purl.
Row 3: Inc into both sts. *(4 sts)*
Row 4: Purl.
Row 5: Inc, k2, inc. *(6 sts)*
Row 6: Purl.
Row 7: Inc, k4, inc. *(8 sts)*
Row 8: Purl.
Row 9: Inc, k6, inc. *(10 sts)*
Row 10: Purl.
Row 11: Inc, k8, inc. *(12 sts)*
Row 12: Purl.
Row 13: Inc, k10, inc. *(14 sts)*
Row 14: Purl.
Row 15: Inc, k12, inc. *(16 sts)*
Cont in st st to fit all along tummy to bottom of chest (approx 60 rows), ending with a p row.
Next row: K2tog, k12, k2tog. *(14 sts)*
Next row: Purl.
Next row: Knit.
Next row: Purl.
Next row: K2tog, k10, k2tog. *(12 sts)*
Next row: Purl.
Next row: Knit.

Next row: Purl.
Next row: K2tog, k8, k2tog. *(10 sts)*
Next row: Purl.
Next row: Knit.
Next row: Purl.
Next row: K2tog, k6, k2tog. *(8 sts)*
Next row: Purl.
Next row: K2tog, k4, k2tog. *(6 sts)*
Next row: Purl.
Next row: K2tog, k2, k2tog. *(4 sts)*
Next row: Purl.
Next row: K2tog twice. *(2 sts)*
Next row: P2tog and fasten off.

Tail

With cr, cast on 7 sts.
Beg with a k row, work 8 rows st st.
Cast (bind) off.

Ear

(make 2 the same)
With cr, cast on 9 sts.
Beg with a k row, work 5 rows st st.
Row 6: K2tog, k5, k2tog. *(7 sts)*
Row 7: P2tog, p3, p2tog. *(5 sts)*
Row 8: K2tog, k1, k2tog. *(3 sts)*
Row 9: P2tog, p1. *(2 sts)*
Row 10: K2tog and fasten off.

Nose

With bl, cast on 4 sts.
Row 1: Knit.
Row 2: P2tog twice. *(2 sts)*
Row 3: K2tog and fasten off.

Eyes

With bl, cast on 4 sts.
Beg with a k row, work 2 rows st st.
Cast (bind) off.

Collar

With mo, cast on 42 sts.
Knit 2 rows.
Cast (bind) off.

To Make Up

Sew in ends, leaving ends from cast on
and cast (bound) off rows for sewing up.
Using mattress or whip stitch, sew up legs
starting at paw. Stuff each leg.

Using mattress or whip stitch, sew cast on
row of tummy to base of back and sew cast
(bound) off row under chin. Ease and sew
tummy to fit body. Leave a 2.5cm (1in) gap
between front and back legs on one side.
Turn right side out, stuff then sew up gap
with mattress stitch.

Sew up seams on top of head, sew sides
of head together. Sew cheeks to neck and
under chin. Stuff head quite loosely.

Sew on ears and tail (folded in half with
purl side as RS) as shown in photograph.
If you want to make the body more wrinkly,
you can thread the end of yarn used to sew
on the tail through the body and catch it to
the head to concertina the body.

Fold nose back on itself as in photograph
and sew tip of nose to centre of middle head
section with whip stitch. Sew chin up under
nose for extra jowl effect.

Using black yarn, sew on eyes. Embroider
a white stitch close to bottom edge.

Sew ends of collar together and slide over
head onto neck.

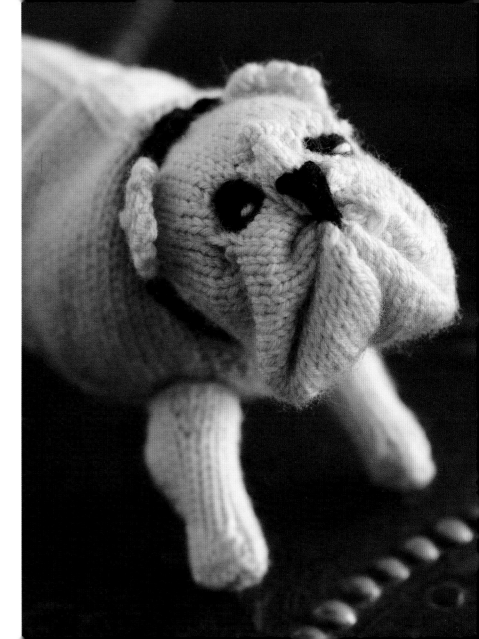

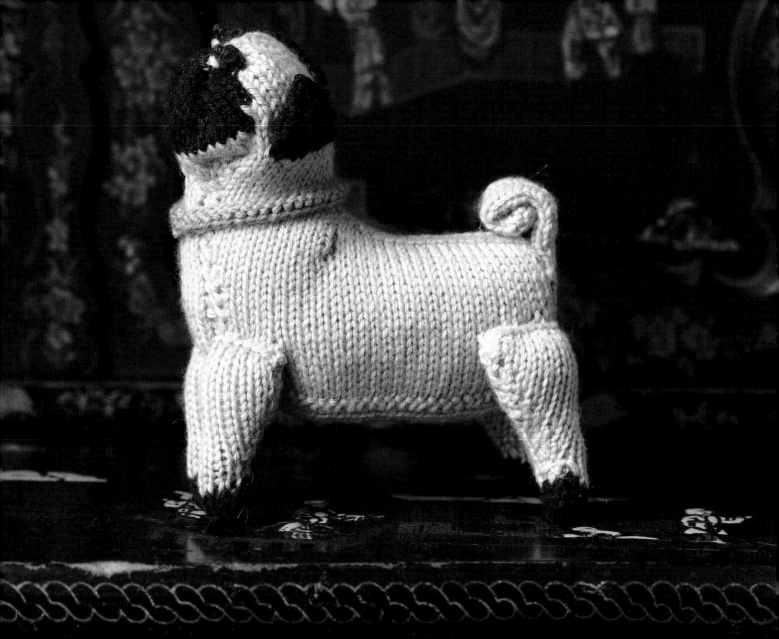

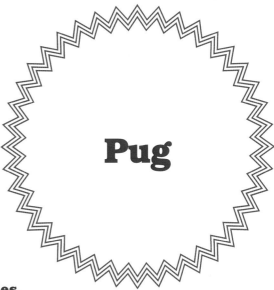

Pug

Hilarious looking and with large personalities, Pugs are known for their playful and charming temperaments. They prefer the company of humans to other dogs and will become anxious if ignored. Pugs are one of the few breeds that perform no function. Originally they graced the laps of Chinese royalty, then in the 16th century moved across the globe to become the European aristocrat's accessory of choice. Queen Victoria had quite a collection, only rivalled by the Duke and Duchess of Windsor who had eleven Pugs who ate off silver plates and wore Miss Dior perfume.

Pug

Take care not to over-stuff the head as it needs to have its characteristic folds.

Measurements

Length: 11cm (4½in)
Height to top of head: 13cm (5in)

Materials

- Pair of 2¾mm (US 2) knitting needles
- 10g (¼oz) of Rowan Cashsoft 4ply in Black 422 (bl)
- 30g (1⅛oz) of Rowan Cashsoft 4ply in Elite 451 (el)
- Small amount of Rowan Pure Wool 4ply in Eau de Nil 450 (ea) for collar
- Tiny amount of Rowan Pure Wool 4ply in Mocha 417 for eyes

Abbreviations

See page 172.

Back Leg

(make 2 the same)
With bl, cast on 8 sts.
Beg with a k row, work 2 rows st st.
Change to el, work 4 rows st st.
Row 7: Inc, k6, inc. *(10 sts)*
Row 8: Purl.
Row 9: Inc, k8, inc. *(12 sts)*
Row 10: Purl.
Row 11: Inc, k4, k2tog, k4, inc. *(13 sts)*
Row 12: Purl.
Row 13: Inc, k3, k2tog, k1, k2tog, k3, inc. *(13 sts)*

Row 14: Purl.
Row 15: Inc, k11, inc. *(15 sts)*
Row 16: Purl.
Row 17: Inc, k13, inc. *(17 sts)*
Row 18: Purl.
Row 19: Inc, k15, inc. *(19 sts)*
Row 20: Purl.
Row 21: Knit.
Row 22: Purl.
Cast (bind) off.

Front Leg

(make 2 the same)
With bl, cast on 6 sts.
Beg with a k row, work 2 rows st st.
Row 3: Change to el, work 4 rows st st.
Row 7: Inc, K4, inc. *(8 sts)*
Row 8: Purl.
Rep last 2 rows 3 times more. *(14 sts)*
Work 8 rows st st.
Cast (bind) off.

Right Side of Body and Head

With el, cast on 23 sts.
Beg with a k row, work 2 rows st st.
Row 3: Inc, k22, cast on 3 sts. *(27 sts)*
Row 4: Purl.
Row 5: Inc, k25, inc. *(29 sts)*
Work 5 rows st st.
Row 11: Inc, k28. *(30 sts)*
Work 3 rows st st.
Row 15: K29, inc. *(31 sts)*
Row 16: Purl.
Rep last 2 rows once more. *(32 sts)*
Row 19: K12, pult (pick up loop below next st on left needle by inserting tip of right needle from back through loop – this stops a hole forming when turning work – then turn, leaving rem 20 sts on left needle unworked).
Row 20: Working chest on these 12 sts only, p2tog (first st of p2tog is loop picked up at end of last row), p11.
Row 21: K12, pult.
Row 22: P2tog, p11.

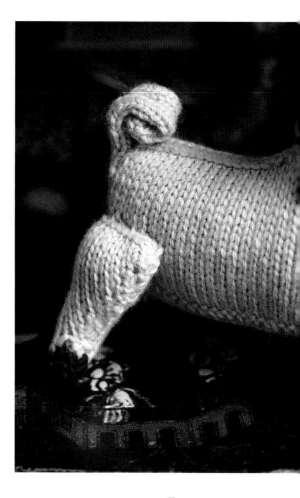

Legs
To get the stuffing right down into the legs you can use a chopstick or something similar.

Row 23: K12, pult.
Row 24: P2tog, p11.
Row 25: K32.
Row 26: Cast (bind) off 15 sts, p to end. *(17 sts)*
Row 27: Inc, k14, k2tog. *(17 sts)*
Row 28: P2tog, p15, cast on 6 sts. *(22 sts)*
Row 29: Knit.
Row 30: P2tog, p19, inc. *(22 sts)*
Row 31: Knit.
Row 32: P9, pult (pick up loop below next st on left needle by inserting tip of right needle from back through loop – this stops a hole forming when turning work – then turn, leaving rem 13 sts on left needle unworked).
Row 33: Working top of head on these 9 sts only, k2tog (first st of k2tog is loop picked up at end of last row), k8.
Row 34: P9, pult.
Row 35: K2tog, k8.
Row 36: P9, pult.
Row 37: K2tog, k8.
Work 2 rows st st. *(22 sts)*
Row 40: P10el, join in bl, p12bl.
Row 41: K12bl, k10el.
Row 42: P9el, p13bl.
Row 43: K13bl, K9el.
Row 44: P2togel, p7el, p13bl. *(21 sts)*
Row 45: K13bl, k8el.
Row 46: P7el, p14bl.
Row 47: K14bl, k7el.
Row 48: P2togel, p5el, p14bl. *(20 sts)*
Row 49: K14bl, k6el.
With bl, dec 1st at each end of every other row twice. *(16 sts)*
Cast (bind) off.

Left Side of Body and Head

With el, cast on 23 sts.
Row 1: Knit.
Row 2: Inc, p22, cast on 3 sts. *(27 sts)*
Row 3: Knit.
Row 4: Inc, p25, inc. *(29 sts)*
Work 5 rows st st.

Row 10: Inc, p28. *(30 sts)*
Work 3 rows st st.
Row 14: P29, inc. *(31 sts)*
Row 15: Knit.
Rep last 2 rows once more. *(32 sts)*
Row 18: P12, pult (pick up loop below next st on left needle by inserting tip of right needle from back through loop – this stops a hole forming when turning work – then turn, leaving rem 20 sts on left needle unworked).
Row 19: Working chest on these 12 sts only, k2tog (first st of k2tog is loop picked up at end of last row), k11.
Row 20: P12, pult.
Row 21: K2tog, k11.
Row 22: P12, pult.
Row 23: K2tog, k11.
Row 24: P32.

Body

The tail is knitted as part of the tummy and curls around on itself to give that unique Pug look.

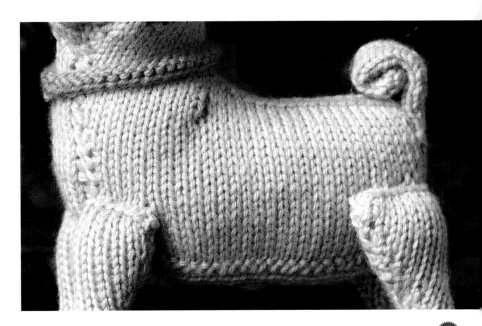

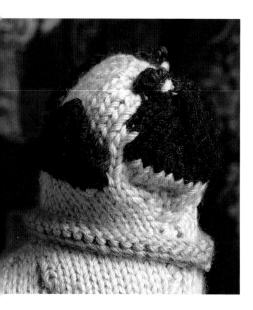

Head

Don't over-stuff the head, then you can press the eyeballs deeply into the head so the knitting folds around them in a Pug-like way.

Row 25: Cast (bind) off 15 sts, k to end. *(17 sts)*
Row 26: Inc, p14, p2tog. *(17 sts)*
Row 27: K2tog, k15, cast on 6 sts. *(22 sts)*
Row 28: Purl.
Row 29: K2tog, k19, inc. *(22 sts)*
Row 30: Purl.
Row 31: K9, pult (pick up loop below next st on left needle by inserting tip of right needle from back through loop (this stops a hole forming when turning work) then turn, leaving rem 13 sts on left needle unworked).
Row 32: Working top of head on these 9 sts only, p2tog (first st of p2tog is loop picked up at end of last row), p8.
Row 33: K9, pult.
Row 34: P2tog, p8.
Row 35: K9, pult.
Row 36: P2tog, p8.
Work 2 rows st st. *(22 sts)*
Row 39: K10el, join in bl, k12bl.
Row 40: P12bl, p10el.
Row 41: K9el, k13bl.
Row 42: P13bl, p9el.
Row 43: K2togel, k7el, k13bl. *(21 sts)*
Row 44: P13bl, p8el.
Row 45: K7el, k14bl.
Row 46: P14bl, p7el.
Row 47: K2togel, k5el, k14bl. *(20 sts)*
Row 48: P14bl, p6el.
With bl, dec 1st at each end of every other row twice. *(16 sts)*
Cast (bind) off.

Tail and Tummy

With el, cast on 3 sts.
Beg with a k row, work 2 rows st st.
Row 3: Inc, k1, inc. *(5 sts)*
Row 4: Purl.
Row 5: Inc, k3, inc. *(7 sts)*
Row 6: Purl.
Row 7: Inc, k5, inc. *(9 sts)*
Row 8: Purl.

Work approx 60 rows st st starting with a k row (measure from under chin to dog's bottom and adjust accordingly), and ending with a p row.
Next row: K2tog, k5, k2tog. *(7 sts)*
Next row: Purl.
Work approx 24 rows st st starting with a k row (measure against body and adjust accordingly, this section forms tail).
Cast (bind) off.

Ear

(make 2 the same)
With bl, cast on 9 sts.
Row 1: [K1, p1] 4 times, k1.
Row 2: [K1, p1] 4 times, k1.
Row 3: K2tog, k1, p1, k1, p1, k1, k2tog. *(7 sts)*
Row 4: [P1, k1] 3 times, p1.
Row 5: K2tog, p1, k1, p1, k2tog. *(5 sts)*
Row 6: [K1, p1] twice, k1.
Row 7: K2tog, k1, k2tog. *(3 sts)*
Row 8: K2tog, k1. *(2 sts)*
Row 9: K2tog and fasten off.

Eyes

With bl, cast on 4 sts.
Beg with a k row, work 2 rows st st.
Cast (bind) off.

Collar

With ea, cast on 40 sts.
Knit 1 row.
Cast (bind) off.

To Make Up

Sew in ends, leaving ends from cast on and cast (bound) off rows for sewing up. Using mattress or whip stitch, sew up legs starting at paw. Stuff each leg. Using whip stitch, sew along top of leg, leaving an end to sew leg to body.
Using mattress stitch, sew down centre back. Sew cast (bound) off row of tummy

and tail by curling it around once and sewing to back to form tail as shown in photograph. Sew the cast on row to under chin at top of chest. Ease and sew tummy to fit body. Leave a 2.5cm (1in) gap between front and back legs on one side. Stuff then sew up gap.

Using whip stitch, sew legs to body as shown in photograph; front legs with seams at back and back legs with seams at front. Fold nose up and curl it in on itself, this will take a bit of trial and error to make it look pug-like. Use the black end from the cast (bound) off row to sew the nose down with whip st. Don't over-stuff the head as it needs to look slightly loose and wrinkled.

Sew ears to head as shown in photograph. Using black yarn, sew on eyes. Embroider a French knot in mocha and a stitch in elite close to bottom edge.

Sew ends of collar together and slide over head onto neck.

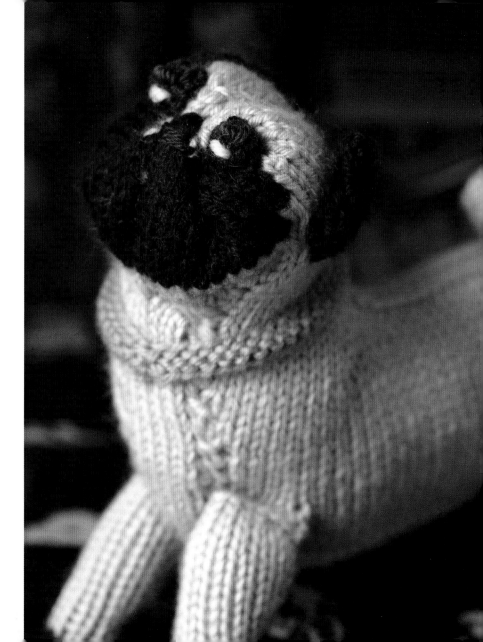

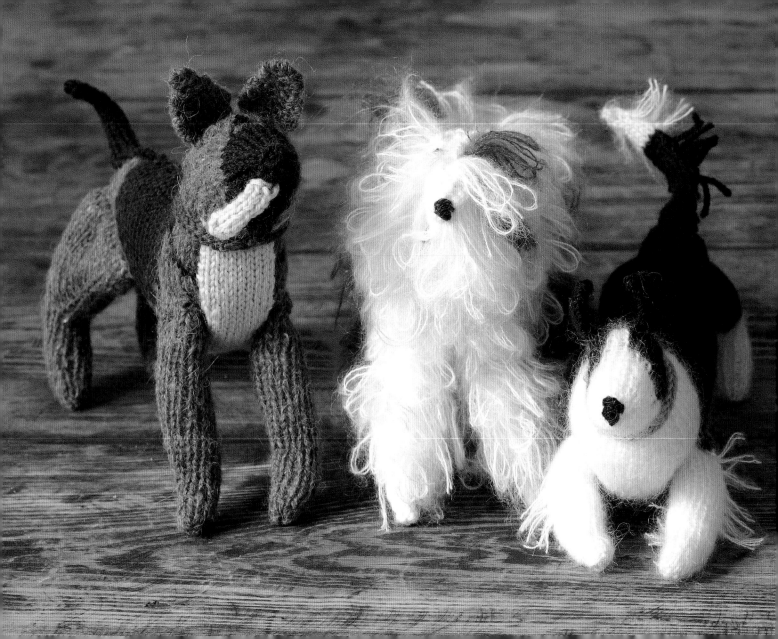

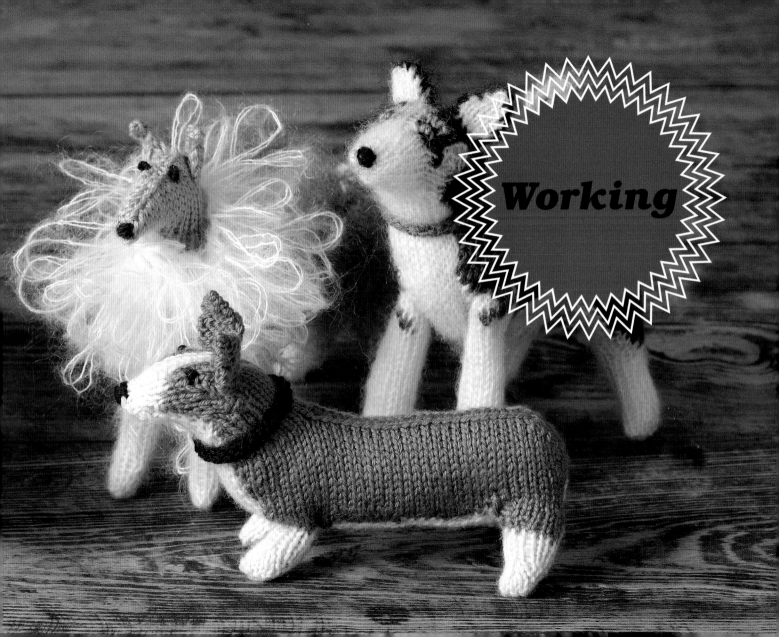

Working

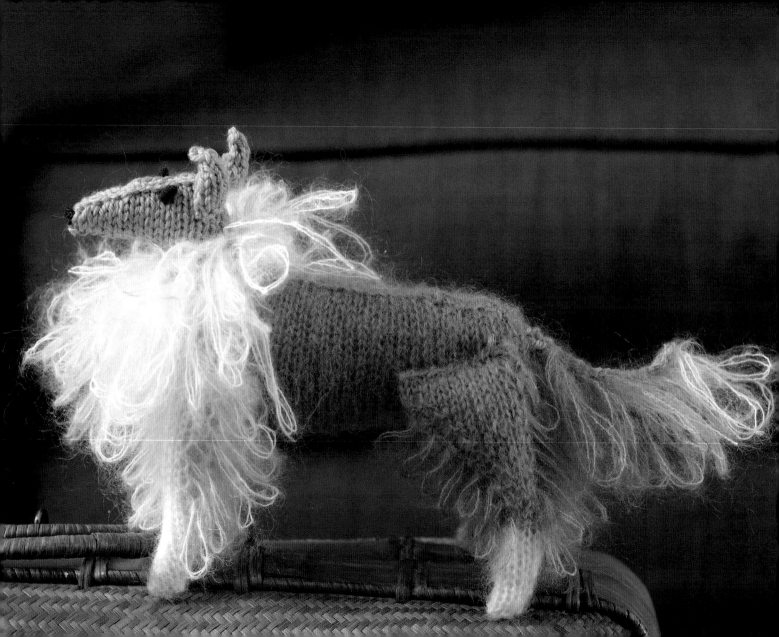

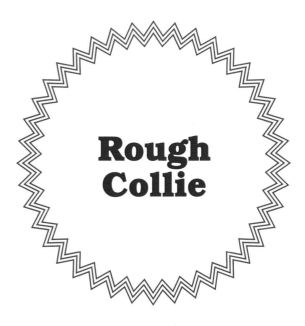

Rough Collie

The Rough Collie is elegant and dignified yet resourceful and intelligent, they were originally bred to herd Highland sheep. Due to their long and luxurious coats, they are most suited for owners who enjoy hairdressing. Lassie, the heroic and courageous fictional Collie, was the hugely popular subject of many films and a TV series. Lassie was always played by a male dog on the somewhat controversial grounds that male Collies were more attractive, but less intelligent than the females.

Rough Collie

Deceptively complex looking, the Rough Collie is fairly simple to make, with the mane being knitted separately.

Measurements

Length (excluding tail): 17cm (6¾in)
Height to top of head: 14cm (5½in)

Materials

- Pair of 2¾mm (US 2) knitting needles
- 20g (¾oz) of Rowan Kidsilk Haze in Cream 634 (cr) used DOUBLE throughout
- 20g (¾oz) of Rowan Kidsilk Haze in Ember 644 (em) used DOUBLE throughout
- 5g (⅛oz) of Rowan Cashsoft 4ply in Savannah 439 (sa)
- Tiny amount of Rowan Pure Wool 4ply in Black 404 for nose and eyes
- Pipecleaners for legs

Abbreviations

*k = make one 2-finger loopy st
See also page 172.
For loopy stitch technique, see page 173.

Back Leg

(make 2 the same)
With cr, cast on 9 sts.
Beg with a k row, work 2 rows st st.
Row 3: Inc, k1, k2tog, k1, k2tog, k1, inc. *(9 sts)*
Work 7 rows st st.
Change to em.
Work 3 rows st st.

Row 14: P1,*k, p2,*k, p2,*k, p1.
Row 15: K2tog, inc into next 2 sts, k1, inc into next 2 sts, k2tog. *(11 sts)*
Row 16: P1, *k, p3, *k, p3, *k, p1.
Row 17: K2tog, inc, k1, inc, k1, inc, k1, inc, k2tog. *(13 sts)*
Row 18: P1, *k, p4, *k, p4, *k, p1.
Row 19: K5, inc, k1, inc, k5. *(15 sts)*
Row 20: P1, *k, p5, *k, p5, *k, p1.
Row 21: K6, inc, k1, inc, k6. *(17 sts)*
Row 22: P1, *k, p6,*k, p6, *k, p1.
Row 23: K7, inc, k1, inc, k7. *(19 sts)*
Row 24: P1,*k, p7, *k, p7, *k, p1.
Row 25: K8, inc, k1, inc, k8. *(21 sts)*
Row 26: P1,*k, p8, *k, p8, *k, p1.
Row 27: K9, inc, k1, inc, k9. *(23 sts)*
Row 28: P1,*k, p9,*k, p9,*k, p1.
Row 29: K10, inc, k1, inc, k10. *(25 sts)*
Row 30: P1, *k, p10, *k, p10, *k, p1.
Cast (bind) off.

Front Leg

(make 2 the same)
With cr, cast on 9 sts.
Beg with a k row, work 2 rows st st.
Row 3: Inc, k1, k2tog, k1, k2tog, k1, inc. *(9 sts)*
Row 4: Purl.
Rep last 2 rows once more.
Work 2 rows st st.
Row 9: Inc, k7, inc. *(11 sts)*
Work 4 rows st st.
Row 14: P1, *k, p3, *k, p3, *k, p1.
Row 15: Knit.
Rep last 2 rows once more.
Rep row 14 once more.
Row 19: Inc, k9, inc. *(13 sts)*
Row 20: P1, *k, p4, *k, p4, *k, p1.
Row 21: Knit.
Rep last 2 rows once more.
Rep row 20 once more.
Row 25: Inc, k11, inc. *(15 sts)*
Row 26: P1, *k, p5, *k, p5, *k, p1.
Row 27: Knit.
Cast (bind) off.

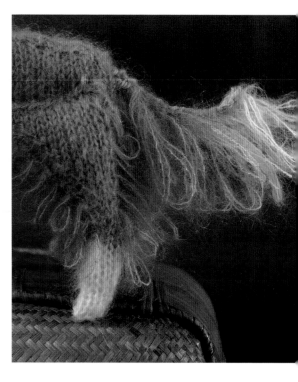

Legs

The legs have uncut loopy stitch edging to give them that feathered look.

Right Side of Body and Head

With em, cast on 8 sts.

Row 1: K8, cast on 6 sts. *(14 sts)*
Row 2: P13, inc. *(15 sts)*
Row 3: K15, cast on 3 sts. *(18 sts)*
Row 4: P17, inc. *(19 sts)*
Row 5: K19, cast on 3 sts. *(22 sts)*
Row 6: P21, inc. *(23 sts)*
Row 7: K23, cast on 3 sts. *(26 sts)*
Row 8: P25, inc. *(27 sts)*
Row 9: K27, cast on 3 sts. *(30 sts)*
Row 10: P29, inc. *(31 sts)*
Row 11: K31, cast on 3 sts. *(34 sts)*
Work 9 rows st st.
Row 21: K32, k2tog. *(33 sts)*
Row 22: P2tog, p31. *(32 sts)*

Row 23: K30, k2tog. *(31 sts)*
Row 24: Cast (bind) off 5 sts, p to end. *(26 sts)*
Row 25: K8, cast (bind) off rem 18 sts.
Change to sa.
Row 26: P8, cast on 9 sts. *(17 sts)*
Work 2 rows st st.
Row 29: K2tog, k15. *(16 sts)*
Row 30: P14, p2tog. *(15 sts)*
Row 31: K2tog, k13. *(14 sts)*
Row 32: P2tog, p10, p2tog. *(12 sts)*
Row 33: K2tog, k10. *(11 sts)*
Row 34: P9, p2tog. *(10 sts)*
Row 35: Cast (bind) off 4 sts, k to end. *(6 sts)*
Row 36: P2tog, p2, p2tog. *(4 sts)*
Cast (bind) off.

Body

The three-finger loopy stitch ruff gives the Collie an exuberant look and you just pop it over its head.

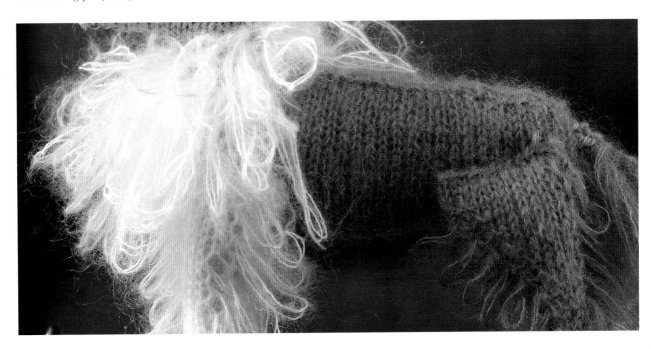

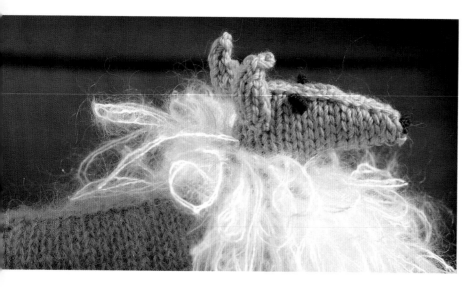

Head

Tweak the ears between finger and thumb so they are upright and perky to give added personality.

Left Side of Body and Head

With em, cast on 8 sts.
Row 1: Knit.
Row 2: P8, cast on 6 sts. *(14 sts)*
Row 3: K13, inc. *(15 sts)*
Row 4: P15, cast on 3 sts. *(18 sts)*
Row 5: K17, inc. *(19 sts)*
Row 6: P19, cast on 3 sts. *(22 sts)*
Row 7: K21, inc. *(23 sts)*
Row 8: P23, cast on 3 sts. *(26 sts)*
Row 9: K25, inc. *(27 sts)*
Row 10: P27, cast on 3 sts. *(30 sts)*
Row 11: K 29, inc. *(31 sts)*
Row 12: P31, cast on 3 sts. *(34 sts)*
Work 9 rows st st.
Row 22: P32, p2tog. *(33 sts)*
Row 23: K2tog, k31. *(32 sts)*
Row 24: P30, p2tog. *(31 sts)*
Row 25: Cast (bind) off 5 sts, k to end. *(26 sts)*
Row 26: P8, cast (bind) off rem 18 sts.
Change to sa.

Row 27: K8, cast on 9 sts. *(17 sts)*
Work 2 rows st st.
Row 30: P2tog, p15. *(16 sts)*
Row 31: K14, k2tog. *(15 sts)*
Row 32: P2tog, p13. *(14 sts)*
Row 33: K2tog, k10, k2tog. *(12 sts)*
Row 34: P2tog, p10. *(11 sts)*
Row 35: K9, k2tog. *(10 sts)*
Row 36: Cast (bind) off 4 sts, p to end. *(6 sts)*
Row 37: K2tog, k2, k2tog. *(4 sts)*
Cast (bind) off.

Ruff

With cr, cast on 4 sts.
Work 2 rows st st.
Row 3: Inc, k2, inc. *(6 sts)*
Row 4: Purl.
Row 5: Inc, k4, inc. *(8 sts)*
Row 6: Purl.
Row 7: Inc, k6, inc. *(10 sts)*
Row 8: Make 3-finger loopy st in every st across row.
Row 9: Inc, k8, inc. *(12 sts)*
Row 10: Make 3-finger loopy st in every st across row.
Row 11: Inc, k10, inc. *(14 sts)*
Row 12: Make 3-finger loopy st in every st across row.
Row 13: K6, turn, work on these 6 sts only.
Row 14: Make 3-finger loopy st in every st across row.
Row 15: Knit.
Row 16: Make 3-finger loopy st in every st across row.
Row 17: Knit. Cut yarn.
Rejoin yarn to 8 sts, cast (bind) off 2 sts, k to end. *(6 sts)*
Rep rows 14–17 on these 6 sts.
Row 18: P across all 12 sts.
Row 19: K2tog, k8, k2tog. *(10 sts)*
Row 20: P2tog, make 3-finger loopy st in each of next 6 sts, p2tog. *(8 sts)*
Row 21: Knit.
Cast (bind) off.

Tail

With sa, cast on 16 sts
Next row: Knit.
Next row: Join in cr, make 2-finger loopy st in next 6 sts, join in em, make 2-finger loopy st in next 10 sts.
Cast (bind) off in sa.

Ear

(make 2 the same)
With sa, cast on 5 sts.
Work 6 rows st st.
Row 7: K2tog, k1, k2tog. *(3 sts)*
Row 8: Purl.
Row 9: K2tog, k1. *(2 sts)*
Row 10: P2tog and fasten off.

To Make Up

Sew in ends, leaving ends from cast on and cast (bound) off rows for sewing up.
Using mattress or whip stitch, sew up legs starting at paw. Turn right side out and stuff each leg, using pipecleaners for rigidity.
Using mattress or whip stitch, sew down centre back and around body. Leave a 2.5cm (1in) gap between front and back legs. Turn right side out, stuff body tightly, then sew up gap with mattress stitch.
Using whip stitch, sew legs to body as shown in photograph, with back legs at an angle.
Slip ruff over Collie's head.
Sew up two sides of head. Sew on ears and tail as shown in photograph.
Using black yarn, embroider the nose using satin stitch and make two French knots for eyes.
If legs are floppy, about 2cm (¾in) down from top edge of leg, sew through leg, body and opposite leg to make dog more stable.

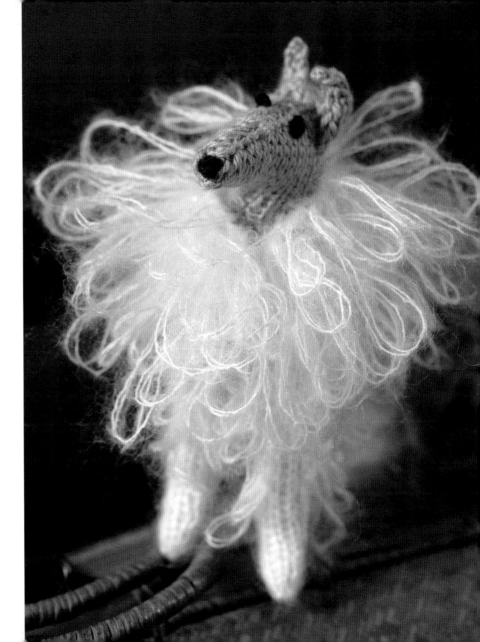

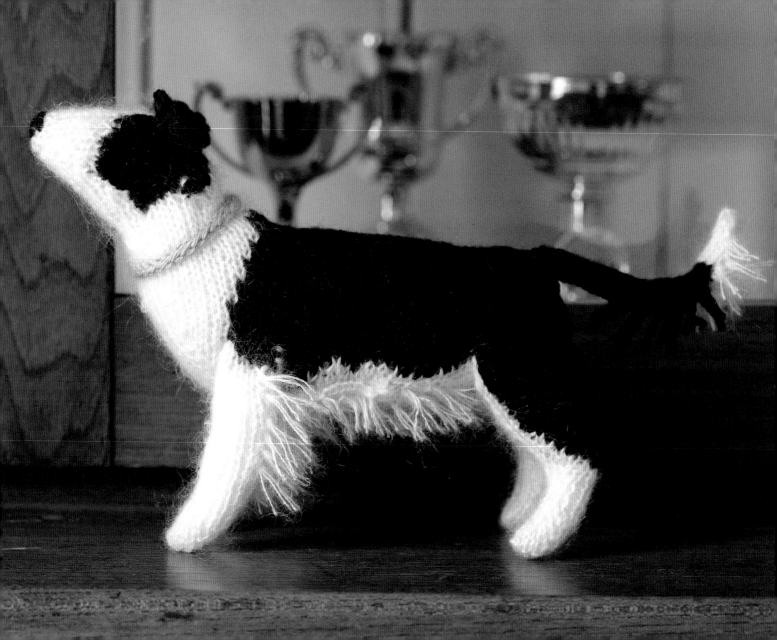

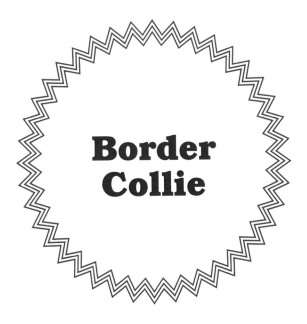

Border Collie

Prized for their honesty, intelligence, integrity and loyalty, the Border Collie is a working dog and likes to be kept busy. They are always on the go, traditionally herding sheep, but will also spend hours retrieving sticks and generally playing. Exercise is essential for this most relentless and eager of breeds and teenage boys just love them. Famous Border Collies are Flye and Rex from the film *Babe*.

Border Collie

Ours has black eyes but you could make them blue or brown, or one blue and one brown.

Measurements

Length (excluding tail): 20cm (8in)
Height to top of head: 13cm (5in)

Materials

- Pair of 2¾mm (US 2) knitting needles
- 2 spare 2¾mm (US 2) knitting needles
- Pair of 2¾mm (US 2) double-pointed knitting needles
- 10g (¼oz) of Rowan Kidsilk Haze in Cream 634 (cr) used DOUBLE throughout
- 15g (½oz) of Rowan Cashsoft 4ply in Black 422 (bl)
- Small amount of Rowan Cashsoft 4ply in Cherish 453 (ch) for collar

Abbreviations

See page 172.
For loopy stitch technique, see page 173.

Right Back Leg

With 2¾mm (US 2) knitting needles and cr, cast on 9 sts.
Beg with a k row, work 2 rows st st.
Row 3: Inc, k1, k2tog, k1, k2tog, k1, inc. *(9 sts)*
Row 4: Purl.
Row 5: K2, k2tog, k1, k2tog, k2. *(7 sts)*
Work 5 rows st st.
Row 11: Inc, k1, inc, k1, inc, k1, inc. *(11 sts)*

Row 12: Purl.*
Row 13: K2togcr, k2cr, inc into next 3 sts cr, k1cr, join in bl, k1bl, k2togbl. *(12 sts)*
Row 14: P4bl, p8cr.
Row 15: K5cr, inc into next 2 sts cr, k5bl. *(14 sts)*
Row 16: P6bl, p8cr.
Row 17: K6cr, inccr, incbl, k6bl. *(16 sts)*
Row 18: P8bl, p8cr.
Row 19: K7cr, inccr, incbl, k7bl. *(18 sts)*
Row 20: P9bl, p9cr.
Row 21: K8cr, inccr, incbl, k8bl. *(20 sts)*
Row 22: P10bl, p10cr.
Row 23: K9cr, inccr, incbl, k9bl. *(22 sts)*
Row 24: P11bl, p11cr.
Row 25: K10cr, inccr, incbl, k10bl. *(24 sts)*
Row 26: P12bl, p12cr.
Row 27: K12cr, k12bl.
Row 28: P12bl, p12cr.
Row 29: Cast (bind) off 12 sts cr, 12 sts bl.

Left Back Leg

Work as for Right Back Leg to *.
Row 13: Join in bl, k2togbl, k1bl, k1cr, inc into next 3 sts cr, k2cr, k2togcr. *(12 sts)*
Row 14: P8cr, p4bl.
Row 15: K5bl, inc into next 2 sts cr, k5cr. *(14 sts)*
Row 16: P8cr, p6bl.
Row 17: K6bl, incbl, inccr, k6cr. *(16 sts)*
Row 18: P8cr, p8bl.
Row 19: K7bl, incbl, inccr, k7cr. *(18 sts)*
Row 20: P9cr, p9bl.
Row 21: K8bl, incbl, inccr, k8cr. *(20 sts)*
Row 22: P10cr, p10bl.
Row 23: K9bl, incbl, inccr, k9cr. *(22 sts)*
Row 24: P11cr, p11bl.
Row 25: K10bl, incbl, inccr, k10cr. *(24 sts)*
Row 26: P12cr, p12bl.
Row 27: K12bl, k12cr.
Row 28: P12cr, p12bl.
Row 29: Cast (bind) off 12 sts bl, 12 sts cr.

Right Front Leg

With 2¾mm (US 2) knitting needles and cr, cast on 9 sts.
Beg with a k row, work 2 rows st st.
Row 3: Inc, k1, k2tog, k1, k2tog, k1, inc. *(9 sts)*
Row 4: Purl.
Rep last 2 rows once more.
Work 2 rows st st.
Row 9: Inc, k7, inc. *(11 sts)*
Work 5 rows st st.
Row 15: **K1, loopy st 1, k7, loopy st 1, k1. *(11 sts)*
Row 16: Purl.**
Rep from ** to ** 5 times more.
Row 27: K1, loopy st 1, k7, loopy st 1, k1.***
Row 28: Join in bl, p2bl, p9cr.
Row 29: K8cr, k3bl.
Row 30: P4bl, p7cr.
Row 31: Cast (bind) off 7 sts cr, 4 sts bl.

Left Front Leg

Work as for Right Front Leg to***.
Row 28: P9cr, join in bl, p2bl.
Row 29: K3bl, k8cr.
Row 30: P7cr, p4bl.
Row 31: Cast (bind) off 4 sts bl, 7 sts cr.

Right Side of Body

With 2¾mm (US 2) knitting needles and bl and cr, cast on 3 sts bl, 5 sts cr.
Row 1: K5cr, k3bl, cast on 8 sts cr. *(16 sts)*
Row 2: P8cr, p4bl, k3cr, inccr. *(17 sts)*
Row 3: K5cr, k5bl, k3cr, k1bl, k3cr, cast on 5 sts bl. *(22 sts)*
Row 4: P10bl, p1cr, p7bl, p3cr, inccr. *(23 sts)*
Row 5: K5cr, k18bl, cast on 11 sts bl. *(34 sts)*
Row 6: P30bl, p3cr, inccr. *(35 sts)*
Row 7: K4cr, k31bl.
Row 8: P31bl, p3cr, inccr. *(36 sts)*
Row 9: K5cr, k31bl.
Row 10: P31bl, p5cr.
Row 11: K5cr, k31bl.
Row 12: P30bl, p6cr.

Row 13: K6cr, k30bl.
Row 14: P30bl, p6cr.
Row 15: K7cr, k29bl.
Row 16: P2togbl, p27bl, p7cr. *(35 sts)*
Row 17: K8cr, k25bl, k2togbl. *(34 sts)*
Row 18: P2togbl, p24bl, p8cr. *(33 sts)*
Row 19: K9cr, k22bl, k2togbl. *(32 sts)*
Row 20: Cast (bind) off 5 sts bl, p18bl icos, p9cr. *(27 sts)*
Row 21: K9cr, k2bl (hold 11 sts on spare needle for right neck), cast (bind) off rem 16 sts bl.

Left Side of Body

With 2¾mm (US 2) knitting needles and bl and cr, cast on 3 sts bl, 5 sts cr.
Row 1: P5cr, p3bl, cast on 8 sts cr. *(16 sts)*
Row 2: K8cr, k4bl, k3cr, inccr. *(17 sts)*
Row 3: P5cr, p5bl, p3cr, p1bl, p3cr, cast on 5 sts bl. *(22 sts)*

Row 4: K10bl, k1cr, k7bl, k3cr, inccr. *(23 sts)*
Row 5: P5cr, p18bl, cast on 11 sts bl. *(34 sts)*
Row 6: K30bl, k3cr, inccr. *(35 sts)*
Row 7: P4cr, p31bl.
Row 8: K31bl, k3cr, inccr. *(36 sts)*
Row 9: P5cr, p31bl.
Row 10: K31bl, k5cr.
Row 11: P5cr, p31bl.
Row 12: K30bl, k6cr.
Row 13: P6cr, p30bl.
Row 14: K30bl, k6cr.
Row 15: P7cr, p29bl.
Row 16: K2togbl, k27bl, k7cr. *(35 sts)*
Row 17: P8cr, p25bl, p2togbl. *(34 sts)*
Row 18: K2togbl, k24bl, k8cr. *(33 sts)*
Row 19: P9cr, p22bl, p2togbl. *(32 sts)*
Row 20: Cast (bind) off 5 sts bl, k18bl icos, k9cr. *(27 sts)*
Row 21: P9cr, p2bl (hold 11 sts on spare needle for left neck), cast (bind) off rem 16 sts in bl, do not break off cr.

Neck and Head

Row 1: With 2¾mm (US 2) knitting needles, bl and cr, and with RS facing k9cr, 2bl from spare needle of Right Side of Body then k2bl, 9cr from spare needle of Left Side of Body. *(22 sts)*
Row 2: P10cr, p2bl, p10cr.
Row 3: K5cr, k2togcr, k8cr, k2togcr, k5cr. *(20 sts)*
Row 4: Purl cr.
Row 5: K5cr, k2togcr, k6cr, k2togcr, k5cr. *(18 sts)*
Row 6: P4bl, p10cr, p4bl.
Row 7: K6bl, k6cr, k2bl, pult (pick up loop below next st on left needle by inserting tip of right needle from back through loop – this stops a hole forming when turning work – then turn, leaving rem 4 sts on left needle unworked).
Row 8: Working top of head on centre 10 sts only, p2tog (first st of p2tog is loop picked up at end of last row), p2bl, p4cr, p3bl, pult.

Body

Use the intarsia technique and a separate ball of each colour yarn, twisting the colours firmly over one another at the joins to prevent holes (see page 172).

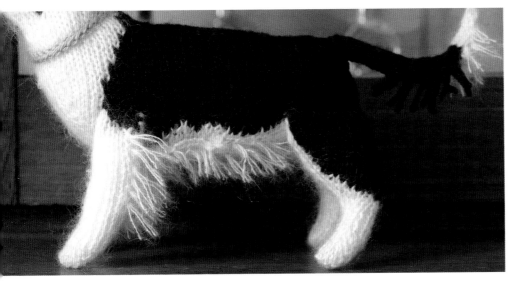

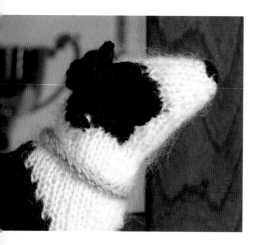

Head

The flyaway ears enhance the Border Collie's keen personality.

Row 9: K2togbl, k3bl, k2cr, k4bl, pult.
Row 10: P2togbl, p9bl, pult.
Row 11: K2togbl, k9bl, pult.
Row 12: P2togbl, p9bl, pult.
Row 13: K2togbl and k to end in bl. *(18 sts)*
Row 14: Purl bl.
Row 15: K2togbl, k14bl, k2togbl. *(16 sts)*
Row 16: Purl bl.
Row 17: K7bl, k2cr, k3bl, pult (leave 4 sts on left needle).
Row 18: Working on centre 8 sts only, p2tog, p2bl, p2cr, p3bl, pult.
Row 19: K2togbl, k2bl, k2cr, k3bl, pult.
Row 20: P2togbl, p2bl, p2cr, p3bl, pult.
Row 21: K2togbl, k2bl, k2cr, k7bl.
Row 22: P7bl, p2cr, p7bl.
Row 23: K2togbl, k2bl, k2togbl, k4cr, k2togbl, k2bl, k2togbl. *(12 sts)*
Row 24: P3bl, p6cr, p3bl.
Cont in cr.
Row 25: Knit.
Row 26: Purl.
Row 27: K2tog, k8, k2tog. *(10 sts)*
Row 28: Purl.
Row 29: Knit.
Row 30: Purl.
Row 31: K2tog, k6, k2tog. *(8 sts)*
Row 32: Purl.
Row 33: Knit.
Cast (bind) off.

Tummy

With 2¾mm (US 2) knitting needles and cr, cast on 6 sts.
Beg with a k row, work 10 rows st st.
Next row: Inc, k4, inc. *(8 sts)*
Work 5 rows st st.
Next row: **K2, loopy st 1, k2, loopy st 1, k2.
Next and foll 3 alt rows: Purl.
Next row: K1, loopy st 1, k1, loopy st 1, k2, loopy st 1, k1.
Next row: K2, loopy st 1, k2, loopy st 1, k2.
Next row: K1, loopy st 1, k2, loopy st 1, k1, loopy st 1, k1.**

Rep from ** to ** twice more.
Work 8 rows st st.
Next row: Inc, k6, inc. *(10 sts)*
Work 15 rows st st.
Next row: K2tog, k6, k2tog. *(8 sts)*
Work 7 rows st st.
Next row: K2tog, k4, k2tog. *(6 sts)*
Work 3 rows st st.
Next row: K2tog, k2, k2tog. *(4 sts)*
Work 2 rows st st.
Cast (bind) off.

Tail

With 2¾mm (US 2) double-pointed knitting needles and bl, cast on 8 sts.
Work in i-cord as folls:
Knit 14 rows.
Next row: K1, loopy st 1, k4, loopy st 1, k1.
Knit 1 row.
Rep last 2 rows 4 times more.
Change to cr.
Next row: K1, loopy st 1, k4, loopy st 1, k1.
Next row: K2tog, k4, k2tog. *(6 sts)*
Next row: K1, loopy st 1, k2, loopy st 1, k1.
Next row: K2tog, k2, k2tog. *(4 sts)*
Next row: K2tog twice. *(2 sts)*.
Next row: K2tog and fasten off.

Ear

(make 2 the same)
With 2¾mm (US 2) knitting needles and bl, cast on 6 sts.
Beg with a k row, work 2 rows st st.
Knit 8 rows.
Next row: K2tog, k2, k2tog. *(4 sts)*
Next row: Knit.
Cast (bind) off.

Collar

With 2¾mm (US 2) knitting needles and ch, cast on 26 sts.
Knit one row.
Cast (bind) off.

To Make Up

Sew in ends, leaving ends from cast on and cast (bound) off rows for sewing up. Using mattress or whip stitch, sew up legs starting at paw. Turn right side out and stuff each leg. Using whip stitch, sew along top of leg, leaving an end to sew leg to body.

Using mattress or whip stitch, sew down centre back and around bottom. At head, fold in half and sew cast (bound) off edges of nose together.

Using mattress or whip stitch, sew down centre back. Sew cast on row of tummy bottom end and sew cast (bound) off row to nose. Ease and sew tummy to fit body. Leave a 2.5cm (1in) gap between front and back legs on one side. Turn right side out, stuff then sew up gap with mattress stitch.

Using whip stitch, sew legs to body as shown in photograph.

About 2cm (¾in) down from top edge of leg, sew through leg, body and opposite leg to make dog more stable.

Sew on tail just where curve of dog's bottom starts. Add a little stitch on underside to keep tail low.

Sew ears to head as shown in photograph, sewing from underside to give ear a little bounce. Fold over ear and mould to shape. If necessary, catch down tip of ear with a stitch to stop it flicking upwards.

Using black yarn, embroider the nose using satin stitch and make two French knots for eyes.

Cut the loops on the loopy st and fluff up. Sew ends of collar together and slide over head onto neck.

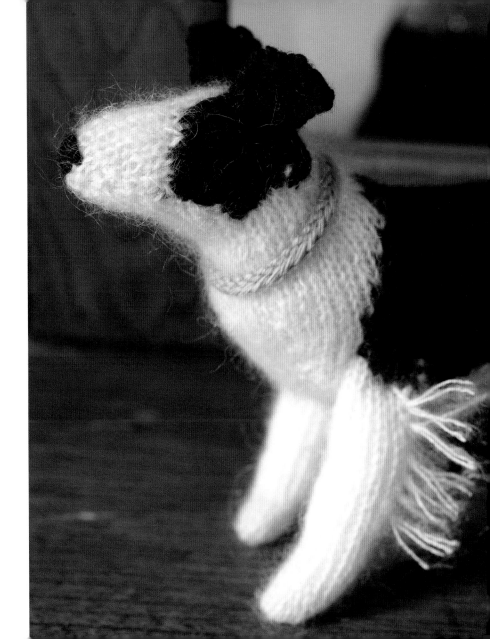

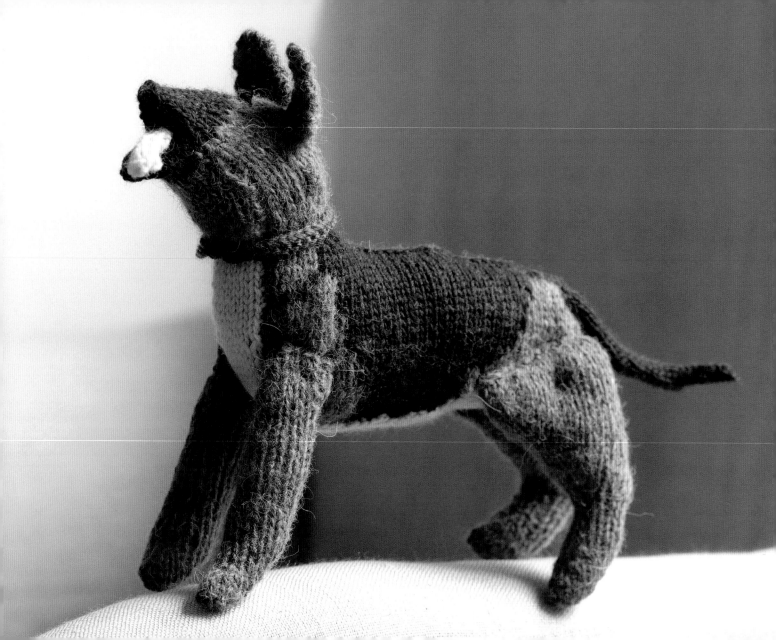

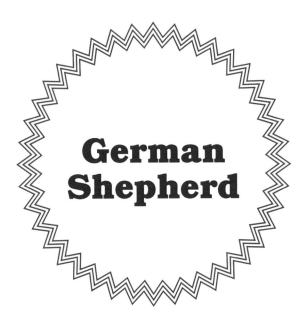

German Shepherd

Bred by Captain Max von Stephanitz, a German cavalry officer, to be the perfect all-purpose working dog. More than any other dog the German Shepherd toils for its keep, they are strong, intelligent and obedient. After World War 1 the German Shepherd was renamed the Alsatian, but since the 1970s has reverted to its original name. Rin Tin Tin was the German Shepherd version of Lassie. Adolf Hitler is reputed to have tested his cyanide capsules on his German Shepherd, Blondi.

German Shepherd

Fairly simple to knit,
but you do need to use
intarsia. This is the only
dog with a knitted tongue.

Measurements
Length (excluding tail): 20cm (8in)
Height to top of head: 17cm (6½in)

Materials
- Pair of 2¾mm (US 2) knitting needles
- 2 spare 2¾mm (US 2) knitting needles
- Pair of 2¾mm (US 2) double-pointed knitting needles
- 10g (¼oz) of Rowan Felted Tweed in Cinnamon 175 (cn)
- 10g (¼oz) of Rowan Pure Wool 4ply in Black 404 (bl)
- 10g (¼oz) of Rowan Pure Wool 4ply in Porcelaine 451 (pr)
- Small amount of Rowan Pure Wool 4ply in Framboise 456 (fr) for collar
- Small amount of Rowan Pure Wool 4ply in Powder 443 (po)

Abbreviations
See page 172.

Back Leg
(make 2 the same)
With 2¾mm (US 2) knitting needles and cn, cast on 11 sts.
Beg with a k row, work 2 rows st st.
Row 3: Inc, k2, k2tog, k1, k2tog, k2, inc. *(11 sts)*
Row 4: Purl.

Rep last 2 rows once more.
Row 7: K3, k2tog, k1, k2tog, k3. *(9 sts)*
Work 7 rows st st.
Row 15: Inc, k1, inc, k3, inc, k1, inc. *(13 sts)*
Row 16: Purl.
Row 17: K2tog, [k1, inc] 4 times, k1, k2tog. *(15 sts)*
Row 18: P2tog, p11, p2tog. *(13 sts)*
Row 19: K3, [inc, k1] 3 times, inc, k3. *(17 sts)*
Row 20: P2tog, p13, p2tog. *(15 sts)*
Row 21: K6, inc, k1, inc, k6. *(17 sts)*
Row 22: Purl.
Row 23: K7, inc, k1, inc, k7. *(19 sts)*
Row 24: Purl.
Row 25: K8, inc, k1, inc, k8. *(21 sts)*
Row 26: Purl.
Row 27: K9, inc, k1, inc, k9. *(23 sts)*
Row 28: Purl.
Row 29: K10, inc, k1, inc, k10. *(25 sts)*
Row 30: Purl.
Row 31: K11, inc, k1, inc, k11. *(27 sts)*
Row 32: Purl
Row 33: K12, inc, k1, inc, k12. *(29 sts)*
Work 2 rows st st.
Row 36: P2tog, p25, p2tog. *(27 sts)*
Cast (bind) off.

Front Leg
(make 2 the same)
With 2¾mm (US 2) knitting needles and cn, cast on 9 sts.
Beg with a k row, work 2 rows st st.
Row 3: Inc, k1, k2tog, k1, k2tog, k1, inc. *(9 sts)*
Row 4: Purl.
Row 5: Inc, k1, k2tog, k1, k2tog, k1, inc. *(9 sts)*
Work 3 rows st st.
Row 9: Inc, k7, inc. *(11 sts)*
Work 24 rows st st.
Cast (bind) off.

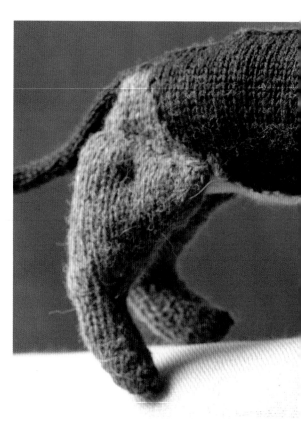

Legs
Position the back legs at a slant to exaggerate the German Shepherd's sloping back.

Right Side of Body

With 2¾mm (US 2) knitting needles and bl and cn, cast on 7 sts bl, 5 sts cn. (12 sts)

Row 1: K5cn, k7bl, cast on 5 sts bl. (17 sts)
Row 2: P12bl, p4cn, inccn. (18 sts)
Row 3: K6cn, k12bl, cast on 3 sts cn. (21 sts)
Row 4: P3cn, p12bl, p5cn, inccn. (22 sts)
Row 5: K7cn, k12bl, k3cn, cast on 12 sts cn. (34 sts)
Row 6: P13cn, p15bl, p5cn, inccn. (35 sts)
Row 7: K7cn, k16bl, k12cn. (35 sts)
Row 8: P11cn, p17bl, p6cn, inccn. (36 sts)
Row 9: K8cn, k18bl, k10cn. (36 sts)
Row 10: P10cn, p19bl, p6cn, inccn. (37 sts)
Row 11: K8cn, k20bl, k9cn. (37 sts)
Row 12: P9cn, p20bl, p8cn. (37 sts)
Rep last 2 rows once more.
Row 15: K7cn, k22bl, k8cn. (37 sts)
Row 16: P2togcn, p6cn, p22bl, p7cn. (36 sts)
Row 17: K2bl, k5cn, k23bl, k4cn, k2togcn. (35 sts)
Row 18: P2togbl, p26bl, p3cn, p3bl, p1cn. (34 sts)
Row 19: K3cn, k2bl, k2cn, k25bl, k2togbl. (33 sts)
Row 20: Cast (bind) off 4 sts bl, p25bl icos, p4cn. (29 sts)
Row 21: K5cn, k24bl. (29 sts)
Row 22: Cast (bind) off 6 sts bl, k18bl icos, p5cn. (23 sts)
Row 23: K5cn, k18bl. (23 sts)
Row 24: Cast (bind) off 11 sts bl, p7bl icos, p5cn, leave yarn attached for neck (hold 12 sts on spare needle for right neck).

Left Side of Body

With 2¾mm (US 2) knitting needles and bl and cn, cast on 7 sts bl, 5 sts cn. (12 sts)

Row 1: P5cn, p7bl, cast on 5 sts bl. (17 sts)
Row 2: K12bl, k4cn, inccn. (18 sts)
Row 3: P6cn, p12bl, cast on 3 sts cn. (21 sts)
Row 4: K3cn, k12bl, k5cn, inccn. (22 sts)
Row 5: P7cn, p12bl, p3cn, cast on 12 sts cn. (34 sts)

Row 6: K13cn, k15bl, k5cn, inccn. (35 sts)
Row 7: P7cn, p16bl, p12cn. (35 sts)
Row 8: K11cn, k17bl, k6cn, inccn. (36 sts)
Row 9: P8cn, p18bl, p10cn. (36 sts)
Row 10: K10cn, k19bl, k6cn, inccn. (37 sts)
Row 11: P8cn, p20bl, p9cn. (37 sts)
Row 12: K9cn, k20bl, k8cn. (37 sts)
Rep last 2 rows once more.
Row 15: P7cn, p22bl, p8cn. (37 sts)
Row 16: K2togcn, k6cn, k22bl, k7cn. (36 sts)
Row 17: P2bl, p5cn, p23bl, p4cn, p2togcn. (35 sts)
Row 18: K2togbl, k26bl, k3cn, k3bl, k1cn. (34 sts)
Row 19: P3cn, p2bl, p2cn, p25bl, p2togbl. (33 sts)
Row 20: Cast (bind) off 4 sts bl, k25bl icos, k4cn. (29 sts)
Row 21: P5cn, p24bl. (29 sts)
Row 22: Cast (bind) off 6 sts bl, k18bl icos, k5cn. (23 sts)

Body

Use the intarsia technique and a separate ball of each colour yarn, twisting the colours firmly over one another at the joins to prevent holes (see page 172).

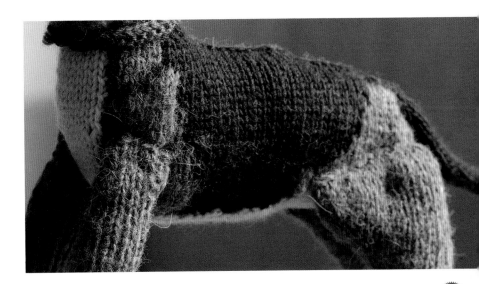

Row 23: P5cn, p18bl. *(23 sts)*

Row 24: Cast (bind) off 11 sts bl, k7bl icos, k5cn (hold 12 sts on spare needle for right neck).

Neck and Head

Row 1: With 2¾mm (US 2) knitting needles and bl and cn, and with RS facing k6cn, k4bl, k2togbl from spare needle of Right Side of Body then k2togbl, k4bl, k6cn from spare needle of Left Side of Body. *(22 sts)*

Row 2: P7cn, p2togbl, p4bl, p2togbl, p7cn. *(20 sts)*

Row 3: K7cn, k6bl, k7cn.

Row 4: P8cn, p4bl, p8cn.

Row 5: K2togcn, k6cn, k4bl, k6cn, k2togcn. *(18 sts)*

Row 6: P8cn, p2bl, p8cn.

Cont in cn.

Work 2 rows st st.

Row 9: K14, pult (pick up loop below next st on left needle by inserting tip of right needle from back through loop – this stops a hole forming when turning work – then turn, leaving rem 4 sts on left needle unworked).

Row 10: Working top of head on centre 10 sts only, p2tog (first st of p2tog is loop picked up at end of last row), p9, pult.

Row 11: K2tog, k9, pult.

Rep last 2 rows once more.

Row 14: P2tog, p9, pult.

Row 15: K2tog, k to end. *(18 sts)*

Work 3 rows st st.

Row 19: K13, pult (leave 5 sts on left needle).

Row 20: P2tog, p7, pult.

Row 21: K2tog, k7, pult.

Rep last 2 rows once more.

Row 24: P2tog, p7, pult.

Row 25: K2tog, k to end. *(18 sts)*

Row 26: Purl.

Row 27: K5, k2tog, k4, k2tog, k5. *(16 sts)*

Row 28: P7cn, join in bl, p2bl, p7cn.

Row 29: K5cn, k2togbl, k2bl, k2togbl, k5cn. *(14 sts)*

Row 30: P3cn, p8bl, p3cn.

Cont in bl.

Row 31: Knit.

Row 32: P3, p2tog, p4, p2tog, p3. *(12 sts)*

Work 2 rows st st.

Row 35: K2, k2tog, k4, k2tog, k2. *(10 sts)*

Row 36: Purl.

Row 37: K2, k2tog, k2, k2tog, k2. *(8 sts)*

Row 38: Purl.

Cast (bind) off.

Tummy

With 2¾mm (US 2) knitting needles and pr, cast on 6 sts.

Beg with a k row, work 10 rows st st.

Next row: Inc, k4, inc. *(8 sts)*

Work 33 rows st st.

Next row: Inc, k6, inc. *(10 sts)*

Work 9 rows st st.

Next row: K3pr, join in cn, k4cn, k3pr.

Next row: P2pr, p6cn, p2pr.

Cont in cn.

Work 10 rows st st.

Next row: K2tog, k2, k2tog, k2, k2tog. *(7 sts)*

Cont in bl.

Next row: Purl.

Next row: K2tog, k3, k2tog. *(5 sts)*

Work 3 rows st st.

Next row: K2tog, k1, k2tog. *(3 sts)*

Next row: Purl.

Knit 3 rows (to make turning edge for mouth).

Beg with a p row, work 3 rows st st.

Next row: Inc, k1, inc. *(5 sts)*

Work 3 rows st st.

Next row: K2tog, k1, k2tog. *(3 sts)*

Work 3 rows st st.

Cast (bind) off.

Tail

With 2¾mm (US 2) double-pointed knitting needles and bl, cast on 8 sts.

Work in i-cord as folls:

Knit 18 rows.

Next row: K2tog, k4, k2tog. *(6 sts)*

Knit 8 rows.

Next row: K2tog, k2, k2tog. *(4 sts)*

Knit 4 rows.

Next row: K2tog twice. *(2 sts)*

Next row: K2tog and fasten off.

Ear

(make 2 the same)

With 2¾mm (US 2) knitting needles and cn, cast on 7 sts.

Knit 6 rows.

Next row: K2tog, k3, k2tog. *(5 sts)*

Knit 4 rows.

Next row: K2tog, k1, k2tog. *(3 sts)*

Knit 3 rows.

Next row: K3tog and fasten off.

Collar

With 2¾mm (US 2) knitting needles and fr, cast on 28 sts.

Knit one row.

Cast (bind) off.

Tongue

With 2¾mm (US 2) knitting needles and po, cast on 2 sts.

Row 1: Knit.

Row 2: Inc into both sts. *(4 sts)*

Beg with a k row, work 6 rows st st.

Row 9: K2tog twice. *(2 sts)*

Cast (bind) off.

To Make Up

Sew in ends, leaving ends from cast on and cast (bound) off rows for sewing up. Using mattress or whip stitch, sew up legs starting at paw. Turn right side out and stuff each leg. Using whip stitch, sew along top of leg, leaving an end to sew leg to body. Using mattress or whip stitch, sew down centre back and around bottom. At head, fold in half and sew cast (bound) off edges of nose together.

Fold black tip of tummy over on itself, using garter st row to make edge for bottom of mouth. Sew along black section on side of mouth only. Using mattress or whip stitch, sew cast on row of tummy to bottom end of dog and sew cast (bound) off row to mouth. Ease and sew tummy to fit body. Leave a 2.5cm (1in) gap between front and back legs on one side. Turn right side out, stuff then sew up gap with mattress stitch.

Using whip stitch, sew legs to body as shown in photograph.

About 1cm (½in) down from top edge of leg, sew through leg, body and opposite leg to make dog more stable.

Sew on tail just where curve of dog's bottom starts. Add a little stitch on underside to keep tail low.

Sew ears to head as shown in photograph.

Using black yarn, make two French knots for eyes.

Sew tongue into back of open mouth.

Sew ends of collar together and slide over head onto neck.

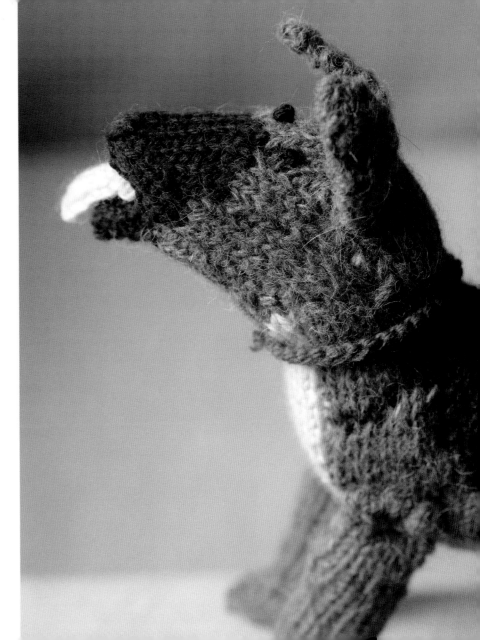

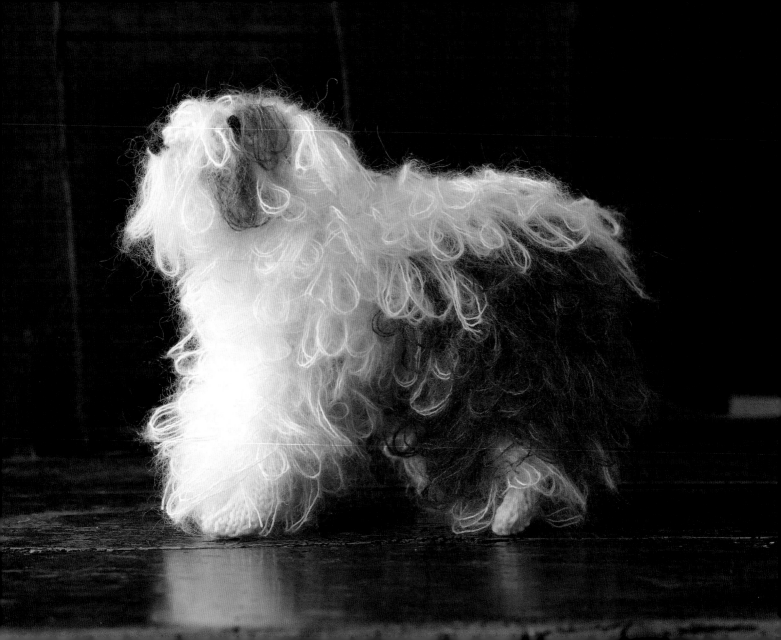

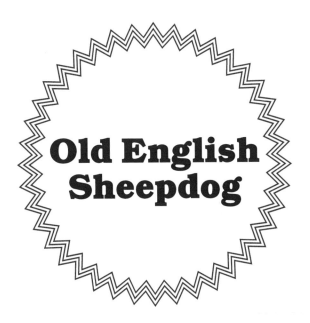

Old English Sheepdog

This large, bear-like dog is the ideal pet if you enjoy grooming. Instantly recognizable, the Sheepdog has been the face of Dulux paints in the UK for years. The most famous Dulux dog, Fernville Lord Digby, was treated like a star, chauffeured to filmsets and trained by Barbara Woodhouse. Paul McCartney's Old English Sheepdog, Martha, was immortalized in the song 'Martha My Dear' on *The White Album*.

Old English Sheepdog

You need to perfect your loopy stitch technique before you tackle this dog.

Measurements
Length: 16cm (6¼in)
Height to top of head: 14cm (5½in)

Materials
- Pair of 2¾mm (US 2) knitting needles
- 30g (1⅛oz) of Rowan Cashsoft 4ply in Cream 433 (cr)
- 20g (¾oz) of Rowan Kidsilk Haze in Cream 634 (mcr) used DOUBLE throughout
- 15g (½oz) of Rowan Kidsilk Haze in Smoke 605 (sm) used DOUBLE throughout
- Tiny amount of Rowan Pure Wool 4ply in Black 404 for nose and eyes
- Pipecleaners for legs

Abbreviations
See page 172.
For loopy stitch technique, see page 173.

Back Leg
(make 2 the same)
With cr, cast on 10 sts.
Beg with a k row, work 2 rows st st.
Row 3: Inc, k2, k2tog twice, k2, inc. *(10 sts)*
Row 4: Purl.
Row 5: Inc, k2, k2tog twice, k2, inc. *(10 sts)*
Row 6: Purl.
Row 7: Inc, k8, inc. *(12 sts)*
Work 5 rows st st.
Row 13: Inc, k10, inc. *(14 sts)*
Row 14: Purl.
Row 15: Inc, k12, inc. *(16 sts)*
Row 16: Work loopy st in mcr in every st.
Row 17: Inccr, k14cr, inccr. *(18 sts)*
Row 18: Purl cr.
Row 19: Inccr, k16cr, inccr. *(20 sts)*
Row 20: Work loopy st in sm in every st.
Work 2 rows st st cr.
Row 23: Inccr, k18cr, inccr. *(22 sts)*
Row 24: Work loopy st in sm in every st.
Work 2 rows st st cr.
Row 27: Inccr, k20cr, inccr. *(24 sts)*
Row 28: Work loopy st in sm in every st.
Work 2 rows st st cr.
Cast (bind) off in cr.

Front Leg
(make 2 the same)
With cr, cast on 10 sts.
Beg with a k row, work 2 rows st st.
Row 3: Inc, k2, k2tog twice, k2, inc. *(10 sts)*
Row 4: Purl.
Row 5: Inc, k8, inc. *(12 sts)*
Row 6: Purl.
Row 7: Inc, k10, inc. *(14 sts)*
Work 8 rows st st.
Row 16: Work loopy st in mcr in every st.
Work 3 rows st st cr.
Row 20: Work loopy st in mcr in every st.
Work 3 rows st st cr.
Row 24: Work loopy st in mcr in every st.
Work 3 rows st st cr.
Row 28: Work loopy st in mcr in every st.
Work 2 rows st st cr.
Cast (bind) off in cr.

Right Side of Body and Head
With cr, cast on 12 sts.
Row 1: Inc, k11, cast on 6 sts. *(19 sts)*
Row 2: Purl.
Row 3: Inc, k18, cast on 6 sts. *(26 sts)*
Row 4: Purl.

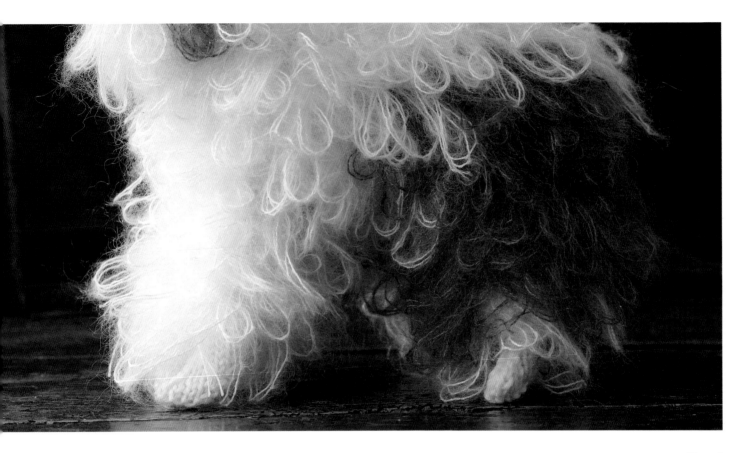

Row 5: K26, cast on 3 sts. *(29 sts)*
Work 2 rows st st.
Row 8: Work loopy st, 10 sts sm, 19 sts mcr.
Row 9: K18cr, k11sm.
Row 10: P11sm, p18cr.
Row 11: K17cr, k12sm.
Row 12: Work loopy st, 12 sts sm, 17 sts mcr.
Row 13: K17cr, k12sm.

Row 14: P13sm, p16cr.
Row 15: K16cr, k13sm.
Row 16: Work loopy st, 15 sts sm, 14 sts mcr.
Row 17: K14cr, k15sm.
Row 18: P15sm, p14cr.
Row 19: Inccr, k13cr, k15sm. *(30 sts)*
Row 20: Work loopy st, 18 sts sm, 12 sts mcr.
Row 21: K12cr, k18sm.

Coat
Don't worry if you make mistakes as
the loopy stitch will hide most errors.

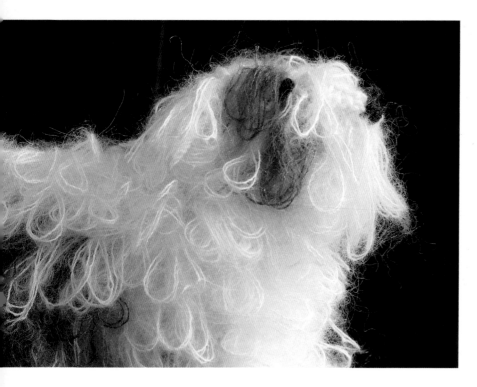

Head

You can give the dog extra personality with careful placing of the ears and embroidery of the eyes and nose.

Row 22: P18sm, p12cr.
Row 23: Inccr, k11cr, k16sm, k2togsm. *(30 sts)*
Row 24: P2togcr, work loopy st, 16 sts sm, 12 sts mcr. *(29 sts)*
Row 25: K27cr, k2togcr. *(28 sts)*
Row 26: With loopy st cast (bind) off 20 sts mcr, work 8 loopy sts mcr icos.
Row 27: Inccr, k7cr. *(9 sts)*
Row 28: P9cr, cast on 6 sts cr. *(15 sts)*
Row 29: Knit.
Row 30: Work loopy st in mcr in every st.
Work 3 rows st st cr.

Row 34: Work loopy st in mcr in every st.
Row 35: Knit.
Row 36: Cast (bind) off 4 sts cr, p9cr icos, p2togcr. *(10 sts)*
Row 37: K8cr, k2togcr. *(9 sts)*
With loopy st cast (bind) off in mcr.

Left Side of Body and Head

With cr, cast on 12 sts.
Row 1: Inc, p11, cast on 6 sts. *(19 sts)*
Row 2: Knit.
Row 3: Inc, p18, cast on 6 sts. *(26 sts)*
Row 4: Knit.
Row 5: P26, cast on 3 sts. *(29 sts)*
Work 3 rows st st.
Row 9: Work loopy st, 18 sts mcr, 11 sts sm.
Row 10: K11sm, k18cr.
Row 11: P18cr, p11sm.
Row 12: K12sm, k17cr.
Row 13: Work loopy st, 17 sts mcr, 12 sts sm.
Row 14: K12sm, k17cr.
Row 15: P16cr, p13sm.
Row 16: K13sm, k16cr.
Row 17: Work loopy st, 16 sts mcr, 13 sts sm.
Row 18: K14sm, k14cr, inccr. *(30 sts)*
Row 19: P14cr, p16sm.
Row 20: K16sm, k14cr. *(30 sts)*
Row 21: Work loopy st, 15 sts mcr, 15 sts sm.
Row 22: K2togcr, k13sm, k14cr, inc. *(30 sts)*
Row 23: P16cr, p12sm, p2togsm. *(29 sts)*
Row 24: K2togcr, k27cr. *(28 sts)*
Row 25: Work loopy st in mcr in every st.
Row 26: Cast (bind) off 20 sts cr, k8cr icos.
Row 27: Inccr, p7cr. *(9 sts)*
Row 28: K9cr, cast on 6 sts cr. *(15 sts)*
Row 29: Work loopy st in mcr in every st.
Work 3 rows st st cr.
Row 33: Work loopy st in mcr in every st.
Row 34: Knit.
Row 35: Purl.
Row 36: Cast (bind) off 4 sts cr, k9cr icos, k2tog. *(10 sts)*
Row 37: Work 8 loopy sts sm, p2togcr. *(9 sts)*
Cast (bind) off in cr.

Tail
With cr, cast on 5 sts.
Row 1: Knit.
Row 2: Work loopy st in mcr in every st.
Work 2 rows st st cr.
Cast (bind) off in cr.

Ear
(make 2 the same)
With cr, cast on 5 sts.
Row 1: Knit
Row 2: Work loopy st in mcr in every st.
Cast (bind) off in cr.

To Make Up
Sew in ends, leaving ends from cast on
and cast (bound) off rows for sewing up.
Using mattress or whip stitch, sew up legs
starting at paw. Turn right side out, stuff
each leg, using pipecleaners for rigidity
if necessary.
Using whip stitch, sew along top of leg,
leaving an end to sew leg to body.
Using mattress stitch, sew down centre back
and around body leaving a 2.5cm (1in) gap.
Stuff body tightly, then sew up gap with
mattress stitch.
Using whip stitch, sew legs to body as
shown in photograph, with back legs
at an angle.
Sew up head and sew on ears as shown
in photograph. Sew tail to dog's bottom.
Using black yarn, embroider the nose
using satin stitch and make two French
knots for eyes.
If legs are floppy, about 2cm (¾in) down
from top edge of leg, sew through leg, body
and opposite leg to make dog more stable.
Shake your Sheepdog to fluff him up.

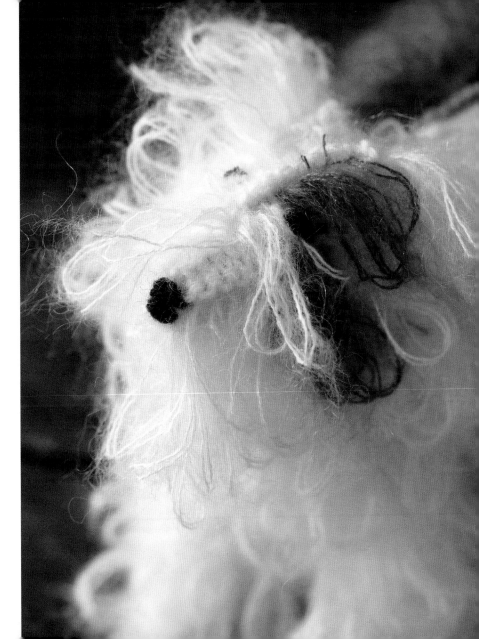

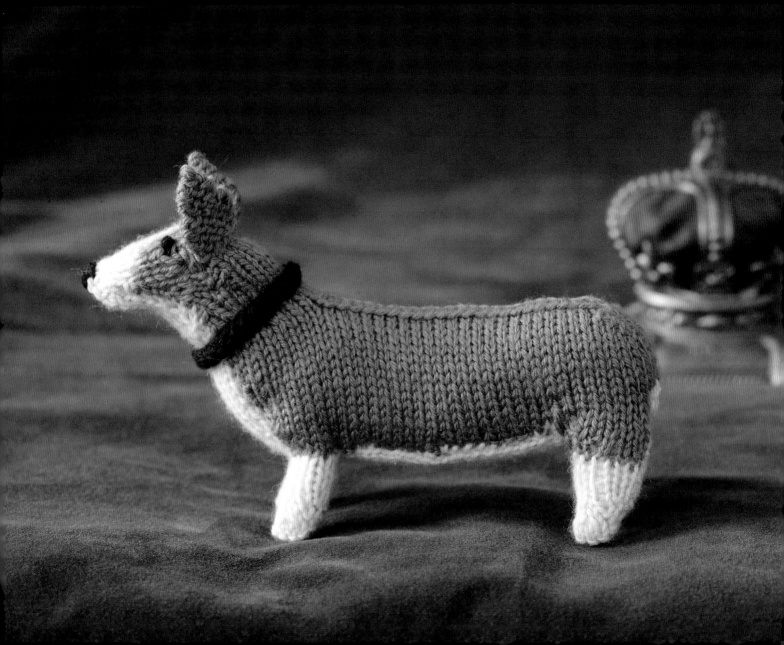

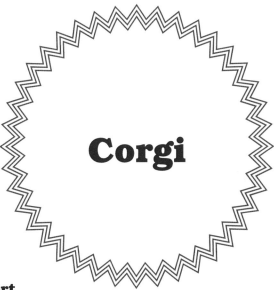

Corgi

The Corgi is a foxy dog, with remarkably short legs and an instinct for herding. Corgis are athletic and use their agility to nip at the heels of sheep and horses. No one seems to know why the Corgi is associated with Wales but there are two types, Pembroke and Cardigan; ours is a Pembroke, identified by having almost no tail. They are much loved by the British Royal Family (sixteen dogs), although there have been stories of the Royal Corgis reverting to their old herding ways with some visitors. Also much loved by my Aunt Joanie (a mere three dogs).

Corgi

This is one of the simplest dogs to knit.

Measurements
Length: 16cm (6¼in)
Height to top of head: 9cm (3½in)

Materials
- Pair of 2¾mm (US 2) knitting needles
- 4 spare 2¾mm (US 2) knitting needles or small stitch holders or safety pins
- 10g (¼oz) of Rowan Cashsoft 4ply in Cream 433 (cr)
- 15g (½oz) of Rowan Cashsoft 4ply in Walnut 441 (wa)
- Small amount of Rowan Pure Wool 4ply in Black 404 for collar and nose and eyes

Abbreviations
See page 172.

Right Back Leg
With cr, cast on 9 sts.
Beg with a k row, work 2 rows st st.
Row 3: Inc, k1, k2tog, k1, k2tog, k1, inc. *(9 sts)*
Row 4: Purl.
Rep last 2 rows once more.*
Work 3 rows st st.**
Row 10: Join in wa, p4wa, p5cr.
Row 11: Inccr, k3cr, k4wa, incwa. *(11 sts)*
Row 12: P4wa, incwa, p1wa, inccr, p4cr. *(13 sts)*
Row 13: K5cr, incwa, k1wa, incwa, k5wa. *(15 sts)*
Row 14: P6wa, incwa, p1wa, incwa, p1wa, p5cr. *(17 sts)*

Row 15: Cast (bind) off 5 sts cr, cast (bind) off 3 sts wa, k to end wa (hold 9 sts on spare needle for Right Side of Body).

Left Back Leg
Work as for Right Back Leg to **.
Row 10: P5cr, join in wa, p4wa.
Row 11: Incwa, k4wa, k3cr, inccr. *(11 sts)*
Row 12: P4cr, inccr, p1wa, incwa, p4wa. *(13 sts)*
Row 13: K5wa, incwa, k1wa, incwa, k5cr. *(15 sts)*
Row 14: P5cr, p1wa, incwa, p1wa, incwa, p6wa. *(17 sts)*
Row 15: K9wa, cast (bind) off 3 sts wa, cast (bind) off 5 sts cr (hold 9 sts on spare needle for Left Side of Body).

Front Leg
(make 2)
Work as for Right Back Leg to *.
Row 7: Knit.
Row 8: Purl.
For right leg: Cast (bind) off 4 sts, k to end (hold 5 sts on spare needle for Right Side of Body).
For left leg: K5, cast (bind) off 4 sts (hold 5 sts on spare needle for Left Side of Body).

Right Side of Body
Work in wa throughout.
Row 1: Cast on 1 st, with RS facing k5 from spare needle of Right Front Leg, cast on 10 sts. *(16 sts)*
Row 2: Purl.
Row 3: K16, cast on 8 sts. *(24 sts)*
Row 4: Purl.
Row 5: Inc, k23, with RS facing k9 from spare needle of Right Back Leg, cast on 2 sts. *(36 sts)*
Row 6: Purl.
Row 7: K35, inc. *(37 sts)*
Work 5 rows st st.
Row 13: Inc, k36. *(38 sts)*

Row 14: P2, p2tog, p34. *(37 sts)*
Row 15: K33, k2tog, k2. *(36 sts)*
Row 16: P2, p2tog, p32. *(35 sts)*
Row 17: K31, k2tog, k2. *(34 sts)*
Row 18: P2tog, using st on right needle as first st, cast (bind) off 23 sts, p to end (hold 10 sts on spare needle for right neck).

Left Side of Body

Work in wa throughout.
Row 1: Cast on 1 st, with WS facing p5 from spare needle of Left Front Leg, cast on 10 sts. *(16 sts)*
Row 2: Knit.
Row 3: P16, cast on 8 sts. *(24 sts)*

Row 4: Knit.
Row 5: Inc, p23, with WS facing p9 from spare needle of Left Back Leg, cast on 2 sts. *(36 sts)*
Row 6: Knit.
Row 7: P35, inc. *(37 sts)*
Work 5 rows st st.
Row 13: Inc, p36. *(38 sts)*
Row 14: K2, k2tog, k34. *(37 sts)*
Row 15: P33, p2tog, p2. *(36 sts)*
Row 16: K2, k2tog, k32. *(35 sts)*
Row 17: P31, p2tog, p2. *(34 sts)*
Row 18: K2tog, using st on right needle as first st, cast (bind) off 23 sts, k to end (hold 10 sts on spare needle for left neck).

Body

When sewing up, match the curve of the tummy with the leg shaping, sewing up one side then the other.

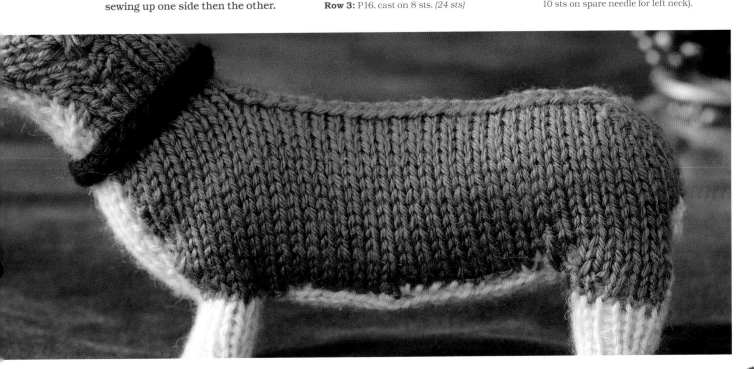

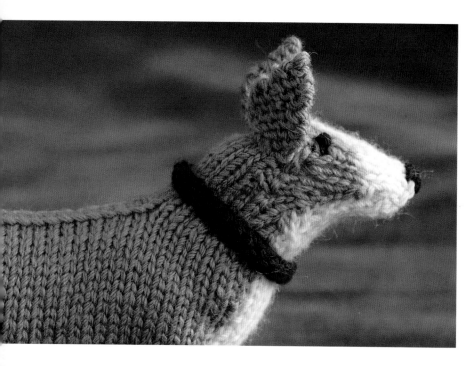

Head

When sewing on the ears, slightly curve the cast on row to give the Corgi its alert expression.

Neck and Head

Row 1: With wa, and with RS facing k10 from spare needle of Right Side of Body then k10 from spare needle of Left Side of Body. *(20 sts)*
Row 2: Purl.
Row 3: K2tog, k16, k2tog. *(18 sts)*
Row 4: Purl.
Row 5: K4, k2tog, k6, k2tog, k4. *(16 sts)*
Row 6: Purl.
Row 7: K13, pult (pick up loop below next st on left needle by inserting tip of right needle from back through loop – this stops a hole forming when turning work – then turn, leaving rem 3 sts on left needle unworked).

Row 8: Working top of head on centre 10 sts only, p2tog (first st of p2tog is loop picked up at end of last row), p9, pult.
Row 9: K2tog, k9, pult.
Rep last 2 rows once more.
Row 12: P2tog, p9, pult.
Row 13: K2tog, k to end. *(16 sts)*
Work 3 rows st st.
Row 17: K2togwa, k5wa, join in cr, k2cr, k3wa, pult (leave 4 sts on left needle).
Row 18: P2togwa, p2wa, p2cr, p3wa, pult.
Row 19: K2togwa, k2wa, k2cr, k3wa, pult.
Rep last 2 rows once more.
Row 22: P2togwa, p2wa, p2cr, p3wa, pult.
Row 23: K2togwa, k2wa, k2cr, k5wa, k2togwa. *(14 sts)*
Row 24: P2tog wa, p2wa, p2togwa, p2cr, p2togwa, p2wa, p2togwa. *(10 sts)*
Row 25: K3wa, k4cr, k3wa.
Row 26: P3wa, p4cr, p3wa.
Row 27: K2togwa, k6cr, k2togwa. *(8 sts)*
Row 28: P1wa, p6cr, p1wa.
Work 3 rows st st cr.
Cast (bind) off in cr.

Tummy

With cr, cast on 6 sts.
Beg with a k row, work 2 rows st st.
Next row: K2tog, k2, k2tog. *(4 sts)*
Work 9 rows st st.
Next row: Inc, k2, inc. *(6 sts)*
Next row: Inc, p4, inc. *(8 sts)*
Work 26 rows st st.
Next row: K2tog, k4, k2tog. *(6 sts)*
Next row: P2tog, p2, p2tog. *(4 sts)*
Work 4 rows st st.
Next row: Inc, k2, inc. *(6 sts)*
Work 2 rows st st.
Next row: Inc, p4, inc. *(8 sts)*
Work 2 rows st st.
Next row: Inc, k6, inc. *(10 sts)*
Work 11 rows st st.
Next row: K2tog, k6, k2tog. *(8 sts)*
Work 3 rows st st.

Next row: K2tog, k4, k2tog. *(6 sts)*
Work 3 rows st st.
Next row: K2tog, k2, k2tog. *(4 sts)*
Work 5 rows st st.
Next row: K2tog twice. *(2 sts)*
Next row: K2tog and fasten off.

Ear

(make 2 the same)
With wa, cast on 6 sts.
Knit 6 rows.
Row 7: K2tog, k2, k2tog. *(4 sts)*
Knit 4 rows.
Row 12: K2tog twice. *(2 sts)*
Row 13: Knit.
Row 14: K2tog and fasten off.

Collar

With bl, cast on 24 sts.
Knit one row.
Cast (bind) off.

To Make Up

Sew in ends, leaving ends from cast on
and cast (bound) off rows for sewing up.
Using mattress or whip stitch, sew up legs
starting at paw. Stuff all four legs.
Using mattress or whip stitch, sew down
centre back, around tail and down bottom.
At head, fold in half and sew cast (bound)
off edges of nose together.
Using mattress or whip stitch, sew cast on
row of tummy to bottom end of dog and sew
cast (bound) off row to nose. Ease and sew
tummy to fit body, matching curves to legs.
Leave a 2.5cm (1in) gap between front and
back legs on one side. Turn right side out,
stuff then sew up gap with mattress stitch.
Sew ears to head as shown in photograph.
Using black yarn, embroider the nose
using satin stitch and make two French
knots for eyes.
Sew ends of collar together and slide
over head onto neck.

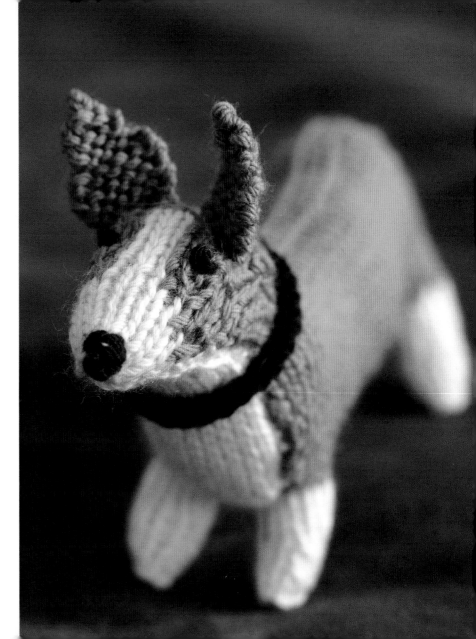

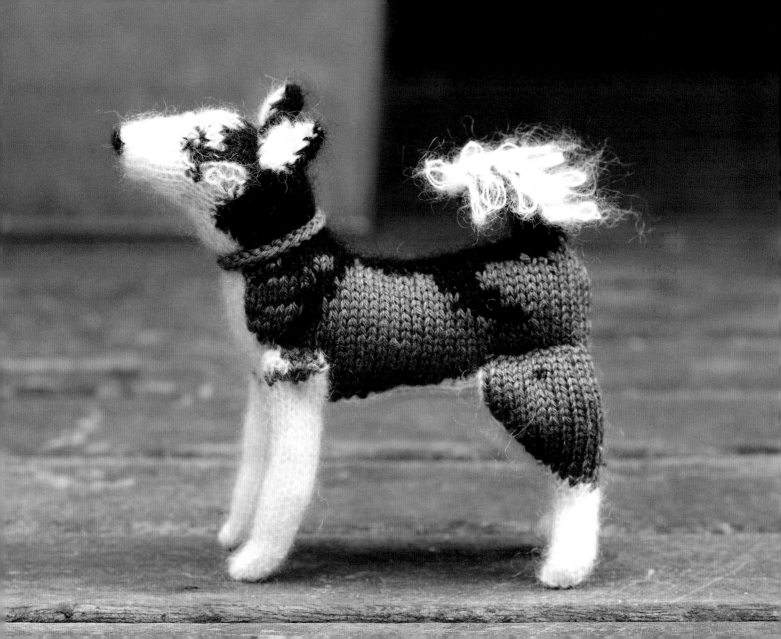

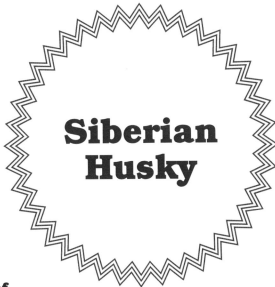

Siberian Husky

Husky is a general term for several breeds of sled dog, ours is Siberian. The Husky is a resilient and energetic breed with outstanding powers of endurance. Their eyes can often be different colours or parti-coloured. They closely resemble their ancestor the wolf and howl rather than bark. A heroic dog, the Husky has helped many explorers to reach the North Pole. A Husky called Balto saved a town from a diptheria epidemic in 1925 by leading a team of sled dogs through the snow with a life-saving serum. He is now stuffed and displayed in Cleveland Museum of Natural History.

Siberian Husky

The Husky uses intarsia knitting, loopy stitch and pipecleaners.

Measurements
Length: 17cm (6¾in)
Height to top of head: 15cm (6in)

Materials
- Pair of 2¾mm (US 2) knitting needles
- 4 spare 2¾mm (US 2) knitting needles or small stitch holders or safety pins
- 10g (¼oz) of Rowan Kidsilk Haze in Cream 634 (cr) used DOUBLE throughout
- 20g (¾oz) of Rowan Cashsoft 4ply in Thunder 437 (th)
- 10g (¼oz) of Rowan Kidsilk Haze in Wicked 599 (wk) used DOUBLE throughout
- A small amount of Rowan Cashsoft 4ply in Fennel 436 (fn) for collar
- Tiny amount of Rowan Cashsoft 4ply in Spa 424 for eyes
- 3 pipecleaners for legs and tail

Abbreviations
See page 172.
For loopy stitch technique, see page 173.

Right Back Leg
With cr, cast on 9 sts.
Beg with a k row, work 2 rows st st.
Row 3: Inc, k1, k2tog, k1, k2tog, k1, inc. *(9 sts)*
Row 4: Purl.
Row 5: K2, k2tog, k1, k2tog, k2. *(7 sts)*
Work 7 rows st st.
Row 13: Inc, k1, inc, k1, inc, k1, inc. *(11 sts)*

Row 14: Purl.*
Row 15: K2togcr, k2cr, inc into next 3 sts cr, k1cr, join in th, k1th, k2togth. *(12 sts)*
Row 16: P4th, p8cr.
Row 17: K5cr, inc into next 2 sts cr, k5th. *(14 sts)*
Row 18: P6th, p8cr.
Row 19: K6cr, inccr, incth, k6th. *(16 sts)*
Row 20: P8th, p8cr.
Row 21: K7cr, inccr, incth, k7th. *(18 sts)*
Row 22: P9th, p9cr.
Row 23: K8cr, inccr, incth, k8th. *(20 sts)*
Row 24: P10th, p10cr.
Row 25: K9cr, inccr, incth, k9th. *(22 sts)*
Row 26: P11th, p11cr.
Row 27: K10cr, inccr, incth, k10th. *(24 sts)*
Row 28: P12th, p12cr.
Row 29: K12cr, k12th.
Row 30: P12th, p12cr.
Rep last 2 rows once more.
Cast (bind) off 12 sts cr, 12 sts th.

Left Back Leg
Work as for Right Back Leg to *.
Row 15: Join in th, k2togth, k1th, k1cr, inc into next 3 sts cr, k2cr, k2togcr. *(12 sts)*
Row 16: P8cr, p4th.
Row 17: K5th, inc into next 2 sts cr, k5cr. *(14 sts)*
Row 18: P8cr, p6th.
Row 19: K6th, incth, inccr, k6cr. *(16 sts)*
Row 20: P8cr, p8th.
Row 21: K7th, incth, inccr, k7cr. *(18 sts)*
Row 22: P9cr, p9th.
Row 23: K8th, incth, inccr, k8cr. *(20 sts)*
Row 24: P10cr, p10th.
Row 25: K9th, incth, inccr, k9cr. *(22 sts)*
Row 26: P11cr, p11th.
Row 27: K10th, incth, inccr, k10cr. *(24 sts)*
Row 28: P12cr, p12th.
Row 29: K12th, k12cr.
Row 30: P12cr, p12th.
Rep last 2 rows once more.
Cast (bind) off 12 sts th, 12 sts cr.

Right Front Leg
With cr, cast on 9 sts.
Beg with a k row, work 2 rows st st.
Row 3: Inc, k1, k2tog, k1, k2tog, k1, inc. *(9 sts)*
Row 4: Purl.
Rep last 2 rows once more.
Work 2 rows st st.
Row 9: Inc, k7, inc. *(11 sts)*
Work 17 rows st st.**
Row 27: K5cr, join in th, k1th, k5cr.
Row 28: P3cr, p2th, p6cr.
Row 29: K7cr, k2th, k2cr.
Row 30: P1cr, p3th, p7cr.
Cast (bind) off 7 sts cr, 4 sts th.

Left Front Leg
Work as for Right Front Leg to **.
Row 27: K5cr, k1th, k5cr.
Row 28: P6cr, p2th, p3cr.
Row 29: K2cr, k2th, k7cr.
Row 30: P7cr, p3th, p1cr.
Cast (bind) off 4 sts th, 7 sts cr.

Right Side of Body
With th and cr, cast on 3 sts th, 5 sts cr. *(8 sts)*
Row 1: K5cr, k3th, cast on 5 sts th. *(13 sts)*
Row 2: P9th, p3cr, inccr. *(14 sts)*
Row 3: K3cr, k11th, cast on 4 sts th. *(18 sts)*
Row 4: P17th, inccr. *(19 sts)*
Row 5: K2cr, k17th, cast on 4 sts th. *(23 sts)*
Row 6: P20th, p2cr, inccr. *(24 sts)*
Row 7: K4cr, k20th, cast on 11 sts th. *(35 sts)*
Row 8: P32th, p2cr, inccr. *(36 sts)*
Row 9: K2cr, k34th.
Row 10: P31th, join in wk, p1wk, p3th, p1cr.
Row 11: K5th, k2wk, k29th.
Row 12: P8th, p4wk, p16th, p2wk, p6th.
Row 13: K6th, k2wk, k14th, k5wk, k9th.
Row 14: P11th, p5wk, p11th, p7wk, p2th.
Row 15: K5th, k4wk, k11th, k4wk, k12th.
Row 16: P13th, p4wk, p9th, p3wk, p7th.

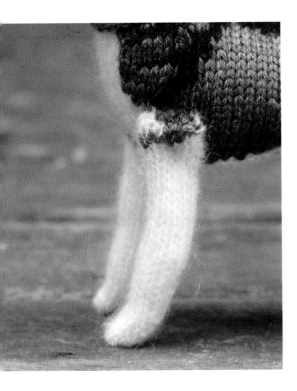

Legs

The Husky has an upright stance.
You can bend the tips of the legs to
make paws.

Row 17: K8th, k2wk, k9th, k4wk, k11th, k2togth. *(35 sts)*
Row 18: P2togth, p9th, p5wk, p2th, p3wk, p3th, p2wk, p3th, p6wk. *(34 sts)*
Row 19: K2th, k5wk, k2th, k2wk, k1th, k18wk, k2th, k2togth. *(33 sts)*
Row 20: P2th, p27wk, p4th. *(33 sts)*
Row 21: K5th, k6wk (hold 11 sts on spare needle for right neck), cast (bind) off 16 sts wk, k4wk icos, k2th (hold 6 sts on spare needle for tail).

Left Side of Body

With th and cr, cast on 3 sts th, 5 sts cr. *(8 sts)*
Row 1: P5cr, p3th, cast on 5 sts th. *(13 sts)*
Row 2: K9th, k3cr, inccr. *(14 sts)*
Row 3: P3cr, p11th, cast on 4 sts th. *(18 sts)*
Row 4: K17th, inccr. *(19 sts)*
Row 5: P2cr, p17th, cast on 4 sts th. *(23 sts)*
Row 6: K20th, k2cr, inccr. *(24 sts)*
Row 7: P4cr, p20th, cast on 11 sts th. *(35 sts)*
Row 8: K32th, k2cr, inccr. *(36 sts)*
Row 9: P2cr, p34th.
Row 10: K31th, join in wk, k1wk, k3th, k1cr.
Row 11: P5th, p2wk, p29th.
Row 12: K8th, k4wk, k16th, k2wk, k6th.
Row 13: P6th, p2wk, p14th, p5wk, p9th.
Row 14: K11th, k5wk, k11th, k7wk, k2th.
Row 15: P5th, p4wk, p11th, p4wk, p12th.
Row 16: K13th, k4wk, k9th, k3wk, k7th.
Row 17: P8th, p2wk, p9th, p4wk, p11th, p2togth. *(35 sts)*
Row 18: K2togth, k9th, k5wk, k2th, k3wk, k3th, k2wk, k3th, k6wk. *(34 sts)*
Row 19: P2th, p5wk, p2th, p2wk, p1th, p18wk, p2th, p2togth. *(33 sts)*
Row 20: K2th, k27wk, k4th. *(33 sts)*
Row 21: P5th, p6wk (hold 11 sts on spare needle for left neck), cast (bind) off 16 sts wk, p4wk icos, p2th (hold 6 sts on spare needle for tail).

Neck and Head

Row 1: With th and wk, and with RS facing k4th, k7wk from spare needle of Right Side of Body then k7wk, k4th from spare needle of Left Side of Body. *(22 sts)*
Row 2: P3th, p16wk, p3th.
Row 3: K1th, k4wk, k2togwk, k8wk, k2togwk, k4wk, k1th. *(20 sts)*
Cont in wk.
Row 4: Purl.
Row 5: K5, k2tog, k6, k2tog, k5. *(18 sts)*
Row 6: Purl.
Row 7: K15, pult (pick up loop below next st on left needle by inserting tip of right needle from back through loop – this stops a hole forming when turning work – then turn, leaving rem 3 sts on left needle unworked).
Row 8: Working top of head on centre 12 sts only, p2tog (first st of p2tog is loop picked up at end of last row), p11, pult.
Row 9: K2tog, k11, pult.
Row 10: P2tog, p11, pult.
Rep last 2 rows once more.
Row 13: K2tog, k to end. *(18 sts)*
Work 2 rows st st.
Row 16: Join in cr, p3cr, p12wk, p3cr.
Row 17: K5cr, k8wk, k2cr, pult (leave 3 sts on left needle).
Row 18: P2togcr, p1cr, p8wk, p2cr, pult.
Row 19: K2togcr, k1cr, k8wk, k2cr, pult.
Row 20: P2togcr, p1cr, p3wk, p2cr, p3wk, p2cr, pult.
Row 21: K2togcr, k1cr, k3wk, k2cr, k3wk, k2cr, pult.
Row 22: P2togcr, p1cr, p1wk, p6cr, p1wk, p2cr, pult.
Row 23: K2togcr, k1cr, k1wk, k6cr, k1wk, k5cr. *(18 sts in total)*
Row 24: P4cr, p4wk, p2cr, p4wk, p4cr.
Row 25: K2cr, k2togcr, k1cr, k1wk, k2togwk, k2cr, k2togwk, k1wk, k1cr, k2togcr, k2cr. *(14 sts)*
Row 26: P3cr, p2togcr, p1wk, p2cr, p1wk, p2togcr, p3cr. *(12 sts)*

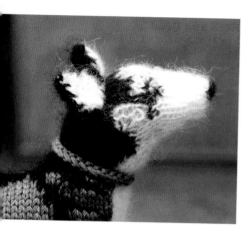

Head

The Husky is the only knitted dog with double ears and blue eyes.

Cont in cr.
Work 6 rows st st.
Row 33: K3, k2tog, k2, k2tog, k3. *(10 sts)*
Work 3 rows st st.
Cast (bind) off.

Tail

Row 1: With th and wk, and with RS facing k1th, k3wk, k2togwk from spare needle of Left Side of Body then k2togwk, k3wk, k1th from spare needle of Right Side of Body. *(10 sts)*
Cont in wk.
Work 3 rows st st.
Row 5: Join in cr, k2togcr, loopy st 1cr, k1wk, inc into next 2 sts wk, k1wk, loopy st 1cr, k2togcr. *(10 sts)*
Row 6: P2cr, p6wk, p2cr.
Rep last 2 rows 4 times more.
Row 15: K1cr, loopy st 1cr, k2togwk, k2wk, k2togwk, loopy st 1cr, k1cr. *(8 sts)*
Row 16: P2cr, p2tog twice wk, p2cr. *(6 sts)*
Cont in cr.
Row 17: K1, loopy st 1, k2, loopy st 1, k1.
Row 18: P1, p2tog twice, p1. *(4 sts)*
Row 19: K2tog twice. *(2 sts)*
Row 20: P2tog and fasten off.

Tummy

With cr, cast on 6 sts.
Beg with a k row, work 10 rows st st.
Next row: Inc, k4, inc. *(8 sts)*
Work 37 rows st st.
Next row: Inc, k6, inc. *(10 sts)*
Work 9 rows st st.
Next row: K2tog, k6, k2tog. *(8 sts)*
Work 5 rows st st.
Next row: K2tog, k4, k2tog. *(6 sts)*
Work 3 rows st st.
Next row: K2tog, k2, k2tog. *(4 sts)*
Next row: Purl.
Next row: K2tog twice. *(2 sts)*
Work 3 rows st st.
Next row: K2tog and fasten off.

Back of Ear

(make 2 the same)
With wk, cast on 6 sts.
Knit 6 rows.
Row 7: K2tog, k2, k2tog. *(4 sts)*
Knit 2 rows.
Row 10: K2tog twice. *(2 sts)*
Row 11: K2tog and fasten off.

Lining of Ear

(make 2 the same)
With cr, cast on 5 sts.
Beg with a k row, work 5 rows st st.
Row 6: P2tog, p1, p2tog. *(3 sts)*
Row 7: Knit.
Row 8: P3tog and fasten off.

Collar

With fn, cast on 26 sts.
Knit one row.
Cast (bind) off.

To Make Up

Sew in ends, leaving ends from cast on and cast (bound) off rows for sewing up. Using mattress or whip stitch, sew up legs starting at paw. Stuff each leg using pipecleaners. Using whip stitch, sew along top of leg, leaving an end to sew leg to body. Cut a pipecleaner 2.5cm (1in) longer than tail, fold over one end of pipecleaner (tip of tail), roll the pipecleaner in stuffing, place on inside of tail and carefully sew up tail from the outside using mattress stitch. There should be about 1cm (½in) of pipecleaner sticking out, which is pushed into the body when sewing on the tail. Using mattress or whip stitch, sew down centre back, around tail and down bottom. At head, fold in half and sew cast (bound) off edges of nose together.
Sew cast on row of tummy to bottom end of dog and sew cast (bound) off row to nose. Ease and sew tummy to fit body. Leave a

2.5cm (1in) gap between front and back legs on one side. Turn right side out, stuff then sew up gap with mattress stitch. Using whip stitch, sew legs to body as shown in photograph.

About 2cm (¾in) down from top edge of leg, sew through leg, body and opposite leg to make dog more stable.

With a black end of yarn and whip stitch, sew black back of ear to lining of ear. Sew ears to head as shown in photograph, sewing cream lining on first and then black back section of ear.

Using black yarn, embroider the nose using satin stitch. Using blue yarn, make two French knots for eyes, in centre of black circles as shown in photograph.

Sew ends of collar together and slide over head onto neck.

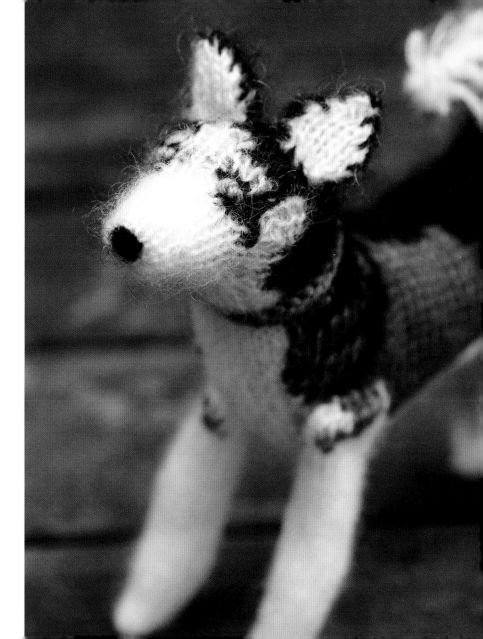

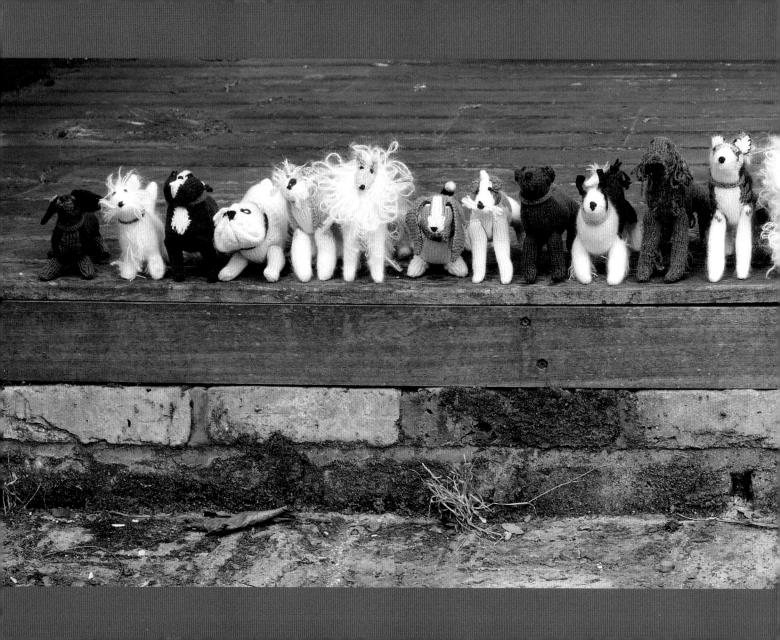

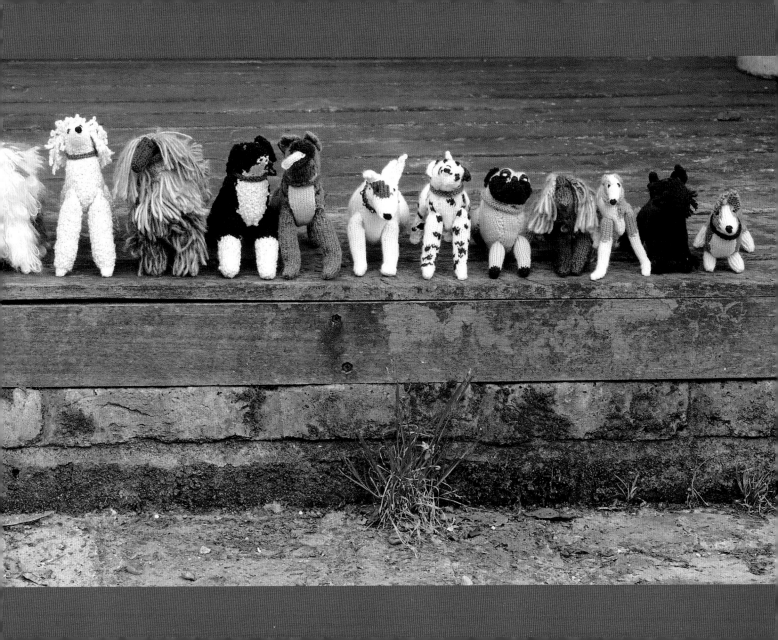

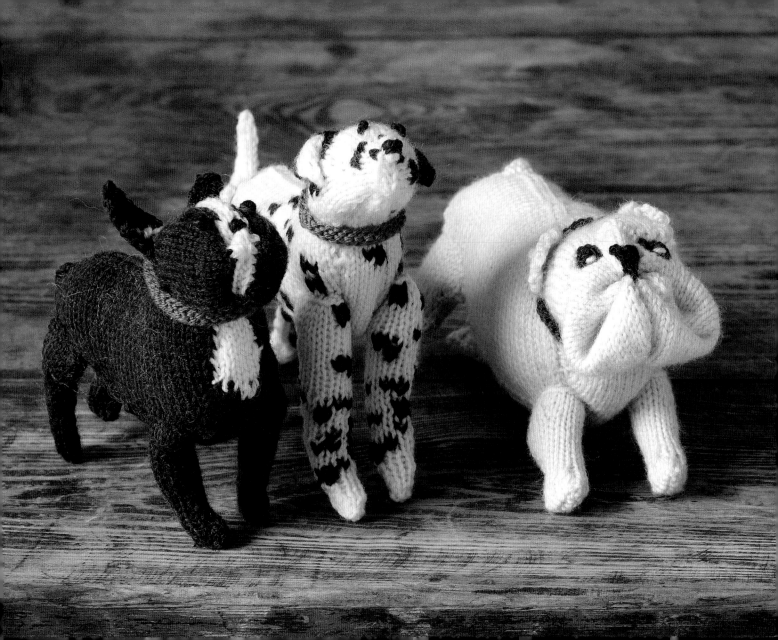

Hints

Choosing Yarns

Alternative yarns can be used – different colours or thicknesses. If using thicker yarns, refer to the ball band for needle size but use a needle at least 2 sizes smaller than recommended as the tension (gauge) needs to be tight to hold the stuffing. The thicker the yarn, the larger the dog will be. We feel that finer yarns create a more refined dog.

Knitting the Body and Head

When holding stitches to use later on in a pattern, use a spare needle, a stitch holder or safety pin.

Holes can develop around the short row shaping at the top of the head. When sewing on the ears, use the sewing up end to patch up any holes. Swiss darning can also be used to cover up any untidy stitches.

Don't worry if the neck of your dog is rather thickset, the collar is handy for giving the neck some shape. If needs be, reduce the number of stitches on the collar.

Stuffing the Dog

Stuffing the dog is as important as knitting it. Depending on the breed, your dog will need either light, normal or dense stuffing. For instance, the Basset Hound needs dense stuffing to give it a sturdy look while the Whippet needs light stuffing to enhance its delicate shape. Refer to the photographs of each dog.

You can completely change the dog's personality by moulding the stuffing. Make sure stuffing goes right to the end of the nose and do not over-stuff the neck. If the stitches become distorted then you have over-stuffed your dog.

We recommend using 100% polyester or kapok stuffing, which is available from craft shops and online retailers. A dog takes 20–40g (¾–1½oz) of stuffing, depending on size.

Sewing and Stuffing Legs

When sewing up thin or loopy stitch legs or tails, use mattress or whip stitch and sew up on the right side of the dog: this means you won't have to turn the leg/tail inside out. Sew on legs with seams facing backwards unless otherwise stated.

Use a knitting needle end or chopstick to push stuffing down to the paws. To smooth out the stuffing in the legs, roll the leg between your fingers.

If the legs are floppy once they have been sewn on, at about 2cm (¾in) down from top edge of leg, sew through the body and legs to make the dog more stable.

If the legs are too bendy, using a pipecleaner within the stuffing will steady them. Cut a pipecleaner to approximately 2.5cm (1in) longer than the leg, bend the ends over to fit the leg (otherwise they'll poke through the knitting), roll the pipecleaner in some stuffing, wrap the leg around it and, starting at the paw, mattress or whip stitch the seam on the right side of the leg. By carefully bending the tips of the legs you can make paws.

These dogs aren't toys, but if you intend to give them to small children do not use pipecleaners in the construction.

Adding Personality

The placing of the ears, eyes and nose needs to be carefully considered. We recommend pinning on the ears to find the perfect position before sewing. For the eyes, experiment with both the size and the placing of the French knots until you are happy with your dog's expression. For the nose, refer to the photograph and work in satin stitch.

Methods

Abbreviations

alt alternate

approx approximately

beg begin(ning)

cm centimetre

cont continue

dec decrease

foll follow(s)(ing)

g grams

icos including cast (bound) off stitch. (After casting (binding) off the stated number of stitches, one stitch remains on the right needle. This stitch is included in the number of the following group of stitches.)

in inches

inc work into front and back of next stitch to increase by one stitch

k knit

k2tog knit next two stitches together

k3tog knit next three stitches together

oz ounces

p purl

pult pick up loop below next st on left needle by inserting tip of right needle from back of work through loop – this stops a hole forming when turning work – then turn, leaving rem (number stated) sts on left needle unworked

p2tog purl next two stitches together

p3tog purl next three stitches together

rem remain(ing)

rep repeat

RS right side

st stitch

st st stocking (stockinette) stitch

tbl through back of loop

WS wrong side

[ ] work instructions within square brackets as directed

* work instructions after asterisk(s) as directed

Colour Knitting

There are two main techniques for working with more than one colour in the same row of knitting – the intarsia technique and the stranding (or Fair Isle) technique.

Intarsia Technique

This method is used when knitting individual, large blocks of colour. It is best to use a small ball (or long length) for each area of colour, otherwise the yarns will easily become tangled. When changing to a new colour, twist the yarns on the wrong side of the work to prevent holes forming.

When starting a new row, turn the knitting so that the yarns that are hanging from it untwist as much as possible. If you have several colours you may occasionally have to re-organize the yarns at the back of the knitting. Your work may look messy but once the ends are all sewn in it will look fine.

Stranding or Fair Isle Technique

If there are no more than 4 stitches between colours you can use the Fair Isle technique: this is good for the Dalmatian, where you have small numbers of stitches between the spots. Begin knitting with the first colour, then drop this when you introduce the second colour. When you come to the first colour again, take it under the second colour to twist the yarns. When you come to the second colour again, take it over the first colour. The secret is not to pull the strands on the wrong side of the work too tightly or the work will pucker.

I-cord

With double-pointed needles *knit a row. Slide the stitches to the other end of the needle. Do not turn the knitting. Rep from *, pulling the yarn tight on the first st so that the knitting forms a tube.

Loopy Stitch

Different dogs use slightly different loop techniques, so do check the one needed before you start knitting your dog.

Border Collie, Portuguese Water Dog, West Highland Terrier, Scottish Terrier, Miniature Schnauzer, Siberian Husky, Poodle

On a knit row, knit one stitch as normal, but leave the stitch on the left needle. Bring the yarn from the back to the front between the two needles. With the yarn in front, loop the yarn around your left thumb. Take the yarn back between the two needles to the back of the work. Knit the stitch from the left needle as normal. You now have two stitches on the right needle and a loop between them. Pass the first stitch over the second stitch to trap the loop, which is now secure. The end of the loop can be cut when finishing the dog.

Poodle (applies only to topknot)

On a purl row, work the loopy stitch knitwise as above. When the loop is complete, slip the loopy stitch onto the right needle, bring the yarn from the back to the front between the two needles. Slip the loopy stitch back onto the left needle, pushing the loop to the back (RS) of the work.

Rough Collie, Cocker Spaniel, Red Setter

Always worked on a purl row. Insert the tip of the right needle knitwise into the next stitch on the left needle. Place the first two (or three) fingers of the left hand behind the stitch and wrap the yarn around the fingers and the tip of the right needle, then knit the stitch without dropping it from the left needle. Keeping the fingers inside the yarn wrap, insert the tip of the left needle from left to right through the front of the stitch just made (on the right needle) and slip this stitch back onto the left needle. Knit the slipped stitch and the next stitch on the left needle together through the back of the loops. Slide the fingers out of the wrap to complete the loopy stitch.

Old English Sheepdog, Afghan Hound

For these dogs the loops are worked in Kid Silk/Tapestry yarn while the base stitches themselves are worked in 4ply yarn. Work loopy stitches knitwise on a purl row in the same way as for the Rough Collie, Cocker Spaniel and Red Setter.

Insert the tip of the right needle knitwise into the next stitch on the left needle. Place the first two (or three) fingers of the left hand behind the stitch and wrap Kid Silk/Tapestry around the fingers and the tip of the right needle, then knit the stitch without dropping it from the left needle. Keeping the fingers inside the yarn wrap, insert the tip of the left needle from left to right through the front of the stitch just made (on the right needle) and slip this stitch back onto the left needle. Using the 4ply yarn, knit the slipped stitch and the next stitch on the left needle together through the back of the loops. Slide the fingers out of the wrap to complete the loopy stitch.

Index of dogs

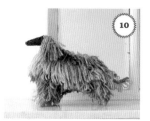
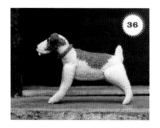
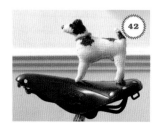
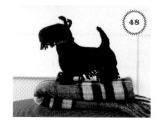
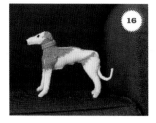
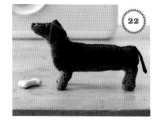
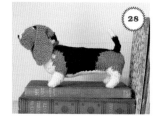
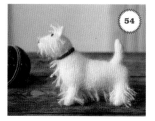
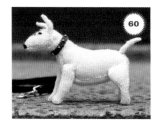
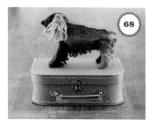
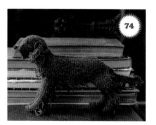

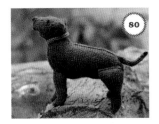

80

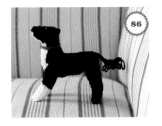

86

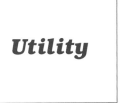

Utility

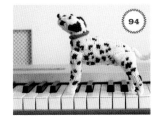

94

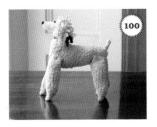

100

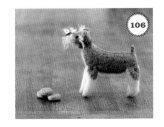

106

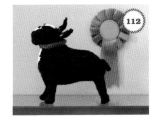

112

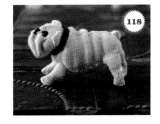

118

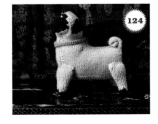

124

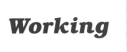

Working

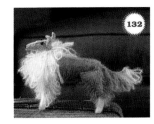

132

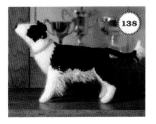

138

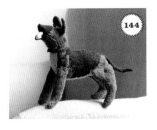

144

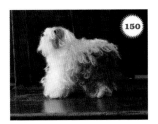

150

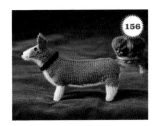

156

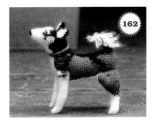

162

Resources

Most of the dogs are knitted in Rowan Yarns; for stockists please refer to their website www.knitrowan.com.

The Poodle and Portuguese Water Dog are knitted in silk bouclé, which you can buy from www.halcyonyarn.com.

We recommend using 100% polyester or kapok stuffing, which is available from craft shops and online retailers. A dog takes 20–40g (¾–1½oz) of stuffing, depending on size.

We are selling knitting kits; in each bag you get a pair of knitting needles, the correct amount of yarn for the dog and collar, a dog tag, a pattern and stuffing.

For those who cannot knit, have no inclination to learn or are too busy, we are selling most of the dogs ready made. You can see the range of dogs and kits on our website, www.muirandosborne.co.uk.

Best in Show

This book offers the unique opportunity to knit yourself a dog. There are 25 different breeds included, from a perky Poodle to a burly Bulldog, a delightful Dalmatian to a loyal Labrador. With Sally Muir and Joanna Osborne's designs you can now knit your precious pet, reproduce your favourite breed, or even knit the dog you have always desperately wanted.

The dogs are surprisingly easy to make. It will only take a few evenings to create a covetable companion for life.

Idiosyncratic descriptions of the various breeds accompany beautiful photography, making this book irresistible for both keen knitters and devoted dog-lovers.

Acknowledgements

Thank you to Rowan Yarns for their generosity.

We are very grateful to Marilyn Wilson and Kate Haxell for their immaculate work on the patterns; it's a hideous job and their enthusiasm and attention to detail has been invaluable.

Many thanks to Caroline Dawnay and Olivia Hunt for introducing us to Katie Cowan at Collins & Brown. We would also like to thank Nina Sharman and Gemma Wilson for their invaluable work on the book and Holly Jolliffe and Ali Bradshaw for the magnificent photographs.

We would like to thank our tolerant families and finally the makers of all television programmes shown between January and March 2010.

The Authors

Sally Muir and Joanna Osborne run their own knitwear business, Muir and Osborne. They export their knitwear to stores in the United States, Japan and Europe as well as selling to shops in the United Kingdom. Several pieces of their knitwear are in the permanent collection at the Victoria and Albert Museum, London. Best in Show is their second book.

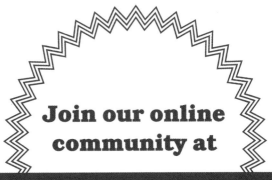

Join our online community at

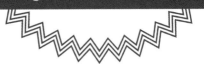

www.knityourowndog.com

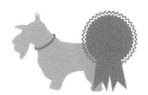

Best in Show

Knit your own dog then enter it into our online knitted dog show!

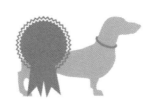

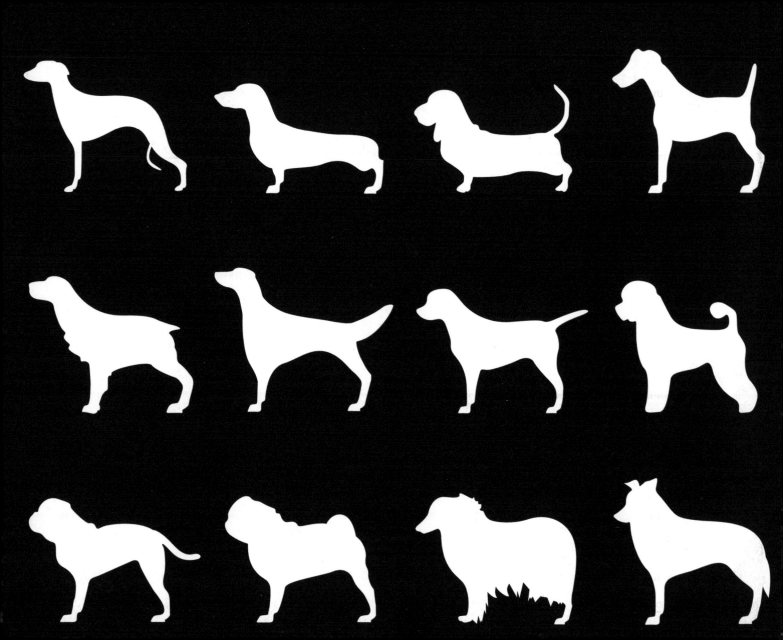